body outlaws

rewriting the rules
of beauty and body image

edited by ophira edut
foreword by rebecca walker

seal press

BODY OUTLAWS: REWRITING THE RULES OF BEAUTY AND BODY IMAGE

Published by Seal Press
A member of the Perseus Books Group
1700 Fourth Street
Berkeley, CA 94710

ISBN-13: 978-1-58005-108-8

A version of "Klaus, Barbie, and Other Dolls I'd Like to See" by Susan Jane Gilman originally appeared in HUES magazine.

A version of "The Butt" by Erin J. Aubry originally appeared in the LA Weekly.

A version of "Padding It: Why I Don't Need a Plus-Size Maxi Pad" by Wendy Shanker originally appeared in Grace Woman magazine's premier issue.

"Parisian Peel" by Joyce Dyer originally appeared in High Plains Literary Review. Copyright © 2001 by Joyce Dyer. Reprint by permission of the author.

Library of Congress Cataloging-in-Publication Data

Edut, Ophira.
Body outlaws : rewriting the rules of beauty and body image / edited by Ophira Edut ; foreword by Rebecca Walker.—2nd ed.
    p.cm.
ISBN 1580051081 (pbk.)
1. Body image. 2. Beauty, Personal--Psychological aspects. 3. Feminine beauty (Aesthetics) 4. Self-esteem in women. 5. Identity (Psychology) 6. Body image.
7. Beauty, Personal--Psychological aspects. 8. Feminine beauty (Aesthetics)
9. Self-esteem in women. 10. Identity (Psychology) I. Edut, Ophira. II. Title.

BF697.5.B63 A35   2003   155.9'1--dc21

2004274170

Cover Design by Lorie Pagnozzi
Text Design by Laura Gronewold

Distributed by Publishers Group West

note to the new edition

note to the new edition

Like most women's bodies, this book has undergone a lot of changes over the years. It was originally published in 1998 as *Adios, Barbie*. A year later, Mattel revolted against our pink and not-so-pretty tales by slapping Seal Press with a trademark infringement lawsuit. (Babs seems to have a lot of those "suits" in her closet, doesn't she?) After being ousted from the Dreamhouse, we settled by changing the book's name to *Body Outlaws* and giving it a new cover. With this new edition, I'm happy to say the book has gained a few healthy inches with the inclusion of nine new essays—including two by men—and a resource guide. It's also gotten a style makeover, because hey, the '90s are *so* yesterday. It's even traveled extensively—*Body Outlaws* has been translated into Greek and Chinese, adapted for the stage and used in college curricula all over the United States.

The world has changed a bit since the book's first edition, too. Back in 1998, body image was but a whisper on the radar of mass social consciousness. Today, nobody has to be convinced that body image is a real issue. Mainstream mags like *Glamour* and *YM* have "Love Your Body!" cover stories, and plus-size fashion has become a legitimate business. At the same time, the pressure to fit an unnatural ideal has stepped up, for both men and women. In 2002, some 6.6 million people had cosmetic surgery, with women making up 85 percent of the patients. Pharmaceutical companies have now beat out fabric softeners and dryer sheets in their quest to rid the world of wrinkles: In 2002, 1.1 million people injected Botox, a serum of botulinum toxin that erases frown lines and furrows for about four months. A friend's mother recently whiled away an afternoon at a Botox party (the modern alternative to Tupperware parties), where guests were treated to hors d'oeuvres and a needleful of the latest youth juice. And last year, I was interviewed by both *Inside Edition* and the *New York Observer* about the disturbing new trend of *teenagers* getting Botox injections. It seems, in our high-tech and anti-aging era, that people are willing to go to new extremes to beat the clock: *Vogue* recently touted the latest non-FDA-approved dewrinklers, including one made from "neo-natal foreskin." (Ugh!) At this rate, we'll have to take our beauty cues from the 1970s sitcom *Mork & Mindy* and move to the planet Ork, where inhabitants aged in reverse.

Yet the question looms larger than ever: How do we stop the insanity while still being responsible for our well-being? Finding that balance between health and obsession is a slippery slope at best, strewn with fad diets, weight-loss schemes disguised as health plans, mixed messages and bogus health studies led by self-interested corporations. One-third of American adults are considered obese (and an additional 20 percent or more are over what doctors consider a healthy weight). Kids are reportedly unhealthier than ever, getting minimal exercise and scarfing down junk food (the in-school vending machines don't help). School systems in a few states have even tried to legislate health report cards, which has caused an anxiety-fueled wave of extreme dieting among kids of all sizes.

When I lecture at colleges about *Body Outlaws,* invariably an audience member asks if the book is promoting poor health choices: "How can you tell people to eat whatever they want, when they're risking heart disease, diabetes, stroke?" It's a valid point. And my answer is that yo-yo dieting puts stress on the heart and other organs, that surgery is an invasive procedure and that body obsession causes psychological stress that diminishes the quality of life. I suggest that people find ways to balance out their hectic lives—efforts that don't usually get a whole lot of societal support. We've yet to discover the perfect balance between health and humanity.

All the while, my own struggles, questions and body issues have gone through more cycles than a raging PMS victim. I was a hopeful twenty-four when I first gathered these essays. Back then, a heady combo of youth and inexperience made it easy for "Love your body!" to be my steady battle cry. At thirty-one, I have months when I rock my rolls, and others when love don't live there anymore. Life in New York City can be tough on a girl whose best shot at a six-pack involves soda, not stomach muscles. And the new wrinkles around my eyes startle me; I seem to forget that youth is something one has to either buy or say goodbye to after a certain age. There are times when even *Sex and the City* and a good issue of *Bust* can't convince me that the "dirty thirties" are hotter than my "twenty and plenty" era.

Trying to find that pinhead-sized place between taking care of myself and selling out is enough to make a girl neurotic. When I recently decided to end a six-month couch-potato campaign by joining a gym, I got stuck at the Overthinkers Anonymous buffet. After recovering from the teenage throes of exercise bulimia (bingeing then exercising excessively) and disordered eating, was I hitting a setback by working out and trying to eat healthy foods? Or was I simply being responsible for my well-being? On one hand, exercise gave me energy and vitality, which I loved. But was I also back in the weight-pumping, carb-counting rat race? It is hard to draw the line between—or even distinguish—where the balance ends and the Balance Bars begin. I want to be fit, energetic and healthy. But I also want to be a body outlaw who coolly rejects the beauty standard and marches to her own chunky, funky beat. I haven't quite mastered that integration.

Trying to be a body image role model (or "roll model," as I say in honor of my love handles) brings another interesting responsibility. I can no longer ignore how my thoughts, words and feelings about my body create my own reality and, thus, affect other people's. It's true for all of us. I believe in the power of energy, and that language transmits energy. Every day, we have the choice to contribute to or to subtract from a bodylovin' world that we're building, one bountiful brick at a time.

Another insight I've developed, and applied with spotty success, is how significantly the myths of our culture influence our lives. Most of us *intellectually* know that fashion ads and airbrushed models are unrealistic and that very few people look like Kate Moss, including the model herself. Yet, emotionally, we're in denial about it. We must be, or we wouldn't spend so much time and money trying to look like something that doesn't even exist. Perhaps there's a deeper layer of mythology that we need to uncover—our own. Most of us haven't quite processed that the many "truths" we hold about our bodies are myths, too. We're all dragging around an invisible history book of tales about our bodies—why we're too much of this and not enough of that—and it's pulling us all down. That's why I hope that reading these stories will help.

I encourage everyone who struggles with self-acceptance to write her or his body story. Don't use it as a reason to justify feeling like a victim (tough job, believe me). Instead, use it as a key to find the wisdom, brilliance, humor and humility in your experiences. Treat yourself to some compassion and understanding. Of *course* you started slouching after that sixth-grade jerk pointed out your "raisinettes" on the playground. Naturally you stopped feeling safe in your skin after a date rape. Pinpoint the choices you made at every turn, honor them and explore some new choices that might empower you today. Enlist your friends to help. Tell them you're stuck in this feedback loop, and you'd love their advice on another approach. Be patient with yourself, experiment and bring a sense of humor.

For most of my life, I've treated my body like a house I'm not quite ready to move into. There are always renovations, home improvements, cleanups done for show. It's hard to remember that I *own* this house, and to step into that responsibility. When I was a young Girl Scout, I hated the "law" (which we recited with three raised fingers) about leaving a place better than the way you found it. My main gripe was that it usually involved scrubbing a campground outhouse. But hey, an organization that makes cookies that delicious might just have a point. Truly owning up to our whole selves—bullshit, baggage and beauty—is a powerful notion.

So no matter how many fashion mags we might buy or how many times we have secretly considered Botox or plastic surgery, in other words how much we buy into the myth, I still believe that we as people crave and respond to one another's honest stories. With this knowledge, I have retained my faith in the power of stories to heal, protect and blaze the path for change.

Ophira Edut
New York City
September 2003

ophira edut   vii

Contents

foreword
rebecca walker

I am a woman obsessed with skin—others' and especially my own. I squint into the mirror, trying not to see the scars left from my bout with the chicken pox, the wrinkles appearing branchlike across my once satiny forehead, the dark spots reminding me of all the times I didn't practice restraint. I turn this way and that in carefully modulated lighting, keeping a fair distance from the looking glass, not wanting to know what it cannot help but say: My skin is not flawless. It ages, chafes, erupts angrily. It sags where I would like it to be taut, pebbles where I want it to be smooth. Ultimately I acquiesce, accept the unacceptable—I am human, a mere mortal like everybody else— and turn out the light.

But there is something else, a remnant of self-hatred that doesn't go away so easily, that doesn't fade when the light dims. This other thing is what makes me cringe when my lover pulls my jeans over my hips in the half-light of our bedroom. It's what makes me burn myself in the sun year after year, and idolize Naomi Campbell no matter how much I commit to honoring my own beauty instead of someone else's. Spots, scars, bumps and keloids just skim the surface of my neurosis. The depth of my obsession with skin revolves around color, and what I perceive to be my lack thereof.

I have always been light. Pale. Honey-colored. Yellow. Near white. Olive. Neon. Sallow. Jaundiced. Pasty. And I have, for most of my adult life, hated being so. While aunts and cousins told me I had "good" hair and was lucky to be light, I felt cheated, like my mother didn't do her part while I was *in utero,* like her melanin gene was no match for my father's hearty Slavic-Jewish stock. Sure there were moments when light wasn't light enough and I wanted to have straight hair and a mom named Jane, but for the most part I have wanted to be darker, with fuller lips and thicker, more chocolatey thighs. Darker is what my mother is, what my lovers often are. Though I'm ashamed to admit to privileging any color over another, darkness is where I have located the beauty that moves me, the beauty that sets my stomach twitching and my mind dreaming. Darkness is graceful, mellifluous, haunting. Darkness is deeper, smarter, more lovable.

This narrative I've attributed to darkness goes on and on, as obsessive fantasy projections often do. It includes words like *community, belonging, stability, justice, righteousness* and *moral superiority.* In weak moments, my mind construes dark skin as a passport that facilitates admittance to cultures that do not disown, that never fail to claim. I imagine that the darkness provides a ready-made identity, a neat sense of knowing as clear and pure and self-evident as skin itself. I think that to be darker is to be on the "right" side of the powerless/ powerful, oppressed/oppressor equation. To be black is to be part of the solution. Black Is Beautiful, remember? But what about beige, I wonder. Is beige beautiful, too? Or am I only half of the thing itself, muddied, watered down and eternally ambivalent?

I'm not the only one reading more into the surface of the body than meets the eye. In our North American culture, and indeed in cultures around the world, the body is a sign, a text to be read and interpreted. For each body part there is at least one widely accepted script already written, a bit of subtext that fleshes out, so to speak, the extremity in question. Long fingers foretell musical agility (and sexual prowess). Big hands and big feet promise a great big juicy you-know-what. Big breasts bespeak fertility. A long neck is elegant. Full lips are sexy. Fat is slothful. A big nose is awkward. Nappy is unhappy. Bald women are unfeminine.

While these scripts purport to be objective observations, they are more often propagandistic narratives, self-serving tracts that operate primarily in the construction of community, be it based on ideology, race, vocation or class, on a local, national or international level. As long as there is a standard of beauty, a set of positive attributes assigned arbitrarily to a particular set of body parts, there are two camps locked in a xenophobic embrace: those who have the "good" parts, and those who do not; those who are on the inside of the community, and those who, tragically, are relegated to its margins.

It has long been the project of the women's, civil rights and gay and lesbian liberation movements to deconstruct this patently problematic relationship and thereby enlarge the community of so-called beautiful people by celebrating exactly those characteristics the dominant culture finds offensive. As a result, in my lifetime not only has pop culture's paradigm of beauty shifted from Farrah Fawcett, Scott Baio and Christie Brinkley to include Erykah Badu, Will Smith, Naomi Campbell, Jenny Shimizu and Alek Wek, but I have seen and participated in the development of entire aesthetic movements that exist and, well, thrive outside the white heterosexual mainstream.

Dyke, hip hop, *cholo,* biker, skater, tribal, punk, Nubian. Whether it's multiple piercings, femme girls with no hair, two-foot-high head wraps, or skin so covered with tats that the whole idea of "clear and blemish free" seems hopelessly naive, it is obvious that as a result of artistic and political movements, new and different scripts are being written. The body, a blank page waiting for words, and beauty, a subjective idea looking for a location, have been liberated to meet up in a variety of unique and often surprising ways. Barbie, with her pert nose and shoulder-length blonde hair, no longer reigns supreme.

Yet as we rapidly approach the millennium, patting ourselves on the back for making it this far, so many of us still struggle to claim our shape and size, color and hue. Why? What compels us to even consider ads exhorting us to reshape, resculpt and remake aspects of ourselves that our parents made just fine in the first place? It would be foolish to minimize the power of societal pressure, the waifish models screaming out from every newsstand and supermarket checkout line, nor can we ignore the self-esteem crisis permeating every cell of our culture. But I think there is something else, too, an overlooked by-product of the hysteria to control and commodify an image of ideal beauty: a crisis of the imagination, a dearth of stories, a shocking lack of alternative narratives.

Where are the stories that challenge the notion that perfect happiness can be found in a "perfect" body? Where are the anecdotes about learning to love parts of ourselves not because of how they look or how they measure up to Cindy Crawford, but because of how they feel to us, or how they tell a unique part of our personal history? Where, in this ongoing discussion of body image, is the story of the lover who celebrated the hips we found too narrow or too wide, and caused us to see ourselves anew; the story of the Jewish nose that connects us to an ancestral past; the testimony about that "extra" thirty pounds that make us feel solid and abundant rather than slovenly and unattractive?

The truth is, we say a lot about how the beauty standard needs to change, but we often forget to give the blow by blow of the personal and painstaking process it takes to make that change happen. We don't take the time to write new scripts based not on what the culture dictates, but on what we have come to know and experience in the intimate moments of our day-to-day lives.

Which is why I am excited to be writing this foreword and adding my story to the others in this collection: This book is full of new scripts! New scripts for body hair, fatness, big butts, celibacy, skinniness, tattooed skin, transsexuality and all manner of other taboos and cultural unacceptables. This diverse and talented group of writers bare their insecurities and self-hatred, as well as their determination to work through them to moments of self-awareness and bona fide self-acceptance. With humor and irony they wrestle with the body in the mirror and the culture—be it Latino, African-American, Anglo, Indian, Arab or Israeli—outside the door. Their stories illustrate a truth we've lost sight of: The body is not limited to one reading but can be the site of many, the most important of which is our own.

Which brings me back to *my* own. For most of my life I have been unable to love my honey thighs, to smile back into my "fair-skinned" face because I lacked an accompanying story I could live with. I hated my proximity to whiteness, the colonizing tinge that marked me as an outsider, and pushed me to the periphery of brown worlds I longed to call my own. Looking down the length of my barely brown body, I felt mainly revulsion, a horrifying lack that ran deep.

But I have finally begun to write a better story. It's far from a complete or cohesive narrative, but it begins and ends with my maternal grandmother. I like to think I take after her—full lips, yellow skin, dark eyes and all. When I look at her photograph, which hangs above my desk, I see a haunting, regal beauty, a smoldering intensity that makes me shudder. Lena Horne is in the story, too, also staring down from a photo above my desk with an awesome fearlessness. She's in her early twenties, out for a day in the country, looking honestly and shamelessly into the camera. Somehow, through my yellow-hating fog, I feel connected to these striking, self-made women, and it helps.

My lover is in the story, too, telling me again and again, as many times as it takes, how sexy I am and how much s/he likes my color and the fact that I'm neither black nor white, but both, some land in the middle s/he doesn't find too threatening to love. These affirming bits are punctuated by moments I have more and more often, when I look down the length of my body and feel not disgust but a tender gratitude for what I *do* have: sensitive, resilient and responsive skin that covers and protects. Skin that glows at its very own frequency. Skin that is supple and warm to the touch, smooth; skin that is mine.

I know I have a long way to go before I can unequivocally groove on my paleness, but I consider getting this far to be a major accomplishment. To look at the ways we judge and contort ourselves is a radical and self-affirming act in a culture where altering oneself for admission and approval is the norm. To do the actual work of reprogramming, rewriting the words that we have been taught go with the picture, is a much more strenuous and exacting task.

But at the risk of sounding too grave, this work is of great significance. At its essence is the struggle to wrest for ourselves the self-esteem that is often denied but which is undeniably our birthright. It is an understatement to say that self-esteem, the elusive belief in our intrinsic worth and beauty, makes and saves lives. For many, that journey to survival is mapped on the body's surface—and begins as we extend to our most hated features the first tremblings of compassion. Though I'm afraid this may be a journey without an end, it's a path I'm grateful to be on, especially in the company of these resilient women and their stories.

Rebecca Walker
May 1998

introduction
introduction
ophira edut

It started with a modest bikini, a waterslide and some love handles.

I'd been spreading the love-your-body gospel for a while when summer retail season arrived, bearing an unexpected innovation called the "tankini." You know, those not-quite-bikinis with the short shorts and halter tops? I'd made plans to go to a water park, and decided it was time to walk the talk, challenge my residual body fears and wear my first bikini since the age of four.

That simple decision created more drama than an off-Broadway revue. You see, the bra-style top of my new swimsuit meant I'd have to expose my stomach. It didn't matter that I was going to an out-of-the-way water park in Allentown, Pennsylvania. I was suddenly flooded with the most outrageous fears. I was a size fourteen, the same dimensions as more than half of American women. Yet, I lived in a world that made me believe baring my flesh—ripples, puckers and all—would shock or disgust people.

Well, I told myself, then I would treat the world to some shock therapy.

I would be a *body outlaw*—a rebel with a cause, willing to step outside my comfort zone to expose people to a body type that had practically disappeared from the cultural imagination.

Hello, ladies and gentlemen, this is what a size-fourteen belly looks like. Sit-ups not included. My abs aren't rocks, they're rolls. And here are my love handles. As my friend John would say, "Can you handle my love?"

Desperate times call for desperate measures. We can't beat society at its own body-bashing game—so we need to become body outlaws. In the old West, outlaws lived on the fringes of society. They were thought to be so dangerous, so threatening to the culture, that they had to be relegated to its outskirts. But why were outlaws such a threat? Perhaps their ideas were powerful. Perhaps their presence was so strong and commanding that it could upturn traditions that weren't serving the people. Perhaps they knew the truths that would set people free.

Think about it. We live in an age where the mere idea of "liking your body the way it is" is so uncommon that the women who do so are considered the freaks—not vice versa. Self-acceptance gets minimal support, while entire industries devote themselves to the constant (and profitable) pursuit of change. Our bodies have become like private correctional facilities, and we their prisoners. Body outlaws are the escaped convicts, their only crime a desire to live free from the confining pressures to achieve a beauty they didn't imagine themselves.

Picture the guy who told Leslie "Big Lez" Segar, now a famous hip-hop dancer, that she was too big to dance. In true body outlaw style, she did an amazing set of back flips across the room, and showed 'em what a thick chick could do. Since then, she's danced in nearly every hip-hop video worth remembering and worked with everyone from Mary J. Blige to Michael Jackson. Think of San Francisco-based fat activist Marilyn Wann, who in 1999 protested a local gym for posting a fat-bashing billboard. Thanks to Wann's efforts, it is now illegal in San Francisco to discriminate against people on the grounds of height or weight in jobs, housing and public access. Then there's plus-size model Kate Dillon (a contributor to this book), who began her career as a food-deprived "straight-sized" model, got sick of it and happily gained back all her weight. Facing scorn and doubt, she returned to the business as a size-twelve model, and went on to be voted one of *People* magazine's "50 Most Beautiful People," because she was both beautiful *and* a body outlaw.

Body outlaws know the truth about happiness. They know it isn't in a plastic surgeon's office, a hair-care product or a miracle diet program. They know happiness is self-acceptance—and they know there's a catch. It doesn't mean self-acceptance *after* you "lose those twenty pounds" or get your roots touched up. It means that no matter how you look, you still gotta work it. There's a greater mission. Body outlaws don't live on the fringes for the sake of doing so. They do it because this very brand of shock therapy is the only way we'll change the culture.

At the turn of the millennium, body image is a global crisis among young women (and recently, a growing number of young men—which is why we've included two male essayists in this edition). Until now, there hasn't been a forum where women of diverse cultures and identities could gather to chronicle their experiences, to tell their tales of living as body outlaws.

And the current national discussion of body image reflects this. To date, most literature continues to popularize the myth that distorted body image is merely a symptom of vanity suffered by bored, middle-class white girls. In 1995, *Newsweek* published results from a University of Arizona study that compared the body satisfaction of black and white adolescent girls. The gap in results was wider than the one between Barbie's thighs: 70 percent of the African-American subjects reportedly liked their bodies, while 90 percent of their white peers did not. While the black girls in the study described an ideal body as "full hips and thick thighs," perfection, according to the white girls, came in waifishly impossible dimensions: five-foot-seven and 100 to 110 pounds. The study's implied conclusion? Black girls have better body image than white girls do.

That didn't sit right with many women I knew. We wondered what would have happened if the study had polled subjects on whether they liked their hair texture, their skin and eye color, their facial features. Moreover, what if the study had asked girls whether they felt safe or powerful in their bodies? The focus on weight failed to connect body image to racism and sexism—to power. Class differences were not mentioned, nor was the history that may have shaped the subjects' varying ideals.

But women's struggle with body image *is* about power. Body image goes far beyond weight, and it runs deeper than skin color. Our bodies have become arenas for feelings we don't deal with, for unresolved traumas and injustices. Scratch away the surface of "I'm so fat" and "I hate my hair," and you'll find a sister treading water in a melting pot simmering with every "ism" imaginable.

This is difficult to articulate today, at a time when society has taken on the rosy blush of progressiveness. Are we empowered young women, or aren't we? Our inability to answer this question definitively is a natural offshoot of a capitalist, media-driven society that serves young people a daily diet of mixed messages. Society adopts the "girl power" mantra but refuses to arm girls with the tools to achieve it. Textbooks glorify violence and war, but schools won't properly educate students about safe sex, reproductive health, self-defense and abuse. Multiculturalism is the new media buzzword, but laws upholding it are dismantled while we read *Vibe* magazine. Young women are encouraged to follow rather than to lead, to become passive consumers rather than active creators of our culture and our destinies.

Our bodies—and our convoluted relationships with them—tell the real story. In a world that offers women challenges along with choices, compromise along with control, our bodies may seem the only realm where we can claim sovereignty. So we focus our power there. We start with what we can control—sorta. Our bodies. Our hair. Our weight. Our breasts. Our clothes. When this control inevitably eludes us, our feelings of powerlessness solidify.

Too often, the endless body chase becomes a distraction from a painful reality. Trauma survivors talk about "leaving their bodies" as a survival tactic during violation. For some women, feeling like we're "in our bodies" convinces us we exist. In a twisted way, intense body focus is the one thin thread connecting us to the material world. But gaining a sense of place in our bodies should ultimately build our sense of place in the world. It should be a means of healing, rather than escaping from pain. We need to feel connected to our bodies, to understand what they can do. Sometimes, this even means pushing them to new comfort zones. Can we do this with balance? That's the big question.

Body outlaws are attempting to answer this question with a resounding "yes" by showing that our bodies can be our allies. Rather than simply shun the idea of being defined by our appearances, young women today include our bodies as part of our multilayered self-definitions. In a world that still tries to assume our identities, we rebel with an outward expression of self. Our passion for the truth, in all its messy complexity, compels us to visibly defy easy categories and sweeping labels, even if they were created from within. We rush to show the world who we are rather than allow it to paint us as one-dimensional characters. So instead of declaring "black is beautiful," a young African-American woman today is more likely to ask, *Why does this world assume I'm "too black" or "not black enough"? Who defines blackness anyway?*

Everything is up for questioning today—the media, our identities, each other, the very concept of beauty. The answer to the body image dilemma can't simply be to allow all women a place in the beauty structure. Sure, it's important to tell women of every size and color that they're beautiful and worthwhile people. But it's also fundamental to offer them a world where they are safe, valued and free from oppression. A world that values healing more than destruction, that seeks balance over domination.

The writers in *Body Outlaws* dare to imagine that world. They fight fire with fire, using their bodies to present a different image of beauty, of self. They risk alienation, harassment, even violence, to live as they truly are. And in doing so, they open up the possibility of a world that values difference instead of ignoring or degrading it, a world that embraces contradictions instead of erasing them.

There are no easy answers proposed, no preachy testimonials or sensationalized stories. Just a collection of recipes for clarity, light, a little self-love. With tremendous honesty and a dash of humor, these women describe their struggles to accept—and celebrate—the parts of their bodies that make them different, distinctive.

In "My Jewish Nose," Lisa Jervis refuses rhinoplasty and keeps her prominent nose *au naturel.* In "The Art of the Ponytail," Akkida McDowell explains the roots of her low-maintenance hairstyle, and weaves them to her African-American "hair-itage." Multiracial rower Allison Torres pieces together a new identity in "At Home in My Body: An Asian-American Athlete Searches for Self," uniting the many dimensions of both body and ethnicity. And in "Becoming *La Mujer,*" Marisa Navarro makes sense of the cross-cultural struggle to be a dutiful Mexican-American daughter while defining sensuality on her own terms.

In a culture still mesmerized by an unnatural beauty standard, these simple tales of self-acceptance are heroic deeds, brave acts of resistance. By daring to speak the truth, these writers treat the world to a dose of shock therapy. Yes, women come in more colors, sizes and flavors than you'll find in a candy store. This book offers just a taste.

I hope that *Body Outlaws* lifts taboos, and ultimately propels women into a firm belief in our entitlement. We are entitled to love our bodies at any size. We are entitled to speak, act, create and feel safe wherever we go. We are entitled to resources, and to a real place in this culture. And we are ultimately entitled to live in a world where liking our bodies makes us normal—not outlaws.

So take an about face, if you will, and confront head-on whatever you're running from. Start at the mirror. Take a good, hard look at the part of your body you fear the most, and tell it who's boss. Then give it all the love you've got. Instead of putting all your resistance into the leg press machine, focus some on the culture that directs our best energies into body-hating pursuits. Life is an opportunity for joy and celebration. How can our lives be full if our stomachs aren't? How can we understand life's gifts when we're too blinded by our own perceived inadequacies to appreciate them?

Body Outlaws reveals a hidden truth: Self-acceptance is not defeat. It's a way of plugging ourselves into the organic process of life. It's the entrance ramp to discovering our true power, which is rooted in who we are. When our bodies and identities are in tune, they reflect each other. This beautiful synchronicity throws the world a much-needed curve. It hums with an energy that affects everything and everyone it touches. It changes the culture.

And that's how body outlaws will rewrite the rules and build a bodylovin' world.

body

outlaws

body outlaws

my brown face
mira jacob

Next time, I'm going to walk into that warehouse and snap my tongue like a honeyed whip. I'm going to unfurl with grace and fury. I will stand in the dead center of the room, and I will say:

Obviously, you were raised in a goddamn barn. Haven't any of you boys ever gotten near a woman, or was your leash too short? Well, I know you've never come close to my kind because you would know better than to hiss "Hey, Indi" at my passing shadow, or try that where-you-from-baby line with that don't-I-know-it look in your eye. And the next time you see me . . .

Welcome to my morning fantasy. It starts about forty feet from my door and continues between Brooklyn and Sixth Avenue, occasionally bubbling to the surface in waves of "goddamn." It keeps me occupied on the subway and preoccupied at my desk, my mind shuffling out the endless possibilities of what I'll do next time. By mid-afternoon I've usually pep-rallied myself into a proud-to-be-

3

Indian state of mind, and by nightfall, in an act of denial or resilience, I've let the whole ritual slip away. Survival of the forgetful.

Worse things have happened in this world, to be sure. A steady tap on my remote control informs me of the multitudes of hell that have yet to befall me. My family hasn't been torn apart by war and disease. I'm not under persecution for my political beliefs, and next to "Mama, Stop Screwing My Boyfriend," even my Ricki Lake potential seems small.

"Mira, you say you feel betrayed by your face?" Ricki asks.

"Yes, I do, Ricki," I reply.

"And can you tell the members of our audience what that means?" she asks, gesturing to the rows of scrutiny, hard gazes and arms folded over chests.

"Well, every morning, the guys on the corner scream 'Indi' at me and ask me what style we go for down there, and some mornings I just can't take it."

"Can't take it. Now what does that mean, Mira? What's the worst thing you've done as a result of this?" Ricki gives me a concerned look.

"Uh, nothing, really, it's a more internal kind of thing."

"Okay," Ricki says, not missing a beat. "Our next guest says she is being poisoned by her six-month-old baby. Give a big welcome to . . ."

No, my problem is straightforward and undramatically simple: I was born with a mysterious face. My deep brown eyes and skin, the thick line of my black eyebrows and the slant of my cheekbones have always been described to me as exotic, haunting, elusive. From the day I hit puberty, my Indian-ness has labeled me a box full of secrets, left me wrapped as a package of woman labeled "the other." Why are Indian women mysterious? To answer that question I would have to be outside of myself, claiming a territory I don't inhabit—American, male, most often white. As all outsiders do, I can only hazard a guess, regurgitating the perceptions fed to me: Indian women are quiet, graceful, serene and tranquilized by a thousand blue-skinned gods. We are bent heads looking slyly downward, almond eyes and lotus lips tender with secret knowledge. We are fabulous cooks cloaked in layers of bright silk, bangles dangling in permanent dance from our lithe arms. We are mystery, waiting to be unfolded.

Seattle, late afternoon. The man on the corner is staring at me. I can feel his eyes traveling up my leg, over my stomach and chest, to my face. A smile spreads over his face, and I give all my attention to the red **DON'T WALK** sign across the street.

"Hey, you're Indian, right?" he asks in greeting, stepping in front of me. I walk around him and wait for the light to turn. "Hey, what's up, you don't speak English? I'm just asking you a question. Where are you from?"

I stare at the stoplight, the row of buildings just beyond it. I stare at the businessmen walking around me and glance down at my watch.

"What time is it? Hey, what time is it, baby?" he asks. A slow pool of people gathers at the corner, and the man talks louder, laughing. "Hey, girl, hey! What time is it where you're from? Nighttime?"

A quick heat rises to my face, and I watch the cars pass. Two men in suits turn their heads slightly, their eyes scanning my face.

"What, you can't speak to me?" he asks, pushing his face next to mine. He smells like mint gum, sweat and city.

The next time I'm going to look right at you. I'm going to stare into your eyes and wait through twenty lights, and when you are finally mute and embarrassed, I'll walk on.

I wait for the light to turn, my stomach churning, the pulse in my ears growing louder.

"You too good to speak to me? That it?"

The WALK sign lights up, and I spring forward, hoping he'll stay behind. He does. "Hey!" he yells after me. "You don't look that good, bitch."

I've been unfolded to the point of splitting. I've had my lid thrust open, my contents investigated by prying eyes, hands, lips. Concealed in compliments, come-ons, gifts, I've been asked to explain the wave of enigma my country of origin arouses in the minds of others.

Indophiles, my Indian friends call the more persistent among them. "Tell me about you," these men ask, the sophisticated version of "Where are you from?" Half listening as I rattle off about anything but my ethnicity, they nod knowingly, more interested in my looks than anything I say. I can see it in them, the hunger for a quiet woman, an erotic encounter, a spicy dish. Some men don't even bother with the formalities, cutting to the chase. "Indian," a man in a bar once said, nodding to me. Then, by way of invitation, his mouth pressed hot against my ear, *"Kamasutra?"*

My mother laughs a tired laugh when I tell her this, her voice weary through the crackling phone line. "Oh, men will do that. You're exciting to them because you're something they do not know, an Indian woman."

An Indian woman. I have been to India several times, and I have watched my aunts and cousins with a mixture of curiosity and awe. I've heard their sing-song chatter and loud-mouthed gossip, watched their deft fingers plucking endless batches of coriander leaves. And while they've never consciously excluded me, my ear cannot follow the lilting mother-tongue conversations, my laugh among them is much too loud. They teasingly call me a tomboy and warn that I may end up marrying my truck, a possibility that repulses them as much as it excites me. Simply put, our graces are instinctually different. My bones and flesh hold the precious truth of a history I can claim more in blood than in experience.

Funny that some men can latch on to a part of me I'm still trying to locate. My brown face has made me the recipient of numerous gifts and cryptic cards, mostly from guys I've met in passing. Broken bird wings, wire necklaces and wine bottles filled with rose petals have all found their way to my doorstep, fervid notes tucked under the windshield of my truck. I once opened up a cardboard box to find shattered mirror pieces glued in careful mosaic inside, my own shocked face staring back at me.

Oh, but those gifts were fun when I was younger, in my teens. Just the thought of some stranger thinking enough of me to plot a course of action had me strutting around like a movie star. I rode the drama bull like a rodeo queen, fancied myself a connoisseur of the slightly deranged and obsessed. Heady stuff—all that desire and frisson, electric connection given in doses. I floated outside my body in a state of awe, imagining something in my very soul conducted the energy around me, leading guys to do things they had "never done before" or "felt before" or "dared to think."

The shift from arousal to fear is as hard to pinpoint as it is unmistakable. As I grew older, these gifts were less appreciated, received on days when I needed to stay in my body and be unaware of it. I couldn't understand the loaded intent behind the presents, and instead I began to realize what was being taken away. That old junkie craving for unseen passion left suddenly, replaced by the certain knowledge that these men were not reacting to me, to my mind or words or wit, but to my face, my brown face.

♌

In Denny's, crying to my best friend Laura over coffee, I struggle to keep my eyes averted from the man in the corner, to answer her questions.

"Did you just hear me?" she asks.

"No. Yes. I can't concentrate, that man is watching me. Don't turn around and look." The man stares straight at me with such a force I wonder if I don't know him. I feel his eyes hotter on my face with every word I say, my voice fading as I realize he isn't going to look away. I'm embarrassed that he can see me crying, embarrassed that I can't concentrate. Relieved when I see him get up to pay his bill and walk out, the pinch in my throat loosens, and Laura and I can finally talk.

Our conversation comes to an abrupt halt when the man returns half an hour later with earrings in hand. Two silver Egyptian pharaohs dangle in my blurred line of vision as he announces, "I've been watching you all night. I don't know much about India, but I thought these would look nice on you. I *had* to get them for you." He searches my eyes with brooding intensity, as though we've just established spiritual connection over my Grand Slam breakfast combo. "If I give you my number, will you call?"

If I give you a black eye, will you take it and leave?

"She's upset," Laura says, her head shaking, eyes wide. "She's crying." The man ignores her, pressing a piece of paper into my palm. "My name is Gil. I think you should call me. You know what I mean." He gives me one last penetrating look, spins on his heel and walks out the door.

God bless my heart of darkness, I think I've stumbled upon a Colonizer Syndrome. It takes seemingly normal men and causes them to lose their minds with brash abandon. It's jarring enough to be snapped in and out of one's body, a phenomenon most women grow accustomed to through experience, resilience. Being sexualized has the remarkable effect of erasing even the most introspective of moments, leaving a woman utterly aware of nothing but her body, while at the same time making her a spectator of herself. But while every woman I know has been cat-called enough to land up on that hot tin roof, or yanked off her train of thought by some whistling dimwit, my brown face pushes me into the region of the unknown. I am left in a place uninhabited by white sisters, mothers, wives, where common courtesy takes a back seat to wild inspiration. I am uncharted territory, ripe for the conquest.

Hearing the word *India* from a stranger leaves me feeling naked and raw, as though something sacred in me has been cheapened through exposure. The word becomes insulting rolling off certain tongues, the poison of intent harder to trace back to "Pssst . . . Indi" than it is to "nice ass." It's harder to yell back at.

But that's what we're known for, we Indian women: bent heads and shut mouths, quiet grace, the Eastern-girl works. I've seen it so many times before, grown up with it hanging over me like a shadow I would eventually step into and unwillingly claim. Men used to follow my mother through the supermarket, mesmerized at the vegetable court, drooling through the detergents. They drew hearts on her palm at the city dump and made her promise not to wash them off before they let her pass through the gates, curiously blind to the rest of her cargo—me and my brother. They chatted with her at our soccer games, small talk leading to a rush of questions. "Where are you from? You're so unusual looking. You're really quite beautiful . . ." this last part said with a furtive glance in her direction. "India," she would mutter, looking away, a cool weight pressing an invisible screen over her eyes. The same heaviness dulled her eyes sometimes while she cooked or, later, in our nighttime bath ritual. It was a look that hung between boredom and frustration, a thin pulse of anger running through it. But my mother never said anything to these men, who would wait for a thank you, a smile, some sort of acknowledgment. "Why don't you ever smile when people tell you you're pretty?" I asked her once, embarrassed by her rudeness. She never answered me either.

Was she weak? Submissive? Clueless? I can't say that about my mother, She of the Wicked Wit and Ever-Dicing Tongue, an Indian version of a pistol-packing mama, sharpshooting and ready for any showdown. In my house, we know my mother is angry when she yells and, worse, disdainfully apathetic when she is silent, leaving us to boil in our own stew. But the intent behind my mother's deadly quiet, a calm I've seen replayed across the features of many of my other female relatives, isn't often recognized by American men. It's our faces, and our supposed mystery, that they tap into.

My late-teens realization about the powers of mystery, or lack thereof, was followed by the keenest silence my lips have ever observed. Just the mention of my "exotic looks" could shut me up for days on end, a phenomenon previously unwitnessed. Yet contrary to my hasty logic (mute girl = bored guy), my silence only perpetuated the enigma, adding the brute element of interpretation. "I think you're avoiding me," I heard at parties, often only hours after being introduced to a guy. "You're scared of our connection, right? I know you can feel it. I felt it the minute I laid eyes on you." And here it was again, the bond, the miracle, the connection associated with my face, the need to be led into whatever temple I had available. I saw desire thrown back to me in fragments of Taj Mahal, *Kamasutra,* womanly wiles. I felt my body turn into a dark country, my silence permission to colonize.

Next time, I will undress in the middle of the room. I will show you the scar of nightmares on my inner thigh and tuck my vision behind your eyelids. This is what you will remember when you wake sweating at night: the sickened Braille of my skin, the emptiness behind my eyes, the blindness of your desire.

Battle tactics—swing hard and low, use the force of motion. My brother taught me that around the time he bought me a thread bracelet for "protection against freaks." I have a mediocre right hook and a prize-fighting tongue, and at age twenty I storm the fort, beginning an all-out war against anything mysterious in me. I begin to talk. Really talk. From the moment I encounter a man, my mouth becomes a vicious running motor, spewing forth indelectable information at a rapid pace. Pauses, silences and ever-sneaky meaningful-eye-contact moments become the perfect stage for an update on my bowel movements and skin abrasions. I curse loudly and often enough to leave me free of a docile stereotype. Too much information becomes my best defense against mystery, rattling off my own lid and investigating my contents in front of anyone who dares to watch. Laden with the ammunition of bodily functions and lewd neuroses, I wreck any sacred shrine I could possibly hold inside me, leaving both me and my audience standing in awkward rubble. With each demolition I am chatterboxing, punching behind my words, swinging fast and hard into conversation with my vicious tongue. With each demolition I am breathless, tired, terrified of being caught off guard.

"I can't stop talking," I confess to Laura over the phone. "I never know where the conversation is going to go." I was exhausted, bone bitten, weary of any man I met, on edge with those I already knew. Every part of my body had been itemized into comedic value, and a mere glance would set me smacking any tender portion into a window display, a caricature.

"I know," Laura said quietly. "I'm worried about you. I don't recognize you sometimes." I was hardening inside, a thick callus growing over my ribs. Any hint that I might soften for a minute, crave something kind, threw me into a panic. I knew she was right. I had become no more than a jumble of body parts, a facade raised in perfect opposition to the white man's Indian woman. "I don't recognize me either," I told her.

And that may be the one sticky truth I have to hold on to: I am not so easy to recognize. I am not so easy to taste, to sample or to know. But this truth, far from being an elusive beckoning to an outsider, or one last boundary for the brave to cross, is a mystery that is only mine. It's the puzzle of how to let myself evolve in a world that will never stop assuming my identity.

In trying to be anything but a brown face, an exotic myth, I almost lost the best part of who I am. I dissected myself into a jumble of Indian and American parts, deeming all things Indian as seductive and weak, and trying to find salvation in being an untouchable "lewd American." And yet, after all of my talking and muting, and general abusing of my body, nothing outside of me had changed. Even if I had opened my mouth and poured every last bit of myself into shifting perceptions and the rest of the cosmos, I was, am and will always be seen as "an Indian woman." So the terror for me is also the one realization that offers me hope: I can't change the reactions that my face triggers. It's not my battle to fight.

I also know that *my* Indian woman isn't the shared secret some men imply, with their hissing "Indis," their darting eyes and spice-hungry lips. She isn't the love of curry or the cool crush of silk beneath greedy palms or "chai tea" served redundantly and by the gallon at Starbucks.

My Indian woman is a work in progress. I find her in the grumbling of my daily subway commute, in the damp green smell of coriander leaves and in late-night drives in my truck. She resides in the thousand small deaths my parents lived through to part from their mother country, in the survival skills they have taught me and in the legendary powers of silence. My Indian woman is not the history of submission, but the history of resilience, of beginning again. It's this woman who is at the center of me, the one the men on the street will never see: this woman who is simultaneously on fire and rising from the ashes.

klaus barbie,
and other dolls i'd like to see
susan jane gilman

For decades, Barbie has remained torpedo-titted, open-mouthed, tippy-toed and vagina-less in her cellophane coffin—and, ever since I was little, she has threatened me.

Most women I know are nostalgic for Barbie. "Oh," they coo wistfully, "I used to *loooove* my Barbies. My girlfriends would come over, and we'd play for hours . . . "

Not me. As a child, I disliked the doll on impulse; as an adult, my feelings have actually fermented into a heady, full-blown hatred.

My friends and I never owned Barbies. When I was young, little girls in my New York City neighborhood collected "Dawns." Only seven inches high, Dawns were, in retrospect, the underdog of fashion dolls. There were four in the collection: Dawn, dirty-blond and appropriately smug; Angie, whose name and black hair allowed her to pass for Italian or Hispanic; Gloria, a redhead with bangs and green eyes (Irish, perhaps, or a Russian Jew?); and Dale, a black doll with a real afro.

Oh, they had their share of glitzy frocks—the tiny wedding dress, the gold lamé ball gown that shredded at the hem. And they had holes punctured in the bottoms of their feet so you could impale them on the model's stand of the "Dawn Fashion Stage" (sold separately), press a button and watch them revolve jerkily around the catwalk. But they also had "mod" clothes like white go-go boots and a multicolored dashiki outfit called "Sock It to Me" with rose-colored sunglasses. Their hair came in different lengths and—although probably only a six-year-old doll fanatic could discern this—their facial expressions and features were indeed different. They were as diverse as fashion dolls could be in 1972, and in this way, I realize now, they were slightly subversive.

Of course, at that age, my friends and I couldn't spell subversive, let alone wrap our minds around the concept. But we sensed intuitively that Dawns were more democratic than Barbies. With their different colors and equal sizes, they were closer to what we looked like. We did not find this consoling—for we hadn't yet learned that our looks were something that required consolation. Rather, our love of Dawns was an offshoot of our own healthy egocentrism. We were still at that stage in our childhood when little girls want to be everything special, glamorous and wonderful—and believe they can be.

As a six-year-old, I remember gushing, "I want to be a ballerina, and a bride, and a movie star, and a model, and a queen . . . " To be sure, I was a disgustingly girly girl. I twirled. I skipped. I actually wore a tutu to school. (I am not kidding.) For a year, I refused to wear blue. Whenever the opportunity presented itself, I dressed up in my grandmother's pink chiffon nightgowns and rhinestone necklaces and paraded around the apartment like the princess of the universe. I dressed like my Dawn dolls—and dressed my Dawn dolls like me. It was a silly, fabulous narcissism—but one that sprang from a crucial self-love. These dolls were part of my fantasy life and an extension of my ambitions. Tellingly, my favorite doll was Angie, who had dark brown hair, like mine.

But at some point, most of us prima ballerinas experienced a terrible turning point. I know I did. I have an achingly clear memory of myself, standing before a mirror in all my finery and jewels, feeling suddenly ridiculous and miserable. *Look at yourself,* I remember thinking acidly. *Nobody will ever like you.* I could not have been older than eight. And then later, another memory: my friend Allison confiding in me, "The kids at my school, they all hate my red hair." Somewhere, somehow, a message seeped into our consciousness telling us that we weren't good enough to be a bride or a model or a queen or anything because we weren't pretty enough. And this translated into not smart enough or likable enough, either.

Looks, girls learn early, collapse into a metaphor for everything else. They quickly become the defining criteria for our status and our worth. And somewhere along the line, we stop believing in our own beauty and its dominion. Subsequently, we also stop believing in the power of our minds and our bodies.

Barbie takes over.

Barbie dolls had been around long before I was born, but it was precisely around the time my friends and I began being evaluated on our "looks" that we became aware of the role Barbie played in our culture.

Initially, my friends and I regarded Barbies with a sort of vague disdain. With their white-blond hair, burnt orange "Malibu" skin, unblinking turquoise eyes and hot-pink convertibles, Barbie dolls represented a world utterly alien to us. They struck us as clumsy, stupid, overly obvious. They were clearly somebody else's idea of a doll—and a doll meant for vapid girls in the suburbs. Dawns, my friend Julie and I once agreed during a sleepover, were far more hip.

But eventually, the message of Barbie sunk in. Literally and metaphorically, Barbies were bigger than Dawns. They were a foot high. They merited more plastic! More height! More visibility! And unlike Dawns, which were pulled off the market in the mid-'70s, Barbies were ubiquitous and perpetual bestsellers.

We urban, Jewish, black, Asian and Latina girls began to realize slowly and painfully that if you didn't look like Barbie, you didn't fit in. Your status was diminished. You were less beautiful, less valuable, less worthy. *If you didn't look like Barbie, companies would discontinue you.* You simply couldn't compete.

I'd like to think that, two decades later, my anger about this would have cooled off—not heated up. (I mean, it's a *doll* for chrissake. Get over it.) The problem, however, is that despite all the flag-waving about multiculturalism and girls' self-esteem these days, I see a new generation of little girls receiving the same message I did twenty-five years ago, courtesy of Mattel. I'm currently a "big sister" to a little girl who recently moved here from Mexico. When I first began spending time with her, she drew pictures of herself as she is: a beautiful seven-year-old with café au lait skin and short black hair. Then she began playing with Barbies. Now she draws pictures of both herself and her mother with long, blond hair. "I want long hair," she sighs, looking woefully at her drawing.

A coincidence? Maybe, but Barbie is the only toy in the Western world that human beings actively try to mimic. Barbie is not just a children's doll; it's an adult cult and an aesthetic obsession. We've all seen the evidence. During Barbie's thirty-fifth anniversary, a fashion magazine ran a "tribute to Barbie," using live models posing as dolls. A New York museum held a "Barbie retrospective," enshrining Barbie as a pop artifact—at a time when most human female pop artists continue to work in obscurity. Then there's Pamela Lee. The Barbie

Halls of Fame. The websites, the newsletters, the collectors clubs. The woman whose goal is to transform herself, via plastic surgery, into a real Barbie. Is it any wonder then that little girls have been longing for generations to "look like Barbie"—and that the irony of this goes unchallenged?

For this reason, I've started calling Barbie dolls "Klaus Barbie dolls" after the infamous Gestapo commander. For I now clearly recognize what I only sensed as a child. This "pop artifact" is an icon of Aryanism. Introduced after the second world war, in the conservatism of the Eisenhower era (and rumored to be modeled after a German prostitute by a man who designed nuclear warheads), Barbies, in their "innocent," "apolitical" cutesiness, propagate the ideals of the Third Reich. They ultimately succeed where Hitler failed: They instill in legions of little girls a preference for whiteness, for blond hair, blue eyes and delicate features, for an impossible *über*figure, perched eternally and submissively in high heels. In the Cult of the Blond, Barbies are a cornerstone. They reach the young, and they reach them quickly. *Barbie, Barbie!* The Aqua song throbs. *I'm a Barbie girl!*

It's true that, in the past few years, Mattel has made an effort to create a few slightly more p.c. versions of its best-selling blond. Walk down the aisle at Toys-R-Us (and they wonder why kids today can't spell), and you can see a few boxes of American Indian Barbie, Jamaican Barbie, Cowgirl Barbie. Their skin tone is darker and their outfits ethnicized, but they have the same Aryan features and the same "tell-me-anything-and-I'll-believe-it" expressions on their plastic faces. Ultimately, their packaging reinforces their status as "Other." These are "special" and "limited" edition Barbies, the labels announce: clearly *not* the standard.

And, Barbie's head still pops off with ease. Granted, this makes life a little sweeter for the sadists on the playground (there's always one girl who gets more pleasure out of destroying Barbie than dressing her), but the real purpose is to make it easier to swap your Barbies' Lilliputian ball gowns. Look at the literal message of this: Hey, girls, a head is simply a neck plug, easily disposed of in the name of fashion. Lest anyone think I'm nit-picking here, a few years ago, a "new, improved" Talking Barbie hit the shelves and created a brouhaha because one of the phrases it parroted was *Math is hard.* Once again, the cerebrum took a backseat to "style." Similarly, the latest "new, improved" Barbie simply trades in one impossible aesthetic for another: The bombshell has now become the waif. Why? According to a Mattel spokesperson, a Kate Moss figure is better suited for today's fashions. Ah, such an improvement.

Now, I am not, as a rule, anti-doll. Remember, I once wore a tutu and collected the entire Dawn family myself. I know better than to claim that dolls are nothing but sexist gender propaganda. Dolls can be a lightning rod for the imagination, for companionship, for learning. And they're *fun*—something that must never be undervalued.

But dolls often give children their first lessons in what a society considers valuable—and beautiful. And so I'd like to see dolls that teach little girls something more than fashion-consciousness and self-consciousness. I'd like to see dolls that expand girls' ideas about what is beautiful instead of constricting them. And how about a few role models instead of runway models as playmates? If you can make a Talking Barbie, surely you can make a Working Barbie. If you can have a Barbie Townhouse, surely you can have a Barbie business. And if you can construct an entire Barbie world out of pink and purple plastic, surely you can construct some "regular" Barbies that are more than white and blond. And remember, Barbie's only a doll! So give it a little more inspired goofiness, some real *pizzazz!*

Along with Barbies of all shapes and colors, here are some Barbies I'd personally like to see:

Dinner Roll Barbie. A Barbie with multiple love handles, double chin, a real, curvy belly, generous tits and ass and voluminous thighs to show girls that voluptuousness is also beautiful. Comes with miniature basket of dinner rolls, bucket o' fried chicken, tiny Entenmann's walnut ring, a brick of Sealtest ice cream, three packs of potato chips, a T-shirt reading "Only the Weak Don't Eat" and, of course, an appetite.

Birkenstock Barbie. Finally, a doll made with horizontal feet and comfortable sandals. Made from recycled materials.

Bisexual Barbie. Comes in a package with Skipper and Ken.

Butch Barbie. Comes with short hair, leather jacket, "Silence=Death" T-shirt, pink triangle buttons, Doc Martens, pool cue and dental dams. Packaged in cardboard closet with doors flung wide open. Barbie Carpentry Business sold separately.

Our Barbies, Ourselves. Anatomically correct Barbie, both inside and out, comes with spreadable legs, her own speculum, magnifying glass and detailed diagrams of female anatomy so that little girls can learn about their bodies in a friendly, nonthreatening way. Also included: tiny Kotex, booklets on sexual responsibility. Accessories such as contraceptives, sex toys, expanding uterus with fetus at various stages of development and breast pump are all optional, underscoring that each young women has the right to choose what she does with her own Barbie.

Harley Barbie. Equipped with motorcyle, helmet, shades. Tattoos are non-toxic and can be removed with baby oil.

Body Piercings Barbie. Why should Earring Ken have all the fun? Body Piercings Barbie comes with changeable multiple earrings, nose ring, nipple rings, lip ring, navel ring and tiny piercing gun. Enables girls to rebel, express alienation and gross out elders without actually having to puncture themselves.

Blue Collar Barbie. Comes with overalls, protective goggles, lunch pail, UAW membership, pamphlet on union organizing and pay scales for women as compared to men. Waitressing outfits and cashier's register may be purchased separately for Barbies who are holding down second jobs to make ends meet.

Rebbe Barbie. So why not? Women rabbis are on the cutting edge in Judaism. Rebbe Barbie comes with tiny satin *yarmulke,* prayer shawl, *tefillin,* silver *kaddish* cup, Torah scrolls. Optional: tiny *mezuzah* for doorway of Barbie Dreamhouse.

B-Girl Barbie. Truly fly Barbie in midriff-baring shirt and baggy jeans. Comes with skateboard, hip hop accessories and plenty of attitude. Pull her cord, and she says things like, "I don't *think* so," "Dang, get outta my face" and "You go, girl." Teaches girls not to take shit from men and condescending white people.

The Barbie Dream Team. Featuring Quadratic Equation Barbie (a Nobel Prize–winning mathematician with her own tiny books and calculator), Microbiologist Barbie (comes with petri dishes, computer and Barbie Laboratory) and Bite-the-Bullet Barbie, an anthropologist with pith helmet, camera, detachable limbs, fake blood and kit for performing surgery on herself in the outback.

Transgender Barbie. Formerly known as G.I. Joe.

susan jane gilman   21

the butt:
its politics, its profanity, its power
erin j. aubry

Unlike the face with its mixture of trickery and pretense, the behind has a genuine sincerity that comes quite simply from the fact that we cannot control it.

—*Jean-Luc Herring,* Rear View:
A Brief But Elegant History of the Bottom

I have a big butt. Not wide hips, not a preening, weightlifting-enhanced butt thrust up like a chin, not an occasionally saucy rear that throws coquettish glances at strangers when it's in a good mood and withdraws like a turtle when it's not. Every day, my butt wears *me*—tolerably well, I'd like to think—and has ever since I came full up on puberty about twenty years ago and had to wrestle it back into the Levi's 501s it had barely put up with anyway. My butt hollered, *I'm mad!* at that point and hasn't calmed down since.

But my butt is quite my advocate: introducing me at parties, granting me space among strangers when I am too timorous to ask for it. It retreats with me only when I am at my gloomiest, when it has no choice, and even then it does so reluctantly, a little sullenly, crying out from beneath the most voluminous pants I own: *When can we go back?* It has been my greatest trial and the core of my latest, greatest epiphany of self-acceptance, which came only after a day of clothes shopping that yielded the Big Three—pants, skirt, another pair of pants. (Floating out the mall doors with bags in hand, I thought, *Veni, vidi, vici!*) I think of my butt as a secret weapon that can be activated without anyone knowing: In the middle of an earnest conversation with a just-met man, I shift in my seat or, if I am standing, lean on one hip, as though to momentarily rest the other side. *Voilà!* My points are suddenly more salient, my words more muscled, and the guy never knew what hit him.

I have come to realize that my butt makes much more than a declaration at parties and small gatherings. Its sheer size makes it politically incorrect in an age in which everything is shrinking— government, computers, distances between people. In a new small-world order, it is hopelessly passé. Of course, not fitting—literally and otherwise—has always been a fact of life for black women, who unfairly or not are regarded as archetypes of the protuberant butt, or at least the spiritual heirs to its African origins.

Now, many people will immediately cry that black women have been stereotyped this way, and they'd be right—but I'd add that the stereotype is less concerned with body shape than with the sum total of black female sexuality (read: potency), which, while not nearly as problematic as its male counterpart, still makes a whole lot of America uneasy. Thus, an undisguised butt is a reminder of that fact, and I have spent an inordinate number of mornings buried in my closet trying to decide whether I should remind other people, and myself, of yet another American irresolution about black folks.

erin j. aubry   **23**

Women tend to talk freely about butt woes—it is simply another point along the whole food-exercise-diet continuum that dominates so many of our conversations, especially in my hometown of Los Angeles. But black women do not so readily consign their butts to this sort of pathology, because that is like condemning an integral part of ourselves; even *talking* disparagingly about butts, as if they existed separately from the rest of the body, is pointless and mildly amusing to many of us.

Sounds like this would be the healthiest attitude of all—but it's not the end of the story, says Gail Elizabeth Wyatt, an African-American psychologist at the University of California at Los Angeles who recently published a book about black female sexuality, *Stolen Women: Reclaiming Our Sexuality, Taking Back Our Lives.* As you might guess from the title, her book—the first comprehensive study of its kind—is an all-out assault on a host of misperceptions and stereotypes about black women, many of which Wyatt believes are rooted in slavery and notions of sexual servitude. Not to my surprise, one survey she cites found that the black woman/big butt association is among the most enduring of female physical stereotypes; it was the only thing the majority of the women polled—black, white and other—agreed upon as being characteristic of black women.

All right, I ask, but don't most black women *have* good-sized butts? Is that, in and of itself, a bad thing? Wyatt says no, explaining that what she objects to is not the butt per se, but how it is negatively perceived by the mainstream and by ourselves. We have all, she says, effectively reduced the black woman to either the "she devil," a purely sexual object, butt prominently in place, or the long-suffering "workhorse" and caretaking "mammy" types, who have no real sexual presence to speak of. To complicate things further, Wyatt says that American culture is increasingly sexualizing its young. "Unfortunately, the very sexual image has moved from magazine pages to school campuses," she says. "But when, say, Madonna puts on that image, it's understood that it's an image. She can move between being a ho' and being a film genius. We don't move that easily." In other words, black women have little or no context to work with.

I recognize the truth of black women's unfortunate history, but I am nonetheless dispirited. If in fact we spend so much time battling myths other people created, if we are always put on the butt defensive, as it were, we'll never have the psychic space to assess how we *really* feel about wearing Lycra—and a woman with a sizable butt *must* have an opinion about it. Another one of Wyatt's findings was that black women, when it comes to the body parts they like most, tend to focus on hair, nails and feet; everything in between is virtually ignored. "We're not dealing with our bodies at all," Wyatt says, by way of interpretation. "We're very conscious of the fact that our image is so bad. We're not dealing with ourselves individually."

The moment of butt reckoning always comes with a mirror—if it's a three-way mirror, you're pretty much standing at the gates of hell. It is a bad day. I freeze my eyes on a spot in the middle mirror that's well above my waist, with no more gut left to suck in or butt left to pull under. I'm trapped with my own excess, which commands my attention though I will myself not to look. The butt swallows my peripheral vision and sops up reserve confidence like it's gravy; it doesn't merely reject my hopes for a size six, it explodes them with a nearly audible laugh that forces the ill-fated jeans back into an ignominious heap around my ankles. My butt looms triumphant, like Ali dancing over Liston: *Don't you know who I am?*

My butt refuses to follow the current trend of black marginalization, nor does it care that we are heading into the millennium with the most collective uncertainty as a people since we first stumbled up out of the dark holds of the slave ships and onto American soil. It proclaims from the miserable depths of the sofa where I lie prone, in a stirring Maya Angelou rumble: *I rise! I rise! Still I rise!* My butt has a reserve of esteem and then some; like the brain, it may even have profound, uncharted capacities to heal.

It also has a social conscience. When I pass a similarly endowed woman in public I relax into a feeling of extended family; I know we are flesh and blood, not Frank Frazetta cartoons.

Recently I got a very gratifying bit of news from an African friend who called to say she had spotted supermodel Tyra Banks in the Century City Bloomingdale's. I was mildly curious: What was Tyra like? There was a significant pause. "Erin," my friend said solemnly, "she has a *big butt.*"

"Oh," I said. "You mean, big by model standards."

"No, no. I mean she has a *big* butt."

"What?"

"Yes. Let me tell you." The finality in her voice had a residue of awe. "A Big Butt."

It took a few moments for it to sink in: She was one of us. She was a famous model. *And* she was rumored to be dating Tiger Woods. I could have wept.

As has happened in many other instances, black people have taken a white-created pejorative of a black image—a purely external defini- tion of themselves—and made it worse. Big butts thus offend a lot of black people as being not just improper, but low-class and ghettoish, the result of consuming too much fried chicken and fatback. "Look at that!" one black woman will hiss in the direction of another shuf- fling past, wearing bike shorts with abandon. *"Mmm-mmm-mmmh.* Criminal. Now you know she needs to do something about that."

In the mind of the black upwardly mobile, the butt may connote a dangerous lack of self-analysis, a loose, unrestricted appetite for food, sex, dances like the Atomic Dog. It's like having a big mouth or no table manners.

Now, we will accept, even expect, generous butts in a select group of black people—blues and gospel singers, for example, whose emotional excess can and should be physically manifest—but for most of us who are trying to Make It, butts are the first to hit a glass ceiling.

I have a friend who's been trying to elevate the butt's social status by publishing a classy pinup calendar called "The Darker Image." It's the black answer to the *Sports Illustrated* version—airbrushed skies, tropical settings—but its models are notably endowed with butts that Kathy Ireland could only dream of, butts that sit up higher than the surf rolling over them and render a thong bikini ridiculously beside the point. My friend said it was hell to get distribution from mainstream bookstores—black, by definition, is a specialty market, black beauty off the retail radar completely—but he finally got it with Waldenbooks and Barnes & Noble. It's a small but potentially significant victory for the butt, a public admission of its beauty and influence that hasn't been seen since the days of the "Hottentot Venus." I want to give America the big payback: posing next year as Miss January.

Let's face it: Sexual sophistication is one of those black stereotypes, like dancing prowess, that is not entirely bad. It implies a healthy attunement to life, a knowingness. At the age of thirteen or so, though becoming acutely butt-conscious, I also became aware of the implicit power in a figure, how it shaped an attitude and informed a simple walk around the block. In sloping my back and elongating my stride, my butt was literally thrusting me into the world, and I sensed that I had better live up to the costume or it would eventually wear me to death. For me this didn't mean promiscuity at all, but a full-blown statement of the fact that I *stood out,* that I made a statement that might begin with my body, but that also included budding literary proclivities, powers of observation, silent crushes on boys sitting two rows over. Which is not to say—which is never to say—that my shifting center of gravity wasn't cause for alarm. I started a lifelong pattern of vacillating between repulsion and satisfaction: My butt branded me, but it also made me more womanly, not to mention more identifiably black. I may have been a shade too light for comfort, but my butt confirmed my true ethnic identity.

As one of those physical characteristics of black people that tend to differ significantly from whites', like hair texture and skin color, the butt demarcates, but also, in the context of the history of racial oppression, stands as an object of ridicule. Yet unlike hair and skin, the butt is stubborn, immutable—it can't be hot-combed or straightened or bleached into submission. It does not assimilate; it never took a slave name. Accentuating a butt is thumbing a nose at the establishment, like subverting a pinstriped suit with waist-length dreadlocks. And the butt's blatantly sexual nature makes it seem that much more belligerent in its refusal to go away, to lie down and play dead. About the only thing we can do is cover it up, but even those attempts can inadvertently showcase the butt by imparting a certain intrigue. (Hmmm, what is that thing sticking out of the back of her jacket?)

It was tricky, but I absorbed the better aspects of the butt stereotypes, especially the Tootsie-Roll walk—the wave, the undulation in spite of itself, the leisurely antithesis of the spring in the step. I liked the walk and how it defied that silly runway gait, with the hips thrust too far forward and the arms dangling back in empty air. That is a pure apology for butts, a literal bending over backward to admonish the body for any bit of unruliness. Having a butt is more than unruly, it's immoral—the modern-day equivalent of a woman eating a Ding Dong in public.

But there are those cases where a healthy butt is an essential endowment. Take Selena, the *tejana* superstar: Would she have been as big a phenom if not for her prodigious, cocktail-table behind, the whispers of possible African origins surrounding it, the mystery? Mexicans complained when Jennifer Lopez was cast as the lead in the Selena bio-pic two years ago, but what else could Hollywood have done? A butt was of prime concern, and Lopez's butt, courtesy of her Puerto Rican heritage, was accordingly considered.

What impressed me most was how Selena so neatly countered that butt—which was routinely fitted in Lycra pants and set off, like dynamite, by cropped tops—with a wholesome sweetness, a kind of wonder at finding herself in such clothes in the first place. She strutted her stuff, but more dutifully than nastily; she was the physical parallel but the actual opposite of young R&B singers like Foxy Brown and Lil' Kim, who infuse new blood into that most enduring (but least discussed) black-woman image of the sexually available skeezer.

Grounded in butt size, this image is too potent to be complicated by wholesome sweetness or benign intent. No matter the age or station of the black woman who dares to wear revealing dress—Foxy Brown, Aretha Franklin, En Vogue, hell, even octogenarian Lena Horne—they're all variations on a dominant theme of sexiness that is hard-wearing, full but embittered somehow; sexiness with a worldly sneer, that dangles a cigarette from its lips and rubs the fatigue from its eyes before it is fully awake. It's Sister Christian vs. the streetwalking Creole Lady Marmalade. Selena bounded from one end of the stage to the other ruminating on the grand possibilities of love, embodied in her boundless rear; Foxy Brown gyrates her hips and grinds all possibility into dust. One seeks knowledge of eros; the other already knows. To the world at large, the black butt tells the entire sordid story.

Black men are famous for their audacity with women, even more famous for their predilection for healthy butts. The celebratory butt songs of the last ten years testify: "Da Butt," "Rump Shaker," "Baby Got Back," more brazen versions of such '70s butt anthems as "Shake Your Booty," "Shake Your Groove Thing" and, of course, the seminal "Bertha Butt Boogie." These songs are plenty affirming—especially the irreverent "Baby Got Back," in which Sir Mix-A-Lot rightly condemns *Cosmo* magazine *and* Jane Fonda for deifying thinness—but they are also vaguely troubling, because most of the praises are being sung these days by rappers, many of whom are as quick to denigrate black women as they are to celebrate them; indeed, some of these artists don't bother to distinguish between the two. As pop music has segregated itself, the ruling butt democracy of the dance floor (over which the explicitly inoffensive KC and the Sunshine Band presided) has given way to a butt oligarchy run by self-proclaimed thugz and niggaz 4 life. Call me classist, but my butt deserves a wider audience. So to speak.

But sometimes all that matters is a captive audience, and black men rarely disappoint. Recently, as I was walking in comfortable anonymity through a clean section of Hollywood, I passed by a homeless black man pushing a shopping cart. He took a look at me, stopped dead in his tracks and shouted in a single breath: "Honey, don't let the buggy fool you! I got means! How about I take you to lunch? Are you married?" I didn't take him up on it, even after he trailed me for half a block, but I had to admire his nerve; I was in fact grateful for it. For all the much-discussed black angst about our war between the sexes, approbation from black men is still very much food for my soul, even from the ones with no means. It breaks the lull of assimilation and makes me remember that, for all the dressing-room nightmares I've lived and will live, I'd rather be successful at fitting comfortably into my own skin than into clothes meant to cover someone else's.

Recently, I had an epiphanic flash: My figure is still the soul of the feminine ideal. It *has* been through the ages. In the '90s it has merely run afoul of this trend of casting what is good and perfectly logical as something suddenly without currency, something that was once a nice idea, but . . . (cf. affirmative action, civil rights, TVs without remotes).

I'll admit: For all of my hand wringing, I'm growing accustomed to my butt. It's a strange and wonderful development of the last six years or so—as I've gotten heavier I've actually gotten more comfortable with how I look. Perhaps it's a function of maturity or a realization that fashions aren't likely to bulk up anytime soon, but I'm much more inclined to reveal myself now than I ever was before. I've finally concluded that there's no clever way around my butt, as there never seems to be a clever way around the truth—whatever you try leads to the most fantastic lies. In the interest of honesty, my butt now gets accent—a lot of stretch, slouch pants, skirts that fall below the navel, platform shoes that punch up my walk. I don't do big and shapeless anymore, not even in the complete privacy of home. I have finally glimpsed the full, unadulterated length of me and don't want to obfuscate the image any more than I already do on bad mornings. I must burn myself into my own memory; my butt is more than happy to help.

So what if America, in its infinite generosity, wants to help me get rid of this bothersome behind with its *Self* magazines and *L.A. Times* "Celebrity Workouts" and the demonizing of complex carbohydrates. More and more, my response has been: I *am* going to eat cake. I *will* wear the things that fit—whatever ones I can find—with impunity. I *will* walk this way. I don't have an issue, I have a groove thing. Kiss my you know what.

the skinny on small
diane sepanski

I was eleven years old in 1978 when Randy Newman's song "Short People" became a hit. I measured exactly four feet, nine inches; I know this because every year on my birthday my father marked my height on the cold grey pillar that supported his basement workroom. Every year I looked forward to the moment when, after Carvel ice cream cake and presents, Dad would chart my physical journey toward adulthood in black Magic Marker. These longitudinal readings are faint now, and the last of them remains the clearest: By 1980 I had sprouted up to a full five-foot-one.

I don't know why my dad and I stopped our ritual. Perhaps my impending entrance into high school signaled a symbolic denouement: Now I was to put aside childish ways, put on makeup and slowly prepare to enter the world, standing tall on high heels. Or maybe it was because, by the tender age of thirteen, I was already hoofing high heels, making precise proportions, if not beside the point, then at least a lot less imperative. I already knew I was short. And I knew I didn't like it.

I'm short and I'm skinny and I'm small-boned. *Petite* is the euphemism. *Little, small, dainty, dinky, elfin, diminutive, miniature, pygmy, Lilliputian, wee, tiny, teeny, teeny-weeny* and *itsy-bitsy* are some of the synonyms. Notice the list degenerating into "baby talk"; the next word in Roget's catalogue is *baby,* and it just gets worse from there: *toy, portable, compact, poky, cramped, no room to breathe, narrow, runty, puny, weak, petty, trifling, inconsiderable, one-horse.* . . until finally we get to the crux of the matter. The last synonym on the list is *unimportant.*

Girls learn early what's important. When I was six I thought it was the height of hilarity that when I tried to make my Barbie walk, her impossibly long and coltish legs inevitably caused her to topple backwards. At thirty, I can joke that the only way I'd ever look like Barbie is if I shrunk her in the dryer and then amputated those coltish legs at the knee. But in 1978, before the concept of *grrrls* was invented, it was desperately important to me to fit in with all the bigger, more developed girls who seemed like Barbies to my Midge. I wasn't the smallest girl in my class—but it was close, and the distance between who was popular and who was distinctly, absolutely and positively *not* could be—and was—precisely measured. Bigger was better (as long as it wasn't too big, but I did say *precisely,* didn't I?); bigger, in short, was power.

Now power in 1978 in my coed Catholic grammar school in my small Long Island town was a lot of things, and most of them spelled *boys.* For those of you who may not know Long Island, it's a place where kids grow up fast. The race was on, and the track back then looked something like this: If you fit in, you were popular, and if you were popular, you got a boy, and the sooner you got a boy, the sooner you became a woman. You can understand, then, why I couldn't wait to grow up. Pun intended. I waited while Megan and Kathleen and Doreen and Suzanne got their training bras and their periods. I waited while they pushed five-five, then five-six, then five-seven. I waited and watched while they played Seven Minutes in Heaven with the cool boys, the boys we all wanted, the boys who sniffed out the scent of approaching womanhood the way a police dog sniffs out drugs.

Still, I played the same game of adolescent dress-up we all did: feathered Farrah Fawcett hair, earth shoes, Bonne Bell Lip Smacker, ears pierced, eyelashes curled. But my velour top drooped on my slight shoulders like a flimsy excuse; when I looked in the mirror, all I saw was a girl looking back at me. This girl felt ethereal, insubstantial, unlikely. This girl got pelted with snowballs and didn't fight back. This girl didn't take up much room. She just looked at her shoes.

I want to tell you about Megan. She and I became best friends in about fourth or fifth grade. Megan was descended from what is probably a long line of raw-boned, chestnut-maned, strong Irish belles. By the time we reached eighth grade, Megan was five-seven, wide-shouldered yet slim-hipped, a couple of bra sizes ahead of me. She looked great in a bikini. Which is why, to the tune of endless cicadas invisibly whirring in a perfect blue sky, I was walking the two blocks to her house on Saturday morning. We would butter ourselves thoroughly with tanning oil and wait to see who "dropped by." Summer on Long Island was all about the perfect body, the perfect tan—and, of course, the perfect boy.

Megan was already stretched out on a deck chair when I arrived. I would say she looked like Xena, Warrior Princess, except that goddess didn't yet exist. So let me settle for an angel: one of Charlie's. I was wearing my favorite sky-blue-trimmed-with-white terry cloth matching shorts and top set over my bathing suit. For some reason I went inside their house, into the kitchen, and Megan followed. Megan's mom was sitting at the table; she looked me up and down and burst out laughing. "You're wearing a diaper," she said, and then Megan started laughing too. "Your shorts look like a diaper!" They snickered for a long time. I don't remember what I said, although I'm pretty sure I said nothing. I went back outside, my eyes squinting against the sunlight's stare, and fastidiously removed my ugly clothes in slow, deliberate motion, as if my body would somehow shatter with any sudden movement, as if I were made of glass.

How can I tell you what the space around Megan felt like? If I close my eyes, the feeling is still palpable—the way she moved through space; acted on it; occupied it; owned it; made molecules of air dance through her fingers. More than boy-attention, what Megan—and Doreen and Suzanne—possessed was a physical power I felt I would never have, no matter how much swimming, bike-riding, running, walking or playing I did. They took their bodies for granted, felt at home in them. What I perceived from those girls, the only word for it, is presence.

Whereas what I felt was a sort of absence: a hyperbolic diminishment conferred on me solely by virtue of my physical being, threatening to converge me to the vanishing point; to lead me, as does my dictionary, from smallness to scarcity to invisibility to—ultimately—disappearance.

Although this absence had always been viscerally defined for me by the visual juxtaposition between my body and those of other girls, and in truth, had begun way before puberty—begun, in fact, in another girl's kitchen, with another girl's mother commenting on my "birdlike" six-year-old appetite—it wasn't until adolescence that it took on a political dimension. I saw clearly society's equation between size and power, and I knew I fell on the wrong side of that equation: Mattel didn't manufacture petite Barbies. I could be Midge, or goofy Thelma from *Scooby Doo,* or Nancy Drew's best friend Bess, but I would always be the sidekick, the buddy, the second banana whose dumb name signaled her unattractive and inferior status. I wasn't just different, I was deficient. I would never be the star of my own show.

How did I know? Randy Newman told me: "Short people got/ no reason/ short people got/ no reason/ to live." So did the salesclerk at Macy's who, when I asked her if she carried that beautiful satin skirt in size two, replied, "I'm sure you can find something you like in the Juniors department." Even strangers felt the need to comment: "Just wait dear, you'll hit a growth spurt in your twenties, I'm sure." It wasn't big of me—maybe it was even a shortcoming—but I hated them, and I sure didn't like myself.

I could easily have disappeared. I had packed my small self in a box marked "fragile," the glass house of my body translucent and easily broken, but soon, without quite realizing why, I decided to throw stones and break out of my prison. My weapon of choice was the only thing big about me: my voice. Naturally loud, an alto by sixth grade, and a smart-ass by nature, I had always been a talker, had already been thrown out of class many times for my gabbing, but somewhere between sixth and eighth grades, the quality of this talk changed, became charged, vital and underscored with meaning in a way I only now understand. Suddenly, I became known for my "big mouth." I was talking, quite simply, to exist.

There were problems. It seems that some people, many of whom were boys, didn't like the fact that when they teased me about my size, I now had something to say about it. I had run into a new obstacle: machismo. We live in a world where anything "big" is seen as the province of men, including a big mouth. As a *small* woman I was twice removed from that most elemental of powers—brute strength—which men have conveniently defined as the basis of *all* power. Nonetheless, I posed a big threat. My existence, embodied in a new way, broke all the old rules of the schoolyard. I wasn't exactly running with the big boys, but I had claimed their swagger as my own, and it felt wild—like flying—like laughing out loud.

What I know now is how perilously close I came to letting others define my existence for me: I *became* small to measure up to society's limited vision of who I am. By opening up my big mouth, I grew into myself, filled myself, in a way I would not have thought possible back in those difficult adolescent years. I no longer wear high heels: At five feet, three-and-one-half inches, I am a large person with an absolutely huge appetite for life. Being born petite taught me to claim a different kind of power. But I'm lucky. I've chosen to work with words, to pursue a profession that doesn't emphasize brawn. For thousands of other women, women whose dreams are to become firefighters, to work in construction or to attend a military academy, size still matters. We need to open our big mouths for those women, to rewrite the definitions.

Big: *grand, substantial, considerable, respectable, weighty, ample, generous, voluminous, capacious, spacious, profound, deep, great in stature, tall, lofty, high, strong, mighty, powerful, influential, intense, superior, of consequence, of consideration, of importance, of concern, crucial, essential, pivotal, central, meaningful, worthwhile, to be taken seriously, not to be despised, not to be overlooked, valuable, significant, necessary, vital, indispensable, irreplaceable, key,*

world-shaking, earthshaking

noisy, loud

soaring, climbing, ascending.

becoming la
mujer

becoming la mujer
marisa navarro

I used to dream that Superwoman would fly into my life, her legs
unshaven and her hair cropped short. She would swoop me up and
take me somewhere that made me feel safe and beautiful—a place
far from the hell I knew as public high school. In this distant place,
I would feel sensual for the first time ever, without feeling dirty. No
one would assume I was destined to be a teenage mom, or that my
brown skin marked me as a criminal. I wouldn't be "too dark" or "too
fat," and my intelligence would never be compromised.

Those were ambitious goals for a Mexican-American girl growing up near East Los Angeles. Every year, the drill team girl had a kid,
then the prom queen. Pregnancy was so common it was almost a game
to guess who the next teenage mother would be. Still, East L.A. is the
only place I've lived where the scent of Aqua Net and overprocessed
hair mingles with the sounds of English, Spanish, Chinese, Korean
and Armenian. There was comfort in being surrounded by hundreds

of other brown people. I missed that when I went away to college and found my skin color and dark hair made me stand out in class.

I was one of the fortunate at my high school, shielded from some of Los Angeles's harshness by college prep classes. My parents stressed education all my life, so I focused on earning good grades, hoping they would be my ticket to a better life. But there was a price to pay. Since many of my female classmates wouldn't make it to graduation (pregnancy or lack of interest leading them to drop out), girls' actions became dichotomized into right and wrong. There were "good girls" (those who went to college) and "bad girls" (teenage mothers on welfare).

Early on, my parents reinforced that message, and there could be no margin of error. "It's out of love we tell you this, *mijita,*" they'd say. "Be quiet. Study hard. Don't have sex. Go to college, and then get married. A good daughter doesn't dress like a slut. A good daughter doesn't pierce or tattoo herself. A good daughter doesn't rock the boat." If I messed up, my whole future would be over. I must be a good *hijita.*

My parents also grew up in East L.A. I never told them what I faced at school, but I'm sure they knew. That made the parental leash even tighter. As an immigrant (my dad) and a first-generation American (my mom), they stressed hard work and success at any cost. It's a drive I don't think any person who is fourth-generation American or beyond can fully understand. Perhaps it's the stigma of the accent fresh in the memory, the blunter racism and the hard labor not even a distant memory. Either way, it fuels parents' determination that their children will not be like them.

In my family, being a good *hijita* meant more than simply being an obedient daughter. It also meant being desexualized. Being of mind but not of body. Wrapped in that word were my parents hopes for me—and for themselves. I was to transcend the racism they'd experienced and to surpass society's low expectations.

My father was the success story in the family, and he was proud of it. He came from a small town in Mexico, graduated from college in the United States and made lots of money. Somehow, my sister and I had to do even better than he had. On top of being supernaturally smart, we had to fulfill his macho idea of sensuality, a classic Madonna/whore tightrope that demanded we be attractive yet pure. We were expected to be skinny, have long hair and wear clothes that showed our womanliness. Yet, we had to carry this off in a way that let men know we were unavailable for sex.

Sex was the biggest threat to my parents' carefully laid plans. Having sex meant I'd impede my chances to succeed, to achieve an American dream greater than the one offered to my parents. It meant I'd inevitably get pregnant and become a statistic, trapped in a community that was slowly falling apart. My body (and what I did with it) could make or break our family's future. The concept of the body as a battleground had much more meaning than even the most radical feminist could conceive. I needed only to keep my legs tightly locked, and everything would be all right.

Eventually, the word *hijita* left a sour taste in my mouth. It meant I was my parents' daughter. I didn't belong to me.

When I hit puberty, my father took on a form of desexualization with me and my sister. Boys were not humans, but the makers of sperm, waiting to plant their seed in us. For some reason my father saw me as extra fertile ground that he was determined be kept fallow. The only way to accomplish this was to forbid boys into the house and into my social life. If a boy called, I was questioned about his intentions. My father would bend down, squint and stare into my eyes to make sure I wasn't lying.

To further the desexualization process, he inspected me before I went out. If I wore lipstick or a tight shirt that showed my breasts, I was criticized and called a slut. I tried being the dutiful, plain daughter, but still I lost. When I cut off my hair and started wearing baggy pants to avoid his scrutiny, my father called me a boy. Where was this invisible line that would win his acceptance? What did it take to be a good *hijita?*

Since I couldn't figure that out, I looked to my older sister. My father always had a special fondness for her. I think it was because she was just so smart—smarter than all the white kids. In high school, she defied him by experimenting with sexuality, sensuality and love. She proved she could be smart and sensual and have neither quality compromised. As an intelligent woman, she was unhappy learning about science and literature while knowing nothing about her body. She innocently assumed our father would be okay with this, since it didn't affect her grades.

Instead, he became enraged. Didn't she know that sex led to pregnancy and pregnancy led to welfare, which led to family dishonor? Although my sister didn't agree with his linear thinking, she was powerless to convince him otherwise. He would not have it. My sister became a bad *hijita* and was kicked out of the house. This terrified me; maybe *la familia* wasn't really about unconditional love after all. And if my sister and my father shared a special relationship that I would never have, what would happen to me if I did the same thing? I was too scared to find out.

I played out my teenage years like a script. More than anything, I felt I dressed in drag throughout high school, wearing clothes that would get boys to look at me, but only with vague interest. Avoiding male attention consumed my thoughts so much that men were all I thought about.

In the end, they won. I was constantly concerned that my outfits were too sensual. I had a hard time looking at my face in the mirror, much less the rest of my body. Everything was wrong with me.

Caught in a paradox, I was always dissatisfied. I hated that men were attracted to me, but I also hated that I didn't have big breasts or a thinner waistline. No guy wanted a fat, small-chested girl.

I lost all sense of ownership and control over my physical self. My memories of that script are vivid, too easy to relive:

Act I: First Year—(Sur)Real World 101

My math teacher walks around the room and then stops and leans his back against mine so that my head and breasts are flattened against the desk. Two boys sitting next to me laugh. I put my head down and silently swear that I'll stick quadratic equations up his ass. Eventually, I stop paying attention in class and drop from an A to barely a B. I chalk it up to the fact that I always hated math.

Act II: Sophomore Year—Boys Will Be Boys

A boy likes me and decides to show it by grabbing me every day. He does it when my back is facing him and I'm trying to be taken seriously. In the beginning, I yell that he's a fuckin' dick/asshole/no good motherfucker. *He smiles and grabs me again. Eventually, I stop reacting, hoping he'll go away if I don't pay attention to his games. He assumes that means I like it and grabs me even more. Sometimes I think I should fuck him to get it over with, because that's all he really wants. Maybe afterward he'll leave me alone. But I don't. Not because I love myself enough not to fuck an asshole, but because the thought of someone seeing me naked is terrifying.*

Act III: Junior Year—Honk If You're Horny

Trying to walk down the street with my head up has become the most political act of my teenage life. I dread major roads and busy intersections because men yell at me or stick out their tongues like deranged lizards. I hate how all they see is long hair and breasts, and how with each honk they take a piece of my self-esteem with them. These are the kind of men that stick silhouettes of women with big tits and tiny waists on their cars. These are the kind of men who smell estrogen and think fuck. *I start to hate everything that makes me look like a woman—the breasts, the hips, the long hair—because I'm getting lots of attention, but no self-esteem.*

Act IV: Senior Year—Stand by Your Man

By now I hate myself for turning men on, for being a "slut." All I want is for someone to love me for my mind. I'm tired of having my body picked apart by my father, being a virgin but made to feel like a whore. I figure since I'm already dirty, having sex won't make it any worse.

In bed, the boy I'm dating pulls my hair and pretends to slap me to make his dick harder. He calls me a slut and a ho'. I lie flat as a board, confused, scared and sexually unfulfilled. I let him fuck me without a condom, without birth control pills, nothing. My body is too dirty to be worth protecting against AIDS or pregnancy. Everything the men on the street and my father told me seems true.

One day the boy laughs and says that the first time he saw me, he thought I looked ugly because my skin was dark. He doesn't want to take me to the beach or lie down in the park because I could get tan again. Another time, he tells me to shut up because I sound "too Mexican." What race does he think I am? I ask. He smiles, caresses my face and tells me he doesn't like to think of me as Mexican. He means it as a compliment. At eighteen, I think if this is love, then maybe I was meant to be alone in the world after all.

Act V: Pomp and Circumstance

The most beautiful song I've ever heard. I collect my diploma like a trophy of war and run far away.

I left Los Angeles for Smith College in Northampton, Massachusetts, knowing the distance of a thousand miles had to release the parental leash. I wanted the power to create my identity, a power that I didn't have before. I purposely chose a women's college because I knew I needed time away from men.

School saved my mind and body. In college, I wasn't anyone's *hijita,* and I wouldn't be anyone's slut. I was able to come out of the closet, first to myself and a year later to everyone else. Women told me I was smart and beautiful; neither quality was ever questioned. When I took up smoking and drinking, I wasn't a bad *hijita.* Good and bad vanished, and I was *la mujer.* That phrase sounded beautiful and empowering to me.

At school I met many different types of women who were smart and proud of their bodies. I had a friend who fought boys. One time she was flyering a concert about a group's homophobic lyrics, and a man shouted "dyke" at her. She grabbed a pool stick, chased him down and threatened to show him "what a real dyke can do." The guy was so dumbfounded that a woman wasn't going to put her head down and take his shit that he hid underneath a pool table and waited for others to calm her down. I met many women who felt comfortable wearing dresses and grabbing their crotches in public. Others recited Marx to their lovers as they prepared to make passionate love.

I thought racing to be a part of the queer community would save me. I enlisted in the dyke world complete with uniform—short hair, overalls, cap on backwards and body piercings. As an extra buffer, I gained twenty-five pounds to make sure men wouldn't be interested in me, and to make sure I didn't have the body of a "slut." I walked down the street with pride, knowing that men no longer honked at me. I was undesirable. There was power in that for me. I thought I was screwing the patriarchy, subverting the status quo of femininity.

I didn't realize, however, that I was still blaming myself. At twenty, I had only run away from my problems and never dealt with them. I still felt as if my body was dirty and shameful. I still believed that the unwanted sexual attention I got in high school had been my fault—as though I'd "asked for it" by trying to fit a narrow prescription of femininity.

Soon, I found myself trying to follow the status quo of a different community, complete with confining norms and stereotypes. Now, instead of wanting to be a good *hijita,* I found myself trying to be a good queer girl and a good feminist. The role was just as confining. The feminist and gay communities still had a white/classist/racist framework—one which did nothing to address the multiple-identity dilemmas that came along with being a queer Latina feminist.

When I looked in the mirror, I felt just as much in drag as I had in high school. Finally, after twenty-one years of confusion, I realized I could be happy only when I defined my own idea of beauty and sensuality. My identity had too many layers for me to wrap it into a convenient package. The most political statement I could make was to look the way I wanted and not be ashamed of it. Today, my closet reflects my philosophy with a feather boa, tuxedo shirt, overalls and platforms all peacefully cohabiting. Such nonsensical words as *butch, femme* and *drag* have disappeared from my vocabulary and my fashion style.

And naked, I'm just as sensual. I can look at myself and not feel ashamed anymore. Sure, I have stretch marks all over my ass, scars all over my body, and my breasts are lopsided. But that's what being a real *mujer* is all about. Real *mujeres* live life intensely—and their bodies show it. They feast on food, drink with revelry and play hard. I look forward to watching my body develop more, to becoming more curvaceous. I'm ready for anything that happens, whether it's cellulite or muscle definition.

Now that I wear whatever I like, I feel sensual. I can go to a club and let the beat lead my hips. That's what I like best about dancing. My mind doesn't think. The rhythms dictate how my hips will sway, how my whole body moves. I don't care if men or women are looking. My sensuality is for me.

I need to discover how my body can move. I need to know me before anyone else can. I thought if I reached this epiphany and expressed my sexuality with freedom, that men would see me as a target. I was wrong. It wasn't my body that made men yell and grab me. It was them.

And, in some ways, I have little power to change that. I can't single-handedly overturn messages telling men that women are sex objects. I can't uproot myths casting women of color as wild and sexually available. I also understand my parents' mistakes. Instead of shielding me from boys and sex, they should have prepared me for what I would come to expect. Instead of "protecting" me by teaching me body hatred, they should have taught me to cherish myself. Had I been proud of my body, I may not have let street harassers bring me down so low. I wouldn't have risked my life sleeping with assholes. I would have known how to defend myself.

I accept this now and fight to unlearn twenty-one years of conditioning. So far, I'm doing pretty well. Without realizing it, I've developed a new body language. When I walked with my head down, men picked up on my powerlessness. I believe that my confident new stride actually scares some of those assholes away. Once in a while, I get catcalls, but now those men are sure to get flipped off, barked at or blown a kiss. I realize why my friend is willing to fight boys, and ultimately, I would fight a man. I spent so many years feeling ashamed of my body that rolling in the dirt might make me feel cleaner.

In the end, no Superfeminist ever flew in from the sky to save me. It took me years to realize that nobody else could rescue me. I didn't have to be a superhero. I just had to allow myself to become *la mujer.*

destination 120
debbie feit

When you're only 4'11-3/4" and weigh over 160 pounds, finding your way down the road to 120 is not something made easier with a call to the Auto Club. Even though it's a road heavily traveled by thousands every year, it's not one you can find on any map. The road down to 120 is long and winding and filled with detours. It's traveling down San Francisco's Highway 1 when you really wanted to take the Autobahn. Its bumps and cracks make the journey difficult; its forks and crossroads make it easy to get lost. Along the way there are ice cream stands and Chinese restaurants and cute little coffee houses with names like The Daily Grind and Spill the Beans and desserts that are almost too pretty to eat.

Almost.

The road I'm traveling is long. But I have others to keep me company. And I've packed well for my trip.

There's my yellow glow worm T-shirt that I wore in the sixth grade. The outline of the worm was raised and puffy, and it really did glow in the dark. I got this T-shirt at the same specialty store in Queens where we bought my favorite clothes-line patterned shirt. Back then, it was where we bought most of my clothes. The store specialized in larger sizes, and though it was a forty-five minute drive from our house in Brooklyn, my parents were always more than willing to make the trip. I liked the clothes I got from the store in Queens. I just didn't like having to go all the way to Queens to get them.

Then there's the bodysuit and leotard I never bought, let alone put on my body. Our sixth-grade class was putting on a play, and our teacher, Mrs. Greenwald, was handing out roles. I was to be one of several trees or bushes or birds or some other generic group of things that didn't require much talking. As one of the quieter kids in the class, I expected such a part. I welcomed it. Until I heard that our costume would be a bodysuit and leotard. Mrs. Greenwald may as well have told me to stand naked in front of the whole school.

I went home crying that day.

But I'm a little fuzzy as to what happened next. My mom claims to have made no phone call; she thinks Mrs. Greenwald was sensitive enough to know I was distraught and simply gave me another part. Whatever the sequence of events may have been, I just know one thing—I never wore a bodysuit and leotard.

The problem with traveling down to 120 or 110 or whatever your final destination happens to be, or whatever you think your final destination should be, is that it's a very long trip. No round of License Plates or Punch Beetle or the Alphabet Game can help to pass the time. It's just you and the road and thirty years worth of baggage crammed in the back seat. Suitcase after suitcase packed with the memories of extra-large T-shirts never to be thrown into the dryer. Unflattering bridesmaid's dresses never to be worn again. And slightly snug sweaters, dresses and pants, all bought in the heat of optimism, never to see more than the inside of the closet.

Packed for my ride is the purple dress with multicolored flying hearts that I wore to my ninth-grade Arista ceremony. Arista was the junior high school's honor society, and getting accepted into it was something I never worried about. I can't say the same about finding a dress to wear to the ceremony.

Our search for a dress began—and ended in failure—at the mall. So my mom suggested having one made. I picked out the fabric, and my mom and the seamstress picked out the style: a simple A-line with a breast pocket, buttons running down the front and a narrow belt that would be worn loosely. The belt was to give the illusion that I had a waist; I don't think Houdini could have pulled it off.

It was a nice dress. The color was pretty. The fabric was soft. And given my short, round, hard-to-fit shape, the cut was as flattering as it could be. Still, one thing was missing: a tag. I was very conscious of the fact that this dress did not come from a store. And while it would be fifteen years before I realized that a custom-made dress was considered a luxury, to an insecure thirteen-year-old, it was a stigma. I was terrified one of my classmates would ask me where I bought the dress. No one did. If they had, I'm sure they would have thought it to be a perfectly innocent question. To me it would have felt like an interrogation leading to my guilty plea; guilty by reason of black and white bakery cookies, barbecue potato chips and Drake's Devil Dogs. Guilty—beyond a reasonable doubt—of being fat.

This is not a single-lane highway I am traveling. I share this road with my mother. My friends. Even Oprah, with her size-ten Calvin Klein jeans packed for good measure, has taken this trip. Often there is disagreement over which route will be the quickest and easiest. So we go our separate ways, hoping to meet again at our final destination. I don't wish to be the last to arrive, but I am traveling a much greater distance than the others. And my car is loaded down with many more bags.

Like the garment bag carefully draped across the back seat. It held my wedding dress, and shopping for it was more stressful than the entire planning of the wedding. Like any other bride, I looked through bridal magazines. But finding a dress I liked was not the same as finding a dress that would fit, let alone one that would make me look thin, reflect my personality and not make me look fifteen years old. (At my height, that's often a problem.) I had to rule out many beautiful dresses. On my body, they would not have been so beautiful.

With my parents, sister and cousin in tow, I went to Kleinfeld's in Brooklyn, the biggest bridal store in the world. My sister had bought her dress there, as had my cousin. Every bride bought her wedding dress at Kleinfeld's. And while my family was excited, I was apprehensive.

I was a blushing bride that day. But it wasn't the thought of my impending marriage that made me glow; it was the size eight dress my size-sixteen-plus body was pinned into that made me blush with embarrassment. Kleinfeld's may have had a big selection of dresses, but all the samples were size eight. The saleswomen literally pin you into the dress. They have to, because in my case, the zippers wouldn't close. I couldn't even fit my arms into the sleeves of some of the dresses I attempted to try on. In those cases, the dress was held up in front of me, its shoulders clipped to my bra straps.

Eventually, we found a dress that was flattering to my figure; the square neckline made me look taller and the empire style gave me a waist. I thought my ordeal was over.

But now the dress needed to be ordered in my size. Out came the measuring tapes and, with them, the ugly reality of my size was recorded on paper. According to the sizing chart of this particular dress, I was, in fact, off the chart. Extra material would have to be ordered, and it would cost $250 more. "No problem," my dad said, whipping out his American Express card. He could handle the extra $250 more easily than I could handle needing the extra material. And on top of all this was my concern that if I lost weight and the dress needed to be taken in, the $250 would go to waste. My mom told me not to worry. She knew I wanted to lose weight; she knew I would be happier if I did. But she also wanted me to have a dress I could be happy with regardless of what I weighed. So the dress—and the extra material—was ordered.

I lost fifteen pounds by the time the big day arrived. But despite everyone telling me how beautiful I looked; despite Dave's tears when he first saw me in my dress; despite my cousins having no difficulty lifting me on a chair during *Hava Nagila,* I still wondered: What would I have looked like if I had lost another ten?

Another reason for my trip? The floor-length, off-the-shoulder, cap-sleeved bridesmaid dress I wore for my friend Glenn's wedding. There was nothing wrong with the dress—if you were tall, thin, and had firm breasts, toned upper arms and smooth skin.

At least it was black.

Kara told me about the dress over the phone—she and Glenn lived in another state—so I went to the bridal salon near my house to see the dress and, I hoped, try it on. Past experience told me that designers of traditional bridesmaid dresses weren't too generous with their sizing, and as I entered the shop I was apprehensive. Would the dress come in my size? Would I have to order extra material? Would they charge me more money for needing a larger size? I was happy for Glenn. But I was fearful that his big day would be my big day of embarrassment.

To my surprise, the sizing chart went well beyond a size fourteen. And the shop even had a sample for me to try on. I wasn't happy that the designer seemed to assign random numbers to the larger sizes.

Maybe they were European. But being told I needed a size thirty-eight—a fourteen or a sixteen if I had been wearing Jones New York or Elisabeth—felt as if someone were going out of his way to remind me, just in case I had forgotten, that I was indeed fat.

Nevertheless, relief washed over me as I felt the zipper easily glide its way to the top. I didn't even have to hold my breath. I assured myself that the worst was over and went home to call Kara. As the nervous bride, she wanted to order all the dresses at the same time from the same store. Perhaps she was even trying to save us some money; I would have preferred to save face. It was bad enough that I needed a size thirty-eight—now I had to share this information with the size-two bride.

But Kara wanted more than just the size; she wanted my measurements. I tried to assure her that the size was sufficient information for ordering the right dress. But she—or maybe it was the shop through which she was placing the order—insisted on having my measurements. And despite my delusion that Kara was purposely looking to humiliate me, I measured myself, wrote down the information and shared it with her over the phone. Fortysomething. Thirtysomething. Fortysomething. Then I threw away the piece of paper.

Months later, a package arrived. I opened the box, tried on the dress, and to my relief, it covered me. For once, a bridesmaid's outfit that didn't squeeze me in and even left me with room to breathe. I figured I was in the clear.

And then I noticed the fitted, full-length gloves.

The road I am traveling has many exit ramps and rest stops along the way. I can end the journey at any time. Many women never make it to their final destination. They're the ones who, part way through their trip, pull over, look around and realize they're happy right where they are, even if it's not the exact spot they originally planned on.

Many women don't even bother pulling out of the driveway; they feel no need to travel. I often wish I could be one of those women. Life on the road is tiring.

Still, it's impossible to spend as much time on the road as I have without looking for a rest stop. Like the turnoff I came upon when I discovered a sharp, two-piece, brown velvet suit. For the first time I could remember, I found myself thinking, *I look good in this. Confident. I might even go so far as to say attractive.* My foot eased off the gas pedal ever so slightly.

I tried on the suit with a cream and brown animal print blouse the saleswoman had suggested. And although the blouse wasn't necessarily my taste, I had to admit that it completed the outfit perfectly. "It doesn't matter if it's your taste," she said. "As long as it fits well."

Part of me had to agree with what she said. My weight was at an all-time high, and I was truly grateful to find, so quickly and painlessly, a flattering outfit I liked. But happy as I was to be finished with my shopping, part of me resented the saleswoman's well-meaning advice. Would she have said the same thing had I been a size eight? Did my clothing size preclude any consideration to my personal preferences simply because of the number on the label?

Truth is, I was relieved to have found this outfit. It reflected my style and flattered my figure. But the sense of gratitude I felt was overwhelming. And I resented feeling that way.

Admittedly, the selection of clothing available in my size has grown considerably since the days my mom took me shopping. And knowing I have more options does make things a little easier. I don't leave the mall in tears as often as I used to. And although I'm still not comfortable with my body, at least I know it can be dressed well.

Still, when you see a place where the people are having a good time, it's only natural to want to join them. And where I'm headed, the people seem happy. Healthy. More popular. They have better weather, successful jobs, fulfilling relationships and fewer problems. Now, I know the reality of this place is miles from my perception. That's okay. I can live with that. Because I know at least one thing is true.

The shopping there is great.

memoirs of an
ex-shaver

memoirs of a
(sorta) ex-shaver
carolyn mackler

By the 1920s, both fashion and film had encouraged a massive "unveiling" of the female body, which meant that certain body parts—such as arms and legs—were bared and displayed in ways they had never been before. This new freedom to display the body was accompanied, however, by demanding beauty and dietary regimens that involved money as well as self-discipline. Beginning in the 1920s, women's legs and underarms had to be smooth and free of body hair; the torso had to be svelte; and the breasts were supposed to be small and firm. What American women didn't realize at the time was that their stunning new freedom actually implied the need for greater internal control of the body, an imperative that would intensify and become even more powerful by the end of the twentieth century.

—Joan Jacobs Brumberg, The Body Project:
An Intimate History of American Girls

Were you aware of the historical tradeoff of women getting rid of one constraint (too much clothing) only to be shackled with a whole new set (de-hairing and dieting) when you started shaving? I sure wasn't. All I knew was that the other girls in my junior high gym class suddenly had legs as smooth as an infant and I celebrated the birth of every new underarm hair by grabbing a pair of scissors and trimming it down. Feeling inexplicably weird about the soft blond peach fuzz coating my legs (that hadn't warranted a nod until the winter of seventh grade), I pounded my mom with questions about shaving: "When could I? How do you? Could I get my own razor?"

"Wait," she cautioned. "Shave once and you'll have black stubble for the rest of your life."

Heeding no warning, I crouched in the tub with a bottle of Johnson and Johnson's baby oil and my dad's old black Gillette. I was focused, driven. Through hell or greasy water, I would have smooth legs. This experimental style (which resulted in awful itching and didn't work very well) was eventually eclipsed by more conventional methods: my own pastel disposable ten pack, a can of Barbosal shaving cream and, a few hours later, a smear of Nivea cream to ease chafing. When I shaved at night, I would lie in bed rejoicing in gloriously silky legs, feeling like a *real* woman.

Oh, I was quite the shaver. I indulged daily, careful not to omit a patch, not even down near my ankles. I bent my knees to scrape them clean and only rarely sliced off some skin in that difficult place in the front where the bone touches so close to the surface. I excised hair as someone would peel tar from the bottom of their feet after going barefoot on a summer road. An impressed family friend once joked she would hire me to shave *her* legs. The guys at school routinely swiped their hands across girls' legs to patrol their shaving prowess and then taunt them if they were slacking off. If I were running late, I'd protect myself by *faux* shaving—just doing the strip between the bottom of my jeans and the top of my cotton socks.

And here I lived, in this world of plastic legs, where moms and daughters, teachers and coaches shaved without a bat of the eye. It was all any of us saw; every woman had smooth legs. It was hygienic, like brushing your teeth or clipping your toenails. I tremble to think of what would have happened if I, a vaguely insecure, overly tall sixteen-year-old, had paraded into homeroom one morning sporting furry legs and an ample bush under each arm. In a town of conformity (where the gossip of the school was that Marta *dared* to have "flat hair"—meaning no perm, no hairspray, no poofed bangs), this would have meant instant death by humiliation. I would have rather stuck my head in an oven.

Desperately suffocated by this clone-ishness (but seeing no way out from within), I jetted off to college at eighteen, with aspirations of hobnobbing among the potpourri of people boasted on the promotional fliers. I imagined a borderless territory for etching out exactly who one was, in the absence of relentless peer police. Granted, things were different. The word was that the college years were a time to get all the nose rings, goatees, crimson hair and bottomed-out Birkenstocks out of your system, to quick-get-it-over-with and dabble in bisexuality and menáges à trois (or at least talk about it), because you'd probably never get another go. So the parameters of conformity had widened, but ultimately, people still navigated within the confines of what was cool and acceptable. And other than on those marginal take-no-shit women, leg and armpit hair was still uncool. Shaving was still the undisputed norm. And the guys were still on hand to check for stubble.

The summer after my sophomore year, something happened that rocked my closely shaven world forever. I took a month-long mountain trek, and with only enough space for essentials, no forecast of running water and no one to impress, I left my razor on the shower ledge at home. And for the first time since I had any hair to speak of, my leg and underarm hair began to grow. And grow. And grow. And the strangest thing was that I actually liked it. Not only did it feel good to be free of that constant bristle, it looked healthy and fuzzy and strong—somehow the way a woman's leg *should* look, not all bald and vulnerable like a little girl's. On the other hand, it felt so bizarre and unfamiliar, like I was this androgynous Bigfoot with hairy legs and pits. Understandably so: I had been around for two decades, and this was my first up-close peek at a woman with body hair! The second I re-emerged into civilization, I shaved away the evidence, but my perceptions had been altered. In other words, I had dipped my hand in the cookie jar, and I liked what I tasted.

In the midst of all this, I had been wading through months of dorm-room body-image rap sessions. It was becoming painfully clear that in our high-powered, image-focused environment, eating disorders ran rampant. To be young and white and female was to have "body issues," as we tenderly referred to them. We all had been afflicted by the bug, in varying ways. We freaked out about our bodies. We paid homage to the Stairmaster and hated it. We opted for salad bar, no dressing, instead of cheesy dining-hall pizza. We gained the freshman fifteen and struggled to lose the sophomore twenty or thirty. Analyzing it ad nauseam was our way of reacting, fighting back and learning to overcome this pressure for physical perfection. Meanwhile, as we shaved/plucked/waxed our body hair away, a dialogue on body hair lay dormant. We didn't see anything political in it.

But isn't body hair yet another image issue dumped in the exhausted laps of women? My mind begins to reel when I ponder the whole de-hairing ordeal:

Eyebrows: *Pluck into symmetrical arches, or at least interrupt the unibrow over the bridge of the nose.*
Mustache (more genteelly referred to as upper lip hair): Bleach, wax

or zap it with electrolysis.

    Chin hair: *Tweeze out ASAP, even if it means using the rear-view mirror at an intersection.*

    Random very **long arm hairs:** *Yank.*

    Rest of arm hair: *Bleach if too dark.*

    Nipple hair: *Tweeze or fry with electrolysis.*

    Underarm hair: *Shave, of course.*

    "Bikini line" hair *(deemed so vile, only a euphemism can be used): Shave (and get a lovely rash), fantasize about being able to afford electrolysis, wear granny-style skirted bathing suits or shorts to the beach.*

    Leg hair: *See* Underarm hair.

    Toe hair: *Pull out while talking on the phone*—owww!

Sound familiar? Women's body hair is apparently so dirty, gross and vulgar that it elicits queasiness in people. It's "excess," meaning it shouldn't be there in the first place. *But it is.* I'll bypass lugging down the hair-as-fur-for-warmth path, because clothes do that trick—but hair has always been there, and it will always be there. It's easy to forget that women have hairy legs and armpits because we never see them in their natural state. In this society, our eyes have actually been retrained to believe that a woman doesn't have body hair. Our memory omits the razors, waxes, creams and bleaches that go into making women hairless. In fact, we *expect* a woman to have smooth legs, et cetera, and are surprised and often repulsed if she doesn't.

    Why has body hair become such a nemesis for women? It poses no health risks. It is not hygienic to remove; it is not cleansing to shave. Rather, the complications arise during the eradication: cuts, infections, rashes, ingrown hairs, dry skin, burning. Is this hairless ideal yet another variation on the tune of "let's take the best (boobs, curves in some places, hair in very few places) and leave the rest (hips, curves in other places, hair in *lots* of other places)"? Or is it: "Let's make women look like eight-year-olds so we can treat them as such"? Or is it: "If women can fill up their extra hours shaving and obsessing about their bodies, then they won't have spare time to plot a world takeover"? Or maybe it's: "Women are *so* grossly overpaid and just don't spend enough on pads, tampons, pantyliners, Ibuprofen, shampoos, conditioners, deodorants, that we should coax them to buy razors, waxes, creams and bleaches." A-ha, it's probably: "How about setting another unattainable ideal for women so they will always fall short of the mark." I mean, what are women if they're not feeling insecure about something or another?

Chewing on all these questions, I returned to campus in the fall and began to test-drive not shaving. I would make a firm decision to quit cold turkey, toss all my razors, and let the hair do its thing. For the first few weeks, I could pass on the bad shaver-stubble ticket. Okay, fine. But after month or so, I found myself eager to answer a question in class, yet halted in my tracks by the horror of exposing my tank-topped hairy underarms to the cute guy across from me! *Ay!* I would settle for wagging my hand around on my desk and vow to stick to T-shirts from then on. But I love tank tops! And here began the eternal debate: Should I shave or should I let it go and feel awkward?

I've finally hit a point where I can hold out through fall, a hairy winter and well into spring. But come summer (lying on bikini-laden beaches, going to the office in a sleeveless dress without stockings, riding a crowded subway and having to reach up to grip the handrail), I start losing steam. At crunchy folk festivals I'm a card-carrying member, but traipsing to a corporate office in midtown Manhattan? Short of bundling up in wool tights and turtlenecks in ninety-degree weather, I feel awfully strange about having hairy legs. I start out by rehearsing witty comebacks. I feel bold and strong for about a day and a half. Then I invent outfits to disguise my hairy legs and underarms. Then the debate rekindles. Finally, I lose my *chutzpah* and shave in defeat.

It's throwing in the towel on all accounts: Besides the strength I derive from rebelling against yet another implicit body pressure, *hair feels good.* Who could have ever imagined the erotic potential in riding a bike or swimming with hairy legs? The breeze ruffles it, the water swishes through it—wow! And sex? Ever sent someone flying out of bed by rubbing your bristly legs against them? Quite the opposite with hairy legs, as it is ultrastimulating to entwine your furry legs with your lover's. This completely uncharted aphrodisiac is scarily reminiscent of women not being encouraged to experience full sexual pleasure (*guys* get the hairy leg turn-on). Add to that, body hair looks incredibly sexy and healthy. We're just not used to seeing it on women.

What body hair needs is more visibility. It needs a publicity agent and a marketing campaign. It needs models and actresses to flounce around with hairy legs and pits. When those trailblazing, unshaven singers and songwriters like Ani DiFranco and Dar Williams stomp onto stage, it sends a loud and clear holler into the hairless vacuum. It propels us to see it, to think about it, to actually make the connection that *this* is a real woman, not the reverse. It cracks open a door that will eventually lead to women having the choice (not the compulsory burden) of whether they want to shave. Maybe someday I'll become a poster child for body hair. For now, I'm just revving up to go an entire summer without shaving, to storm the office in a sundress and sandals, to wear whatever the hell I want to the beach, to not feel ashamed to show my hairy armpits to the world. Every summer I get a little closer. Maybe this time I'll make it.

my jewish nose
lisa jervis

I'm a Jew. I'm not even slightly religious. Aside from attending friends' *bat mitzvahs,* I've been to temple maybe twice. I don't know Hebrew; when given the option of religious education, my junior-high self easily chose to sleep in on Sunday mornings. My family skips around the Passover Haggadah to get to the food faster. Before having dated someone from an observant family, I wouldn't have known a *mezuzah* if it bit me on the butt. I was born assimilated.

But still, I'm a Jew—even though my Jewish identity has very little to do with religion, organized or otherwise. I'm an ethnic Jew of a very specific variety: a godless, New York City–raised, neurotic middle-class girl from a solidly liberal Democrat family, who attended largely Jewish, "progressive" schools that thought they were integrated and nonracist. Growing up, almost everyone around me was Jewish; I was stunned when I found out that Jews make up only two percent of the American population. But what being Jewish meant to me was that on Christmas day my family went out for Chinese food (some years, Indian) and took in the new Woody Allen movie. It also meant that I had a big honkin' nose.

And I still do. By virtue of my class and its sociopolitical trappings, the option of having my nose surgically altered was ever-present. From adolescence on, I've had a standing offer from my mother to get a nose job.

"It's not such a big deal." "Doctors do such individual-looking noses these days, it'll look really natural." "It's not too late, you know," she would say to me for years after I flat-out refused to let someone break my nose, scrape part of it out and reposition it into a smaller, less obtrusive shape. "I'll still pay." As if money were the reason I was resisting.

My mother thought a nose job was a good idea. See, she hadn't wanted one either. But when she was sixteen, her parents demanded that she get that honker "fixed," and they didn't take no for an answer. She insists that she's been glad ever since, although she usually rationalizes that it was good for her social life. (She even briefly dated a guy she met in the surgeon's waiting room: a boxer having his deviated septum corrected.)

Even my father is a believer. He says that without my mother's nose job, my sister and I wouldn't exist, because he never would have gone out with Mom. But I take this with an entire salt lick. My father's a guy who thinks that dressing up means wearing dark sneakers; that pants should be purchased every twenty years, and only if the old ones are literally falling apart at the seams; and that haircuts should cost ten dollars and take as many minutes. The only thing he notices about appearances is to say, "You have some crud . . . " as he picks a piece of lint off your sleeve. But he cared about the nose? Whatever.

Even though my mother was happy with her tidy little surgically altered nose, she wasn't going to put me through the same thing, and for that I am truly grateful. I'm also unspeakably glad that her comments stayed far from the "you'd just be so pretty if you did" angle. ("Yours isn't as big as mine was," she would say. "You don't *need* it.") I know a few people who weren't so lucky. Not that they were dragged kicking and screaming to the doctor's office; no, they were coerced and shamed into it. Seems it was their family's decision more than their own—usually older Jewish female relatives: mothers, grandmothers, aunts.

What's the motivation for that kind of pressure? Can it be that for all the strides made against racism and anti-Semitism, Americans still want to expunge their ethnicity from their looks as much as possible? Were these mothers and grandmothers trying to fit their offspring into a more white, gentile mode? Possibly. Well, definitely. But on purpose? Probably not. Their lust for the button nose is probably more a desire for a typical, "pretty" femininity than for any specific de-ethnicizing. But given the society in which we live, the proximity of white features to the ideal of beauty is no coincidence. I think that anyone who opts for a nose job today (or who pressured her daughter to do so) would say that the reason is to look "better" or "prettier." But when we scratch the surface of what "prettier" means, we find that we might as well be saying "whiter" or "more gentile" (I would add "bland," but that's my personal opinion).

Or perhaps the reason is to become unobtrusive. The stereotypical Jewish woman is loud, pushy—qualities that girls really aren't supposed to have. So is it possible that the nose job is supposed to usher in not only physical femininity but a psychological, traditional femininity as well? Ditch the physical and emotional ties to your ethnicity in one simple procedure: Bob your nose, and become feminine in both mind and body. (This certainly seems to be the way it has worked with someone like Courtney Love, although her issue is class more than ethnicity. But it's undeniable that her new nose comes on a Versace-shilling, largely silent persona, in stark contrast to her old messy, outspoken self.)

Thankfully, none of the women I know have become meek and submissive from their nose jobs. But *damn,* do they have regrets. One told me it was the biggest mistake of her life; another confessed to wanting her old nose back just a few short years after the surgery. They wish they'd stood up to their families and kept their natural features.

Even though I know plenty of women with their genetically determined schnozzes still intact, women who either refused or never considered surgery, sometimes I still feel like an oddity. From what my mother tells me, nose jobs were as compulsory a rite of passage for her peers as multiple ear-piercings are for mine. Once, when I was still in high school, I went with my mother to a Planned Parenthood fundraiser. It was a cocktail party–type thang in some lovely apartment, with lovely food and drink and a lovely short speech by Wendy Wasserstein. But I was confused: We were at a lefty charity event in Manhattan, and all the women in attendance had little WASP noses. (Most of them were blond, too, but that didn't really register. I guess hair dye is a more universal ritual.)

"Why are there no Jewish women here?" I whispered to my mother. She laughed, but I think she was genuinely shocked. "What do you mean? All of these women are Jewish." And then it hit me: We were wall-to-wall rhinoplasties. And worse, there was no reason to be surprised. These were women my mother's age or older who came of age in the late '50s or before, when anti-Semitism in this country was much more overt than it is today. That kind of surface assimilation was practically the norm for Jews back then, and those honkers were way too, ahem, big a liability on the dating and social scenes. Nose jobs have declined since then. They're no longer in the top five plastic surgery procedures performed, edged out by liposuction and laser skin resurfacing. (I guess now it's more important to be young and trim than gentile, what with societal forces of youth-and-beauty worship replacing post–World War II fear and hatred . . .)

I don't think it's a coincidence that I didn't consider my nose an ethnic feature growing up in New York. I didn't have to, because almost everyone around me had that feature (and that ethnicity) too. It wasn't until I graduated from college and moved to California that I realized how marked I was by my nose and my vaguely ethnic, certainly Jewish appearance. I also then realized how much I liked being marked that way, being instantly recognizable to anyone who knew how to look. I once met another Jewish woman at a conference in California. In the middle of our conversation, she randomly popped out with, "You're Jewish, right?" I replied, "With this nose and this hair, you gotta ask?" We both laughed. I was right: The question was just a formality, and we both knew it.

Living in California, I'm particularly in need of those little moments of recognition. I know that a Jew living in, say, Tennessee might laugh at me for saying this, but there are no Jews in California. I feel conspicuously Semitic here in a way that I never did anywhere else (not even at my small Ohio liberal arts college—after all, that place was filled with New York Jews). Few of my friends are Jewish, and those random "bagel and lox" references just don't get understood the way I'm used to.

Only once did I feel uneasy about being "identified." At my first job out of college, my boss asked, after I mentioned an upcoming trip to see my family in New York, "So, are your parents just like people in Woody Allen movies?" I wondered if I had a big sign on my forehead reading, "Big Yid Here." His comment brought up all those insecurities American Jews can have about our ethnicity that, not coincidentally, Woody Allen loves to play on—and overemphasize for comic effect: Am I *that* Jewish? Is it *that* obvious? I felt conspicuous, exposed. But regardless of that incident, I'm glad I have the sign on my face, even if it's located a tad lower than my forehead.

See, I don't have a whole lot of Jewish heritage to hold on to. My family's name was changed—it's not as if "Jervis" is particularly gentile, but it sure is a lot less obvious than "Jersowitz," which my grandfather jettisoned before my father can remember. Temple was never a part of my life—I'm an atheist. I don't know what Purim is about. Hell, it takes me a minute to remember how many candles go in the menorah—and last week I used mine for a candlelight dinner with my husband-to-be, a half-Christian, half-Buddhist Japanese American whose thoughts on God's existence are along the lines of "I don't know, and I don't really care."

But in a larger sense, Judaism is the only identity in which culture and religion are supposedly bound closely: If you're Irish and aren't a practicing Catholic, you can still be fully Irish; being Buddhist doesn't specify a race or an ethnic identity. African Americans can practice any religion, and it doesn't make them any less black. But "Jewish" is a funny ethnicity. Is it a race; is it a set of beliefs? Color doesn't have much to do with it. In fact, the question of whether or not Jews are white can be answered in as many different ways as there are people who have an opinion on the topic.

To me, being a Jew is cultural. But for me it's a culture tied only marginally—even hypothetically—to religion, and mostly to geography (New York Jews are different from California Jews, lemme tell ya) and sensibility/temperament (hyperintellectual, food-lovin', neurotic, worrywartish, perfectionistic). So the question for me is: What happens when Jewish identity becomes untied from religion? I don't know for sure. And that means I'll grab onto anything I need to keep that identity—including my nose.

lisa jervis   67

to apu, with love
bhargavi c. mandava

Shortly after arriving in New York in 1971 from Hyderabad, India, I remember skipping ecstatically behind my father as he carried a naked, used, black-and-white Zenith television through the streets of Astoria, Queens. Since he hadn't learned to drive yet, there was no candy-apple-red Impala to transport the beast. And we couldn't afford to take a taxi—a rickshaw, certainly, but not a taxi. So my father crouched into an Atlaslike stance, and up went the TV onto his shoulders.

"Can you see?" my mother asked him nervously. "Careful, it's wet over there. Are you breathing?"

Her voice faded as I became lost in the appliance teetering above me. Soon, this innocuous gray box would become my savior in a new country where I had no grandfather to tell me stories, no rickshaw drivers to take me for rides, no evening walks with my mother and sister to pluck jasmine blossoms for our hair.

It didn't matter that the channel featuring *The Wonderful World of Disney* was a mess of lines and squiggles. At four years of age, I sat with my ear to the speaker, using the TV like a giant radio and listening raptly to the magic dust spilling from Tinkerbell's wand. When I think about it now, I know it was a blessing in disguise that I had to fashion my own images of Snow White and Sleeping Beauty.

One day, after a healthy dose of that wascally wabbit, I discovered that NBC was coming in loud and *clear.* Finally, I could put pictures to words! Little did I know that fairy skin was a smooth and hairless alabaster—or that fairy hair was blond and flowing.

And so marked the start of my re-education.

During the year's wait to enroll in nursery school, I sat glued to the TV set, a bowl of Spaghetti-Os in hand, and absorbed the world inside the tube. By day, I was bombarded with pitches for Barbies in evening gowns and townhouses and for giant doll heads on which I could smear Avon pinks and blues. By night, my one-eyed doll Judy and I slept in between my parents, my head reeling with wishes that my sister and brother would soon come live with us and that I could play on *Romper Room.*

Well, one of those wishes came true when my siblings joined us in New York a couple years later. I welcomed their companionship, which I had sorely missed. My sister and brother, who are seven and six years my elder, respectively, were flung into the turbulence of an alien culture rather suddenly, since they had to start school as soon as they arrived.

While whisking them off to the local Salvation Army for school clothes, my mother and I bestowed bits of American culture. We taught them English (according to Bugs Bunny) and how to ride the subway (never get on the train going into Manhattan) and which foods were "safe" to eat (pizza and peanut butter and jelly sandwiches). What we couldn't quite impart to them was the scoop on American style.

bhargavi c. mandava   **69**

My mother, who had always been a step ahead of the Hyderabad fashion world, was still contemplating whether the ruffles on a pair of American-made panties went in the front or the back. In India, we all had our clothes custom-tailored to suit my mother's tastes. In Astoria, thrift stores became our fabric shops and my mother, the family tailor.

Silently, we were all going through some kind of transformation, which we faced with a mixture of resistance and naive enthusiasm. While my parents struggled to support us, my sister and brother were trying to fit in at Junior High School 141 and I was wending my way through Public School 122. At first, there were the usual complaints of not having many friends or not receiving any Valentine's Day cards. But by kindergarten's end, I started to feel a visible separation between myself and the rest of the children. Through the third grade, I complained that I never looked like the other kids, that my mother didn't know how to dress me, that my hair was ugly. My mother never denied her cluelessness about kindergarten couture. However, what she absolutely couldn't understand was my fervent hatred for what she saw as a thick head of beautiful, satiny black hair.

In India, she had massaged oil into my scalp and plaited my hair into two ribboned loops. That practice continued even though we were on another continent.

"But no one in school puts oil in their hair," I would argue.

"That's because they don't have such thick black hair like yours," she would reply. "Don't you want it to grow longer and more beautiful?"

Longer? It was quickly approaching my ass; pretty soon, I'd be able to sit on it. Although there was a healthy mix of ethnicities at P.S. 122, I was the only Indian kid going there at the time. No one else's mother wore a *sari* to pick them up from school.

Wasn't she listening to me? I wanted hair with springy waves. I wanted Dippity-Do curls and bangs, and that cropped, tousled look. Anything but straight, black, boring hair.

My mother finally succumbed to my miserable whining and cut my hair into a shoulder-length *That Girl* flip. Unfortunately, this only fueled my pining to meet Hollywood's narrow definition of beauty. The truth was, there was no going back until the demon seed planted by the Breck Girl had played itself out in my beating heart.

As I stood poised with a hammer and chisel, ready to crack the dark brown stone and unearth the more beautiful American me sculpted in glowing white marble, my mother stood vehemently in the way. I couldn't fully comprehend why her ideals of beauty didn't match up with society's. At the time, I felt her insistence that I keep my hair long and avoid the sun was ridiculous—more absurd than my fantasies of waking up white and blonde.

Still, somewhere beyond our many battles over hair, a new seed was planted. I was able to grasp that by eschewing my heritage, I would not be losing something precious, but giving it away. And what was that something—that *it?* That was the question.

So, I started growing my hair again.

The fourth grade was one of my most pleasant school years, mostly because of my teacher Mrs. Rodvien. She was a wonderfully alert and caring woman who nurtured her students' strengths. She picked up on my writing interest and enticed me to include a poem with each of my reports. No one else had to write a poem about Spain or the Middle Ages, but I did so anyway. I was rewarded with a glimpse beyond the physical into the intriguing beauty that lay within me.

Perhaps that precious experience gave me strength to face the times ahead—the changes that menstruation would bring by the fifth grade. Along with this rite of passage arrived hormonal imbalances and a disinterest that shifted my priorities from playing basketball with the boys to gawking at them from the sidelines. I stepped back and looked into the mirror, wondering what the hell was going on with my body.

Actually, I was excited about getting my period and growing breasts, because it proved that there was nothing wrong with me—that everything was going according to plan. Or so I thought. But then my true hair problems began. No, not with the hair on my head, though my mother still insisted on parting it down the middle and tightly plaiting it into two braids. The problem was the hair growing—with more ferocity every day—all over my fifth-grade body. It wasn't so much the sprouting of pubic and underarm hair that concerned me. It was all the *other* hairs rearing their ugly heads—between my eyebrows, above my upper lip, around my jawline, down my neck, around my new breasts, down my front to my navel, over my arms and knuckles, right down my legs to my toes. I didn't recall ever seeing a woman shaving her face and "taking it all off" on that Noxema commercial. None of the other girls at school appeared to be walking carpets.

It wasn't long before a bully picked up on my insecurities and dubbed me an inhabitant of the Planet of the Apes. When I complained to my mother and my sister, they said not to worry about it and to concentrate on getting good grades.

"Did you know that when you were born, your head was already covered with hair?" my mother said proudly. "It's perfectly natural. Your hair shows up more because it's black, that's all."

"So, what you're telling me is this is some kind of birth defect?" I asked with terror.

"No, Nana, you have good genes," she said with a laugh.

That didn't help. Neither did Marcia bonking her nose with a football or Jan's hatred of her freckles; Tabitha's spells or Jeannie's magic; not even Mr. Softie bomb pops.

So what if my mother, a doctor, was telling me I was healthy?

The rest of the world was telling me otherwise. I had to take action.

While doing my homework in front of the Sony Trinitron (my father had traded in the black-and-white Zenith), I took my cue from a Nair commercial. Happily singing, "Who wears short shorts," I slathered the stinky goop on my arms. When my skin started burning, I panicked and quickly washed it clean. After toweling off, I gaped in horror at my arms, which were all patchy. I grabbed a Bic razor and shaved the skin.

My peace, however, was short-lived.

In the lunch line the next day, Susan screamed after brushing past me. "Eww! What happened to your arms—they're prickly!"

Everyone turned and stared. I wanted to crawl under the table. I wanted to grab that blond cheerleader ponytail, wrap it twice around her neck and yank. I wanted to choke the last drop of sky from her heavily-lined eyes. But I didn't say or do anything. For the next few weeks, I just wore a hooded zip-up sweatshirt to school.

Despite my mother's predictions, my arm hair grew in much thinner than before. I was thankful for that, but was still quite disconcerted about my facial hair. I couldn't very well cover it up. Would it ever stop growing? Would it vanish one day as mysteriously as it had appeared?

I became distracted from my hair problems when my parents announced we were moving to Long Island. I left the warmer, melting-pot ambiance of Astoria and was thrust into the cold, suburban homogeneity of green lawns and swimming pools. My parents were on their way to fulfilling the American Dream, and who was I to question it?

So I bucked up. I tried to ignore that people's jaws dropped when I walked into the lunch room, that I was the darkest kid in my junior high school, that they told me I talked funny, that all eyes were on me.

Hanging up my street-smart, blue-and-gold Pumas, I tried to get excited about the latest Sassoon and Jordache jeans. I tried to fit in, but how could I with all that hair? I was wearing it down now, pinned up at the sides with Goody barrettes. The long locks fanning out behind me served to draw some attention away from my facial hair, but I still wasn't happy.

This time, I turned to my college-bound sister and Jolene Bleach. Naturally, the bleached facial hair provided an interesting contrast against my chestnut skin. My new vanishing act was particularly noticeable when the sun hit my face during a game of field hockey.

"Hey, you got blond hair on your face. It's so weird!"

"Big deal," I responded coolly, stalling for an ample retort. "What would you know about it? I got a cousin with blue eyes."

I guess some of the girls and boys at my junior high honestly believed that Indians had jet-black hair on their heads and golden hair on their faces, and that some of us even had blue eyes. More stupid questions and more stupid answers were to follow.

And so began the re-education of my fellow students.

I should have been happy to get them off my back, but my explanations only sufficed to buy me time. Through high school, I focused most of my energy on SATs rather than dating, but I silently floundered to make sense of those much sought-after adjectives: beautiful, gorgeous, sexy, hot.

New York University and the death of my father dumped me into the abyss of an identity crisis. Soon, I was attempting to eradicate societal norms and expectations by cutting my long tresses into a short buzz and donning asexual clothing. Enraged by all the lies I had been radiated with since I stepped on American soil, I spurned fashion, nutrition, television, medication, transportation and mechanization. I delved into an underground world of the non-glamorous, the non-plastic and that hyper-reality New York City is known for.

As I moved past the anger and on to resolution, I toyed with formulas inspired by college Zen courses: Education + Faith + Truth = Beauty. I committed myself to my writing and it propelled me into a deeper search for the purpose of my existence. I realized that with the wink of an eye, we could render ourselves blind or restore our vision. It was as easy as clicking off the television—not just the ones in our living rooms, but the ones droning in our heads. The '70s had brought us Nair; the '80s, electrolysis; and the '90s the "miracles" of laser technology. The one constant has been that droning from television and print advertising—and eventually our own heads—a droning that makes us feel thirsty, hungry and in dire need of looking like "the Other," whatever or whomever that might be. So we continue to shave, bleach and dye our way toward an ideal.

At a local hangout, a female bartender wears a baseball cap etched in glitter with the words "Sexy M.F." *Why not sexy M.F.A.?* I muse. My chuckle is cut short when I spy the glint of something on her forehead. It's a sparkling *bottu* perched on her Third Eye. The same symbol of Hindu faith that propels bigoted groups like the Dot-Busters to commit hate crimes against Indians? The same little thing that made me cringe whenever people stared and pointed at my mother in a mall? It's hard to believe the sacred *bottu* is flaunted by goddess wannabes these days. Wearing crucifixes was popularized by rock musicians, and now it's Hinduism's turn, I suppose. Sipping a club soda, I consider if it's a positive or negative thing that the *yarmulke* hasn't been honored so.

With 1997 marking India's fiftieth year of independence from

Britain, I have to wonder if all the hype further exoticized Indians, or if it pulled us from obscurity and pinned us under a small cultural limelight? After all, it was also the year that Mother Theresa's funeral was televised; the year that Arundhati Roy, the author of the Booker Prize–winning novel *The God of Small Things,* was lionized in the media; the year that Deepa Mehta's film *Fire* put a spin on Indian domesticity; and the year that the ancient art of *mehndi* was translated explosively into temporary tattoos for the fashionably enlightened and the culturally fashioned. Is America caught in the full-blown phase of exoticizing Indian people, or is it in the next phase of re-exoticizing them? And if so, when will the deconstruction of this stupidity begin?

On that same Sony Trinitron from my Astoria days, I watch Apu (the only regular cast member of Indian origin on a prime-time sitcom) have an arranged marriage in Springfield on *The Simpsons,* and *Seinfeld*'s Elaine (wrapped in a *sari* and sporting a pierced nose and jasmine flowers in her hair) attend a love marriage in India. Over the next week, the episodes pop up in conversations with people, and I laugh.

These days, I meet people who tell me how much they love my skin and hair, which, by the way, is once again long. "You have such a nice complexion," they say. "Aren't you glad you don't have to lie out on the beach? You're so lucky. I'm *sooo* jealous."

My partner, like most people I've met in my post-college world, doesn't find the hair covering my body out of the ordinary. I suppose this has every bit to do with the fact that I don't either anymore.

Instead, he compares three white hairs streaking the black around my temples to comets in a night sky.

"Do you see them?" he asks.

"I see constellations on your shoulder," I reply, stroking my index finger across his freckles and moles.

"Oh, I have old Jew skin," he mumbles.

"I love your skin," I say.

"Here they are," he says, as he touches my forehead. "Beautiful."

"Yes," I say as I kiss his shoulder.

fishnets, feather boas and fat
nomy lamm

I tend to overdramatize my life in the telling. A friend of mine once told me that the stories I tell him always sound so outrageous and unreal that it seems like I lead a life full of nonstop drama, intrigue and excitement. He always wondered why such amazing things never happened when he was around, until he realized it was probably just the way I told the stories that made them seem so exciting and if he had been there when the amazing thing took place, perhaps he wouldn't have thought it so amazing after all.

Well, I don't know; it's not like I would try to lie about something to make it sound cooler, so I guess it means I'm a good storyteller. And now, thinking about my life these days, the major themes and ideas that have been on my mind, things seem to fall into place. Anything can make a good story. All you have to do is tell someone.

♌

I happen to be lucky enough to live in a city that has fostered some of the greatest bands ever. Me and my friends dress up, we wear our lingerie, the rubber bustier I made for myself, feather boas, fake fur, blue velvet, fishnets, stinky shoes. We shove our way to the front when our favorite bands play, smelling like armpit and cunt. I might feel a twinge of guilt for pushing in front of other people in the audience, but when the snotty girls in fur coats look down their noses at me and try to block my path to the front, I think to myself that they can fuck off, cuz all they're gonna do is stand there, nod their heads and look cool anyway. Whereas me and my friends, despite the rules of cool that dominate our school, wanna have some fun. We heckle the band, dance our asses off, bump and grind and flirt and line-dance and act like big ol' dorks.

The city where I live, which is hardly a city at all but is bigger than a town, is a mythical place. I personally had no part in creating or perpetuating the glamour and mythos that seem to surround Olympia, Washington, seeing as I have lived here my entire life and it never seemed very cool to me until I read about it in *Sassy* magazine. All I know is that Olympia is the city where I grew up, went to school, did musical theater, was *bat mitzvahed* and became a punk.

The main point of this part of the story, however, is not to discuss Olympia's mythological stature, but rather to point out what has become a very important, self-affirming and critical aspect of my life, and that is *fashion.* Like many a young lass, I am a slave to fashion.

You may think this is strange for a 250-pound, twenty-two-year-old disabled woman, especially when the "message" I've been spreading for the last five years has often been diluted into "We shouldn't judge people by the way they look." I myself have never expressed that sentiment, but when you tell people they need to re-examine their attitudes about fat (and fat people), that's often

nomy lamm   79

what they come up with.

No, I say to hell with not judging by appearance. When I spend an hour getting ready to go out, painting on fake eyelashes and a Valentino mustache, doing my hair in the most glamorous of 1940s styles, using my creative energies to design the perfect outfit, do you suppose I want people to look at me and think absolutely nothing?

No, I want them to look at me and think, *She's hot.* I want them to think, *What a freak.* I want them to think, *That woman is totally captivating, and I can't stop looking at her.*

Not that this necessarily happens, but what I'm saying is that perhaps my fashion obsession is a type of guerrilla activism, an act of rebellion against a punk scene that has conveniently adopted the same beauty standard that dominates the rest of the world. A punk scene where it seems like people no longer have to bond about having been social outcasts in high school. A punk scene made up of former cheerleaders and athletes who get to be popular in high school, and then, when they get tired of that, they can be popular in the punk scene. A punk scene where the beauty standard is not only thin (which it always is) but also, you know, big boobs, high heels, fancy clothes (oh, but bought at a thrift store, of course), makeup, nicely styled hair . . . By being a totally unabashed fat freaky diva, I am "subverting the dominant paradigm," as the college activists say.

I truly believe that redefining the terms of beauty, sexuality and attractiveness is a simple and vastly rewarding act, and I feel sorry for people who have so little imagination that they just do what they're told. For most of my life, I've been told that fat people are gross and ugly and could never be desirable. And, of course, there are times when that demon still lives in me, but there are plenty of times when I am out in the world feeling totally irresistible, and plenty of times when I look at a fat woman and think, Well, damn, there you go: *Zaftikeh moid* (Yiddish for "plump, sexy girl").

Already, at age twenty-two, I've spent five years of my life on this mission, trying to convince people that it's okay to be fat—to convince people that what they've been told by the mainstream media (and their friends and the radical left and just about everyone else) about fat and health, fat and beauty, fat and self-worth has all been bullshit. Trying, with my limited research skills, to make connections between the oppression of fat people and the development of capitalism—how the industrialization of our society and economy has affected our bodies, and how an advanced capitalist culture keeps us relegated to the role of pathetically needy consumer base, forever in search of the miracle diet that will change our lives.

Over and over I've repeated the information that changed my life five years ago:

"Fat doesn't make you unhealthy, diets do."

"The diet industry makes over $30 billion a year, relying on your fear and hatred of fat. They don't care about your health and happiness; they care about your money."

"Good health is not about being thin; it's about doing things that are good for your body. You can be fat and healthy."

I didn't come up with this stuff on my own. I'm no scientific genius—I just read it somewhere, and now I'm letting people know what I've learned. And, on one level, I know that each person I talk to about fat oppression, each person who reads something I've written about fat oppression and fat liberation is an important part of what I once deemed "the fat grrrl revolution"—the revolution that will overthrow the tyranny of thinness and make room in this world for all our bodies and all our experiences.

But, you know, I don't always feel like upholding this serious, committed public persona. It's exhausting, spreading a message, repeating the same shit over and over. Sometimes I wanna say, "God-damn, get over it already, will you people? I wanna go dancing and pick up some chicks."

It gets so boring, trying to convince people that fat is normal, when I really couldn't give a shit either way if I am normal. While I spend day after day trying to get people to challenge their stereotypes and assumptions about fat people, I realize that I am a living replica of a popular stereotype: the fat, hairy, disabled Jewish dyke who is out to destroy the State. And you know what? That's a great thing to be. Let the Delta Burkes of the world break stereotypes by being corporate seductresses. I say: "Fine, I accept that I'm a freak. I'm a fat, sleazy, one-legged anarchist dyke, and I'm a total hottie."

It's an easy attitude to uphold when I'm with my friends, safely within the boundaries of my community of perverts and freaks, pirates and anarchists, feminist sex workers, s/m dykes, trannies, high-school dropouts, artists and activists. It's when I'm forced to go outside that comfort zone to a place where there are no people like me, where people don't know who or what I am, that things get tricky. I may be the girliest girl on the block when I'm at a party in Olympia, but when I get into totally non-queer, normal-person space, it becomes so obvious that I'm not a real woman in the way the rest of the world expects. And not just because I'm not interested in the male-female mating ritual, although that would be enough. Surrounded by "real" women, I seem like an exaggeration—bigger than other women, louder, hairier, my makeup too thick, my clothes like costumes. I feel like a parody—not even a parody of a real woman, but a parody of a drag queen.

The positive images of big women that feminism offers have failed to make me feel any more at home. I'm certainly not some earthy goddess figure, ample-bosomed giver of life, mother and caretaker. I tried that one on for size, but it didn't fit. Sure, I'm fat, I don't shave, I eat tofu and organic produce and I love my cat, but that doesn't mean I don't care for some thigh-high fishnets and a slutty low-cut dress when I go out. I care far too much about appearances to ever be some crunchy earth mama.

Do we need other choices? Hell yes. Of course I don't want to be expected to live up to some unattainable ideal established by the media and diet industry, but I don't want to be pressured from the other direction either. I don't want to feel like I can't embellish my natural appearance, have fun with it, be a total girl if I wanna, rather than having to fill another role that's been prescribed for me. It's called self-determination.

I grew up thinking that to be a feminist you had to not care what you looked like. But to me, the idea that if I care what I look like then I'm buying into the patriarchy is laughable. I don't give a shit what men think of the way I look—I have never gotten their validation, and I have no reason to believe I ever will. However I choose to present myself, I do it for me and the ladies—that is, those who get it and wanna play along. I dress up for fun, for play, so I can act out a role for a night or externalize whatever I'm feeling. Yeah, I still play dress-up, and I'm making up for all those years I wore J.C. Penney's version of a feedsack, thinking I was too fat to wear the clothes I really wanted.

As for body image, that important feminist issue, I always find myself confused in the middle of the discussion. When people ask me to write or speak about body image, I always worry that they'll be disappointed. Body image has never really been my *schtick*. I talk about fat. There's a difference. In my experience, the words *poor body image* usually refer to the plight of thin women who think they are fat—something I certainly don't identify with.

What if I were to say I often picture myself as thinner than I really am? Does that mean I have a good body image or a bad one? I suppose that the goal of those working for better body image is to know and accept the reality of their bodies—and that's an admirable goal, but I just wanna be sure this acceptance is open to women who really are fat. I hope I live to see the day when my thin friends will stop telling me and other fat women that they feel gross and fat. I figure, if I can accept myself—when the body I have been given is probably your worst nightmare—then I know you can do the same.

I'm always asked, "But where did you get the strength to accept yourself as you are?" There are days when I shake my head and wonder, "What makes you think I'm that strong?" Other days I say, "Well, what other choice do I have?" Some days I tell them it's a constant struggle, and others I say it just comes naturally to someone as totally awesome as myself.

It would be the easy thing to look at what makes me "different" as a bunch of marks against me, as burdens heaped on me by some unseen and unfair force, just to make my life harder. In middle school especially—the only time in my life when I truly wanted to be a part of the status quo—I remember wishing so hard not to be a Jew, not to be disabled, not to be a queer and above all (funny how things prioritize themselves in a young teenager's mind) not to be fat. But on some level, even when I thought I totally hated who I was, I also knew I was an extraordinary person—that my mind was capable of great things, that I had a wide range of artistic, literary and musical talents, that I had a deeply spiritual side and that I was a loving and devoted friend, sister and daughter. Of course, most of those things seemed irrelevant to me at the time, and I would've gladly traded it all in to be a shallow, conventionally pretty, popular girl.

Luckily, I never fully succumbed to the mind control of middle school. I got out with most of my identity still intact, and now I realize that I haven't changed a bit since I was five years old. It's all part of the package, you know. I have always been the fat freaky femme that I am today: the little princess in the pink rosebud dress, my hair in ten ponytails all over my head. I was the kid who loved Barbie, who begged my parents for a pink carpet and who wanted to wear my hair to school in a ponytail under my chin. Fourth grade queen of the side ponytail, the asymmetrical haircut, the red and black studded fake-leather dress and green fishnets. I worshipped Cyndi Lauper and the movie *Grease,* imagined myself the hot new teen sensation, top of the pops, before Tiffany even dreamed of covering that '60s song and doing a U.S. tour of the malls.

Well, fame didn't come to me in the way I thought it would. I never did a tour of the malls, and the pop song I wrote and recorded at age ten (chorus: "When, oh when will it happen? When? Ooh oh no oh—when? When? Double you-H-E and N. When when, ooh ooh.") never hit the charts. Who could have predicted I would become famous for being fat? Not that I'm famous in the Tiffany way, but the irony of what fame I have received has far outweighed the glory.

Recently, I went on the Internet and found a list of questions with no heading or title other than "Anorexia/Bulimia." Question number three is: "What is Nomy Lamm's revolution? Is Lamm's use of profanity effective? What purpose does it serve? Does Lamm sound angry, and if so, should she? Is she turning off potential supporters through her language? Would she care if she was?"

I have no idea what this list of questions is for, but it sounds like it's for some college class or something. I picture a group of college kids sitting around discussing why I say the word *fuck.*

Her use of profanity is indicative of the times we live in—it is a reaction against a society that rejects her. And so, in turn, she rejects society.

Yes, but her message is diluted by her anger. Is it her intention to drive people away?

Exactly! She wants others to feel the pain of her alienation!

Yeah, experience my pain. *Fuckity fuck fuckaroo fuckaroni.* It's amusing to me to realize that to many people, just saying *fuck* is some big form of rebellion.

Well, like I said before, it's all part of the package. I was always a freak rebel in the ways I knew I could choose to be: the James Dean/Danny Zucco girly girl, a cigarette danglin' from my lip, hair all fucked up, telling anyone who thinks they have authority over me to fuck off. What I wished I could get rid of was what made me feel deep inside like I really was a freak. I feared, yet identified with, the kind of freaks you see in *Guiness Book of World Records.* The thousand-pound man, too fat to get out of bed, or the people with weird congenital deformities, a foot growing out of their side or a head the size of a beach ball. The bearded ladies and "hermaphrodites." The mounds and mounds of flesh, the twisted arms and legs that supposedly give people the right to stare aghast in horror and pity.

No, I never got to choose to be a freak in the ways that make people pity or fear me, look through me like I'm invisible or stare like I'm a zoo animal. I never chose to be fat (despite what Susan Powter or Jenny Craig might say), and I never chose to be born with one leg all fucked up or to get my foot chopped off when I was three. I never chose to like girls (though I did choose to admit it to myself, and I can't see how I'd be happy any other way) or to feel like a not-really-a-woman.

But what makes me so arrogant as to think I'd be happier if I were a freak only in ways that are acceptable to society? And what the hell is a socially acceptable freak? I wanna be more marketable? I wanna see myself on MTV, part of the X-yeah-bore-me-to-death generation? That's not a freak, and it's not a rebel. It's a decoy.

I guess I'm lucky I was made a freak before I could choose to be one, cuz I got no illusions about that pseudo-rebellion that's being marketed to my generation. Here in Olympia, home of riot grrrl and indie rock, the fashion-conscious often find themselves emulating the images we created, images that were stolen and then sold back to us in watered-down form. But the media and the corporations will always be a step behind life, and the true rebels, freaks and queers (and there are many) continue to write our own stories, to paint our own lives, to sew our own clothes and to sow our own seeds. We are the ones choosing to be our free and freaky selves, always making a scene in the most inappropriate places, spitting defiantly in the face of authority and its values, wearing our Friday-night best, dancing like fiends toward revolution. Life is a cabaret, my friends.

the chosen people
tali edut

When I was ten years old, my hometown of Oak Park, Michigan, was chosen to be wired for cable television. My technophobic parents, who had refused to buy me and my sisters an Atari game system or let us watch *Charlie's Angels,* consented uncharacteristically to the added fifty channels.

There was one condition, of course. A "lockbox" would be installed so they could use "parental discretion" to deny our access to HBO and Cinemax. Although my mother had read us *How Babies Are Made* before we had even wondered how they were made, called our private parts by their proper medical names and talked openly about her "Auntie M" (menstruation) coming to visit, she felt that R-rated movies would steal away our youth before its time.

Before the lockbox discussion, I knew little more of sex than the ova and the swimming sperm illustrated in *How Babies Are Made.* And the loving, hand-drawn couple that resembled my parents . . . well,

I just didn't want to think about that one. My sisters and I had been sent out of the room once when *Coal Miner's Daughter* was on network television and had wondered what in the world the big deal was. "Neeeeeevermind," my father shouted, shooing us from the country-fried dramatization of Loretta Lynn's life. I knew there was something more. Something fruity and forbidden. I wanted a taste. I wanted to know.

Shortly following the installation, my sisters and I slipped the lockbox key from its "hiding place," pedaled furiously to the hardware store for a duplicate and returned the stolen treasure unnoticed. With that simple act of theft, The Summer of Soft Porn was born.

The plan went like this: First, the three of us would pore over the TV guide for premier R-rated showings. Our interest remained focused exclusively on movies that had words like *Nudity* and *Adult Content* printed in italics next to the title. If, say, *The Last American Virgin* was on HBO one warm Wednesday night, we would strategically beg to sleep in the living room, where the air conditioner and, of course, the cable-wired TV were located. If we got the thumbs up, the sofabed would be pulled out and we would lie in wait for our parents to go to sleep. When the coast was clear, the spare key would be produced, the remote control engaged, the volume lowered. With our eyes locked to the TV, we waited eagerly for a kiss to become the unsnapping of a bra, the unzipping of a fly. These were the things we never knew men and women did together—seduction, deceit, adultery, one-night stands; and all this as they tore each other's clothes off.

As I watched women run screaming and naked through the locker room upon discovering the peeping pranksters of *Porky's*, I wondered—is this my future? Will I be the type of chick who hangs around naked after gym class? Will I be as desirable as Betty Chiles in *Revenge of the Nerds*, the girl whose naked picture boys paid big bucks to lick whipped cream off? Will I smolder with such sexiness

tali edut   89

that Lionel Richie will watch me unnoticed as I sculpt his face, and then dial my number singing, "Hello. . . . Is it me you're looking for?"

Well, I think you can guess the answer to that one. When I finally started growing the things that made the R-rated starlets sexy, they didn't quite come together in the same way. I had the personality without the personalititties. The drive without the self-esteem. My wishes screamed *Risky Business,* but all I had was a subscription to *ym.* I wanted the cable TV fantasy cruise. I wanted to be a goddess.

There was one problem, though. I had to wait to be chosen. Because that's how it works for women. A woman has to be chosen before she can choose. She has to wait for ten guys to pursue her, and in the security of this knowledge, she is then allowed to choose one, and only one, Mr. Right. Men go out and choose, conquer, collect a harem of devotees. A notorious player will still have girls fighting over him on *Jerry Springer,* screaming "he's mine!" while he sits back and smokes a mental victory cigar.

A woman who considers asking a guy out on a date worries endlessly about being too "forceful," which, we're told, makes men feel pressured, nagged, fenced in. Instead, we tempt, we scheme, we ask his brother's best friend to do a little digging around. We normally don't wake up one morning, pick a potential boyfriend, walk up to him and say, "Dude, I think you're attractive and was wondering if I could invite you to dinner sometime." Words like these make his balls shoot up into his abdomen faster than a space shuttle on a launch pad. They "emasculate," taking away all that's supposedly fun about being a guy—the chasing, the conquering, the trophy-collecting. Basic message: Easy is bad. Easy leaves you alone with no assets. The opposite of easy is hard. And hard, we know, is how men like it. So that's how we have to make it for them. And since it's a man's world, that makes it hard for everyone.

90   the chosen people

Women, we just want to do the right thing. It's so easy for us to make the "wrong" choice, but so hard for the world to forgive us for our social sins. We're so busy worrying about shit like this, that we forget to worry about what we want.

Sometimes all we want is to be held. To be told that we are the most beautiful, desirable, amazing, smart, sexy woman on the planet. To be, in essence, Chosen, made beautiful and whole by the approving nod of the Boyfriend.

At fourteen, I started hitting the bottle. It was Clairol semipermanent color in "Strawberry Blond." It seemed I had two choices when it came to my looks: I could be invisible (read: wear comfortable clothes and no makeup, spend weekends baby-sitting) or on full digital display (read: wear uncomfortable clothes, wake up one hour earlier to curl my bangs, be noticed for more than my answers on a pop quiz). I chose the latter. And, a few months later, I was chosen for the first time. It was hardly an easy match on paper: He was an awkward saxophone player from a languid, blue-collar Southern family that ate Kentucky Fried Chicken on every major holiday; I, an artsy, misfit Israeli-American Jewess whose family dinners usually turned into screaming, finger-waving arguments. In a lot of ways, I was more attracted to the idea of him liking me than the reality of who he was.

I had a subscription to *ym*, so I knew what I was supposed to do. But, for the first two months, every time I sensed him homing in for a kiss, I would discover something phenomenal 180 degrees away from his lips. Finally, after personal pep talks, I gave in. It wasn't that I wanted to kiss him necessarily—what was important was that he had chosen me out of 163 other freshman girls, that there was one guy on the planet who found me attractive. The magic moment I'd waited for had arrived. And I was scared out of my Sassoons. But, I closed my eyes and went for it. And it was weird. After a few days of practice it wasn't half bad. And soon enough, I started to enjoy it.

That kiss set the stage as we moved from one proverbial base to the next. I wasn't sure I wanted him to unfasten my bra or my belt, but I let him do it anyway. Inside, I was frozen with uncertainty. Fooling around became a game of resistance and surrender. I wasn't really taking, I wasn't really giving. But I wasn't really stopping him either. My mind was saying, *Who do I think I am to say no? I'm not really pretty. I'd better be happy someone likes me at all.* And my body just went along with it. At sixteen, I lost my virginity. Not because I wanted to, not because I didn't want to. It just seemed to follow the irresponsible, noncommunicative pattern we had established of "just doing it."

It never crossed my mind that I could tell him to slow down or stop. Kissing, touching, sex—it was all supposed to be a little traumatic and out of control for women. All the romantic classics I'd read in English class confirmed the historical accuracy of this idea. In fact, we never really talked about our physical activity at all; we didn't even talk while we were messing around. I just closed my eyes, shut my mouth and did it.

Society had set me up to victimize myself. The sexual starlets of the silver screen were the women with the ultimate power; but outside Hollywood, it still wasn't safe or respectable for me to be that kind of woman. So to be sexually active meant to be secretive. Which meant to be silent. Which meant to be silenced. Which meant choice, negotiating, communicating about sex was next to impossible. I felt like my own rapist, stealing my own voice, my own choice, my own power from myself.

Sometimes, while we were doing it, my mind was whirling: *What am I doing? Is this really happening?* Other times, I was as concentrated as a professional athlete, totally focused on the knock-down, drag-out flesh fests that consumed so many hours of my teenage years.

Strange things started happening as a result of this "code of silence." I began to develop two identities: There was the sweet girlfriend who cooed "I love you" and played more miniature golf than she'd care to remember. Then there was the silent sex goddess who kept her mouth busy kissing, never uttering a word while she rolled around under a blanket in his parents' basement. The girlfriend me was the one I chattered about with my sisters and friends. The sexual me, well that was a different story.

I was both addicted to her and ashamed of her. His sexual attraction to me gave me a strong rush of power. This was what I had been waiting for since that fateful Summer of Soft Porn. I was the starlet, riding the wave of desirability; the girl whose skirt guys wanted to peek up. I made him a stud, the envy of his Dungeons & Dragons–playing boys. He brought me into the realms of social acceptability, the envy of my prom-dateless girls. I rebuilt my self-esteem, placing him at the epicenter. I would leave his house feeling lighter than air, powerful and desirable after eight hours of making out. Back at home, the high would swiftly wear off. A thousand doubts would swirl through my head. I would crash, feeling ugly, undesirable, frustrated and depressed. Why did I feel as if my mind and body existed on separate planes? Why did I feel so damn out of control, so unable to connect these two sides of my personality? How could this relationship, which was supposed to be the savior of my awkward inner child, make me feel like such a tool?

Frustrated, I would call him, forcing the conversation to escalate into a petty argument over trivial dating affairs. Inevitably, I'd start crying and feeling rejected, and then he would console and validate me by saying he loved me. This cycle repeated itself until I couldn't stand to be around myself anymore. I was dizzy from rotating on his axis: *I want to feel powerful. I want to feel respected. I want to feel like even though I'm sixteen and having sex that you don't think I'm a slut. I want to be the kind of woman who doesn't care what you think of me. I want to be able to have a voice, but I'm afraid to say the wrong thing because then you might leave me and then who will be the center of my universe?* Exhausted by the high highs and the low lows, I ended the relationship after two and a half years. I had gone from blinking virgin to seasoned sex addict, and I couldn't even vote yet. I had some advanced sexual skills under my belt. And yet, I was clueless about so many of the basics.

I wish I could say that after the breakup I transformed into a glib sexual ambassador who simply started blurting out everything on my mind. But going from chosen to chooser is a process, one that will likely continue throughout my life. As I'm discovering, each level of life brings a new way of challenging a woman's self-esteem. Just when I think I can relax, the rules change. So, the most important choice I've made is to ignore the rules as much as possible.

It's funny how one thing feeds into another. As I learn to feel more comfortable basing my self-esteem inside of me, I become more secure with voicing my thoughts. In turn, I feel a greater sense of control in relationships because I know what I'm getting myself into. My relationships have become less he-loves-me/he-loves-me-not and more I-love-him/I-love-him-not. And my mind and my body are moving closer with each step. I'd rather leave the drama to Aaron Spelling.

Nevertheless, I'm not quite a poster child for duty-free self-esteem. I still tense up with self-consciousness when a guy unbuttons my clothes for the first time. My idea of mood lighting is dim to pitch black. The other day, I caught myself getting excited when I realized I could produce the appearance of cleavage by lying on my side and letting my "east/west" boobs scrunch together. And I wasted a bit of time on this revelation before I noticed how uncomfortable it was leaning on my elbow.

94   the chosen people

I guess it's like the old saying sort of goes, dammit. *You can take the girl out of the R-rated movie, but you can't take the R-rated movie out of the girl.* Still, whether my sex life is rated PG, R or XXX, I want a leading role. I want lines. And, most of all, I want it to be self-directed.

food for our souls
dyann logwood

When my father died a few years ago, the house was filled with visitors. My dad was a gentle person who picked cotton as a teenager, served in the military and worked thirty years as an auto plant supervisor. He was well loved in the community. On Sundays, he took the pulpit regularly at our Pentecostal church, preaching about the ways that kinship and a righteous life would save black people's souls. His early passing hit our congregation hard.

It was no surprise, the September week that the cancer took him, when the cars piled into my mother's gravel driveway. Doors swung open, delivering family and well-wishers, each newcomer bearing a lovingly prepared dish of home-cooked food. Fried chicken, glazed hams, buttered rolls, fruitcakes, cupcakes, homemade cookies. Comfort food. Soul food. As my spirit wept and my plate was piled higher, I truly understood what that meant.

Two months later, I swept the last crumbs from our refrigerator, feeling hollow and tired. At a time when I needed some spiritual strength, my beliefs no longer offered solid ground. I always thought that if you didn't drink or smoke, you'd live a long life. But at age forty-nine, my father, who did neither, got cancer, and at fifty-one he passed away. Witnessing that rocked my security and shook my faith in the strong, loving community that once sheltered me.

I grew up among black working- and middle-class, churchgoing folks who loved to eat. No matter what the occasion—family reunion, graduation, holiday or funeral—food was the guest of honor. It was also our resistance. Eating with zest and abandon was like turning centuries of oppression upside down. What's known today as soul food was once our *sole* food—scraps rejected by white plantation owners because they were considered unfit for consumption. That these recipes are now considered cuisine testifies to the ingenious ways that African Americans have always "made a way outta no way." By virtue of collard greens, pigs' feet and chitlins, we declare, "See, we won't starve. We won't allow you to steal the joy from our lives. In fact, we'll have second, third and fourth helpings just to prove it."

As a girl, I was encouraged to eat and to get some meat on my bones. Rounding out was considered healthy. And as I got older and began to develop into a woman's shape, my opinions rounded out, too. My increasing physical presence had a profound effect on the men around me. My precocious remarks, which were "cute" when I was little, were suddenly deemed inappropriate. It was clear my elders felt I needed to be put back in my place. But my place had expanded with my size. I took up more space and fought with anyone who dared to tread too far across those boundaries.

Filling up space was important to me. It meant that in a larger world that might want to keep a black girl silent, I could not be ignored. As my body filled out, I got louder, smarter and bolder. My hand shot up in class, and I became known for being, well, a little bit cocky. It helped that I was born with a deep, distinctive voice. It was low and powerful, and I knew from my father's Sunday morning example how to dramatically project and inflect it in a way that made people stop and take notice. In high school, my favorite teacher, Trudy Adams, encouraged me to enter local speaking contests. After a while, my voice filled the tall shelf in our living room with trophies, blue ribbons and plaques.

It was strange sometimes, getting up in auditoriums to speak about racism and Martin Luther King, Jr.'s legacy, often to a mostly white audience. In some ways, I now realize it was kind of brave. But my full stomach helped me use my full voice, and I delivered impassioned, fifteen-year-old diatribes with a steady gaze and an even tone.

Still, it wasn't enough for me simply to be heard—I wanted to be seen, too. Since my height peaked just under five feet, I decided to make up for my "shortcoming" by filling out in the other directions. My body was happy to cooperate. Between my own version of the four food groups—sugar, fat, salt and caffeine—and some sturdy genes, I became one thick soul sistah. People joked that they could tell I wasn't starving. But their teasing was meant as a compliment, for it implied that I was taking care of myself.

I became proud of my body, because I was beginning to resemble the women I admired at my church. Although it would take me years to adopt their poised sashays and proudly cocked heads, I looked in the mirror and felt thick, confident and strong. (I would later be told by my doctor that I was "chubby, anemic and unhealthy"—but more on that in a little while.)

Food has always been something of a status symbol in the black community, suggesting that a new day has arrived for African Americans to rejoice in abundant "health" and prosperity. I never thought for a moment that the hearty meals I enjoyed the most, meals that were part of my culture, could be harmful to my body. I just thought I was eating well.

I once went on a dinner date with a football player who was on a low-fat diet. He was under the impression I was a "salad and water only" kind of gal. At the Italian restaurant I ate three plates of food and he ate one. The waiter looked at my clean dishes in amazement and asked if he could wrap up my date's unfinished dinner. I spoke up and told the waiter that would not be necessary, as I planned to finish his dinner as well. "It's always the little ones who love to eat," my date joked. I told him I had been raised with, "Always clean your plate, and if it's a free dinner, eat all you can." He laughed, but, needless to say, we never went out to a restaurant again.

One thing I learned from that experience is that women are not supposed to be able to eat comfortably around men. We're supposed to sacrifice our pleasure and suppress our desire to be full. If we're full, we're satisfied—and we can think and produce. When women starve, we become weak, dependent on men for strength and stability. Hungry women are silent and invisible. Their wants, needs and desires go unaddressed. What I didn't realize was that unhealthy eating habits can be as dangerous as not eating at all.

Although my parents forced me to eat fruits and vegetables as a child (a practice I abandoned in my teens), they never taught me what a proper diet really meant. Today, magazines like *Heart and Soul* and *Essence* devote themselves to encouraging a new culture of nutrition, fitness and health among African Americans. And although this trend is growing, we keep these strange new values at safe distance from our most sacred and authentic spaces. Nobody from my hometown would dream of suggesting, say, a vegetarian church picnic. And while I've heard talk of local churches educating their congregations about diabetes, cancer and heart disease, few people will go whole hog to quit the chitlins, ribs and ham hocks.

But my father's death was a wake-up call for me. The emotional toll left me fatigued and depressed, and my own health began to break down. Some days, I didn't have enough energy to get out of bed, or I was beset with headaches so intense I could hardly see.

Finally, I went to the doctor and discovered that I was anemic and dehydrated. I didn't know much about dehydration—I figured I got some water in my system when I drank soda and fruit juices. "You mean to tell me I have to drink eight glasses of water a day?" I asked my doctor in shock. "And add fruit and vegetables to my diet—*and* take iron pills—in order to function?"

In spite of my dismay, I gave nutrition a chance. As I moved through the grieving process, I needed the energy to get out of bed every day. Food that tasted good didn't necessarily make me *feel* good after I ate it. Healthy food helped me to heal.

I was surprised at how quickly my body responded to the new regimen. I took garlic pills to strengthen my immune system and drank herbal teas that reduced my migraine headaches. I also drank lots of water and carrot juice, which boosted my energy and helped me stay awake without caffeine. I even tried tofu, which I had once scorned, refusing to believe that it could taste as good as beef or chicken. (Well, that may be true, but when prepared well, it ain't half bad.) And there was something culturally reminiscent in my new *au naturel* lifestyle: My grandmother could throw a handful of herbs into a pot and make a tea that would cure any ailment in no time.

Gradually I added new regimens: I joined a gym, bought vitamins and even went to counseling. I know the stereotype: "Black people don't need counseling—that's for crazy white people!" But my soul needed more than literal food. I believed strongly that my body and my soul were interconnected, and I wanted to take a holistic approach to my healing.

The change showed up on the outside: I lost about twenty pounds.

It was never my intention to get smaller, but that's what happens when you cut junk food out of your diet. Funny, as the pounds came off, my family began to worry that I was unhealthy. Their main concern was that I "wasn't eating right."

Black people have a way of discussing weight, I've noticed, as a metaphor for well-being. For us, "You're so thin" often translates into "Are you okay?" Thinness doesn't always imply privilege or that we have leisure time on our hands to work out and obsess over calories. Usually, it's taken as a telltale sign of a sister who's overworked, burdened, burning out—someone who's not quite holding it all together. Even in the fitness-crazed '90s, the sight of a thin black woman still invokes a lot of questioning.

Sure, black women come in all shapes and sizes, but it's no coincidence that what we call "healthy" is exactly what white America considers the opposite—twenty pounds "overweight" and yes, "fat." Even the naturally thin among us will scorn that flat, dimensionless body type that the fashion magazines wave in our faces. After all, it reminds us of a mold that 99.9 percent of us will never fit, even with the "right" body. Save for a Tyra or a Naomi, most black women intrinsically know we'll always be "too much" of this or "not enough" of that to fit the American beauty standard.

But what, really, is a healthy African-American body? Somewhere in the struggle to reclaim what is uniquely ours—that real or imaginary physical difference from our oppressor's image—black women have forgotten to define our health on our own terms. Even as we continue to embrace the diversity of sizes among us, we must ask, what does a healthy body *feel* like? It's a loaded issue that carries the threat of loss, or cultural alienation. If we abandon our foods and our notions of health, what do we put in their place?

At the brink of the millennium, being healthy may be the most rebellious act a black woman can commit. If we develop healthy body *image,* without developing healthy *bodies,* it's a hollow victory. We can't survive as a people if we're dying young. We need a cultural prescription for well-being—one that will give us the energy to continue the fight.

It's a challenge for sure, and one that often begins at the back of the buffet line. My willpower was put to the test last summer when I dropped by my cousin's graduation barbecue. Surrounded by platters of honey-baked ham and mounds of potato salad and with savory steam rising from the backyard grill, I felt a nostalgic pull toward the serving table. Sitting quietly on a picnic bench, my Styrofoam plate bearing a meager heap of collard greens and skinless chicken, I felt more than conspicuous. I was caught in the act of culinary treason, deserting my culture like the oft-caricatured Ph.D. who comes back to the 'hood and is met with hostile suspicion.

Not that anyone was hostile toward me. Bewildered, perhaps, or a little amused. A few people even nodded in encouragement when I explained my new health credo, mumbling affirmations as they spooned up potato salad swirled in tangy barbecue sauce. Mostly, I think they just felt sorry for me, because I was missing out on all that delicious food—the joyous bonding ritual, the ecstasy of each perfectly seasoned bite. By my glum face, they could tell I knew it, too.

Still, I stuck to my resolve—and continue to do so to this day. I was fueled recently after watching the movie *Soul Food,* which was based on the premise that traditional food can unite a black family. Although my mouth watered through most of the footage, I also hoped for a message—one that would support prevalent statistics about the detrimental effects of a high-fat, high-cholesterol diet. Instead, when the matriarchal grandmother passes away from diabetes, her next of kin gather over fried chicken, collard greens, cornbread and dessert.

This year, I graduated from college—and you *know* food was a guest at the celebration. Naturally, my friends arrived expecting the table to be set with all the usual suspects. Instead, they were greeted with platters of cut fruits and vegetables, as well as a few traditional dishes prepared in a healthier fashion. I knew they were a little weirded out by it, so I encouraged them to fill their plates and gather around the various couches and chairs.

Funny, since food wasn't the party's focus, people started to talk. In the past, they would clean their plates and then want to go home for a nap. This time was different; and the recipe, it seemed, was a success. Our mouths weren't too stuffed to sit and reminisce, talk, bond—which we did, for hours. Our voices lifted the delicate sweetness of memories, the juiciness of laughter, the tenderness of loving spirits that seasoned our culture with a rich and wonderful flavor.

strip!
diana courvant

If you ever want power: Strip.

Now, I wouldn't strip in a smoky, dim club for men who like to exercise control from the shadows—too often using more than just imagination or money. But I live every day in a misunderstood body, and I have never had a day that taught me more confidence, more self-love or more power than the day I stripped.

Five years before that day, no one would have noticed anything exceptional about me. Being clean, white, tall and thin, I looked like the picture of an average American—an average American man. But that picture was one without a history.

As a four-year-old, I was convinced I would grow up to be a mother. As a seven-year-old, I fought urgently for girls to be admitted to boys' games. I took their exclusion personally, in a way that other children couldn't quite understand. But it was vital, even visceral to me. Perhaps those feelings were even more important to me because

I couldn't explain (or forget) them. In that sense, they were similar to the pain that had been in my joints for as long as I could remember. When I was young, that pain was dismissed, along with my visions of motherhood, as a phase. But I never outgrew either.

With my first lover, a woman I met in high school, it was both eerie and wonderful to feel excitement in my breasts and nipples, an excitement that seemed to come from above and within me at the same time. Closing my eyes, the boundaries of a body that would enclose all those feelings shone whole and real on the backs of my eyelids.

My facial hair came in late, thin, blond and patchy. Hating the ritual of shaving, I found the hairs easier to ignore. After a week or two, my skin itching, I would take them off, sometimes with a chemical hair remover, sometimes with a razor, but always with a mixture of unease and amusement at the idea of a beard on my face. When I began to work, to look for a career, I planned it around the vision of myself as a mother. As I walked along a sunny sidewalk, blond hairs on my chin, pregnancy plans rolling through my head, and pain ever worsening in my knees, it hardly occurred to me that I might be seen as anything like an average man.

Over the next year, as I came to acknowledge my transsexual identity, others did begin to see me as less and less average, taking clues more from my new openness than from any changes in my body. Though I planned to go through electrolysis, then hormone therapy and, finally, surgery, those steps all required money and time. Instead, or in anticipation, I came out to each of my friends. Some were confused or denied my experience, thinking that because I had dated women, that I couldn't *be* a woman. So, in coming out trans, I also had to come out as a lesbian. My best friend, a bisexual woman, was the most supportive. She bought me a "dyke" pin and gave me a copper pendant in the shape of a goddess. I wore both everywhere. And, I named myself Diana.

I had long been depressed, but my self-image was improving. I used my rising energy to break out of unemployment and take a job conducting surveys over the telephone. Though it felt good to use my new energies and to work for the money I needed for my transition, every time I met a new co-worker or spoke to a stranger over the phone I felt nervous. I knew the discordance between my name and my body or voice would conjure images of drag queens in sequins and heels.

Though I felt more whole than at any other time in my life, many would assume I must have a second, separate life filled with Cover Girl makeup and matching handbags. Actually, I had long preferred loose silk shirts or cotton T's in neutral colors worn over jeans or slacks. It was an androgynous look that felt comfortable to me, especially since most of my clothes were years old and broken in just how I liked them. Even if I had had the money for clothes, I would have spent most of it on new copies of favorite clothes that were pulling slowly apart at the seams. In a culture with a decades-long Barbie fetish, only my friends in the lesbian community could understand how I could claim a feminine identity without adopting dominant feminine beauty standards. Acquaintances or strangers would often ask why, if I were a woman, I didn't have on a dress. I wondered, but didn't ask, if they couldn't see all the other women on the street wearing slacks or shorts or sweatpants.

On the streets, my unease at meeting new people often turned to outright fear. Though I was six-foot-three, something in my body language would cause people who saw me from behind to call me ma'am or miss. If I turned around, my scattered, scruffy facial hair convinced most they had made a horrible mistake, for which they would apologize abjectly, calling me sir. Then, if I were introduced, my name would elicit a second disconcerted apology. Some took my androgynous looks and clothing in stride, but others would stare with hostility, as if I had intentionally caused their confusion and embarrassment.

Because a political campaign against queers had sparked threats and violence throughout the state I lived in, my fear grew to a point where I could feel the eyes of anyone looking at me. Hypervigilant, I read each pair to discover whether I would disgust or offend them because I was not the Diana they expected. Would they hate me? Would I be seen as a freak?

It wasn't long before I found out. I began pursuing a medical transition to a body that for years had been my self-image. But I was required to get a psychotherapist's approval for each step: hormone therapy, changing the designated "Sex" on my driver's license, sex reassignment surgery and, eventually, recognition in a court of law. Because the entire process takes years to complete, I wanted to begin hormone therapy right away.

I picked out a therapist who advertised in a women's resource directory as a specialist in "gender issues." A telephone call confirmed that she treated trans clients and that she recommended hormone therapy for some of them. Within the first hour of my initial evaluation, she told me she wouldn't write the letter of recommendation I needed to begin hormone therapy until I had the money in the bank to pay for sex reassignment surgery. "Anyone," she went on, "with breasts and a penis is a freak." Well, there it was, and it was *not* very reassuring. Not only was I an official freak, but I was only going to get freakier.

Though I wasn't ashamed of being a trans woman, I began to realize the safety issues inherent in my growing visibility. Being a freak was dangerous. I didn't know how people would react to me— would their hatred and discomfort move them to violence? Never sure of the answer, I would vacillate between claiming my identity and withdrawing from people. More and more I wanted to hide, to blend in. Though jeans and flannel were usually too "butch" for me, I sometimes wore the more butch clothes from my closet to be more anonymous.

Not that I felt safe even then: The gender police were always on patrol. Flat chested/small breasted? Wearing jeans and a T-shirt? Maybe a pair of earrings? Here they come. "You a fag?" "Dyke!" "Hey babe, you tryin' to be a man?" I've heard it all: twice. I could have gone crazy trying to figure out what makes a woman "normal" and what makes her a freak.

When you play the gender game by everyone else's rules, you can only lose. So, I stopped listening to the taunts and the slime. If I was going to be a freak, at least I'd be my own freak, making my own choices.

Linen slacks, denim jeans, velvet dresses: I started wearing whatever I wanted. As electrolysis and hormones moved me further into androgyny, it became obvious that people had an incredible ability to ignore the obvious when deciding my gender. "Dyke" pins, height, breasts, facial hair: Most people felt they had to ignore something, since I had to be male or female, didn't I? But there were no tall, bearded women or breasted, dykey men in American gender vocabularies. Most people would simply pretend that parts of me or my personality didn't exist, that they could still use simple categories to describe me. It was amazing how many familiar strangers—regular passengers or drivers on the buses I rode, grocery clerks in the neighborhood stores, servers in my favorite restaurants—were sure I was a man, while just as many were sure I was a woman. No matter how hard I worked to keep myself from getting tagged a freak, I realized that most people looking at me worked even harder.

But wearing whatever was in my closet, using whichever bathroom felt safest, every one of those choices painted me as a target. Still, they were choices I was willing to make, chances I was willing to take . . . until the next time I was stalked by a man with a vicious leer as I walked home from the bus stop. Those stalkings were society's unsubtle reminders that if you wear a target, someone will shoot at you. Sooner or later, someone will shoot.

In that respect, some good came from my fading visibility. As my joints deteriorated further and my pain increased, walking became so excruciating that I chose to use a cane. Though thinking of myself as disabled came slowly, the cane made an instant difference in my visibility. Bus drivers would pull away from the curb without noticing that I was rising from the bench. Shoppers began to reach right in front of me to get bread or cereal off grocery store shelves. If I borrowed my housemate's electric scooter to carry home grocery items like juice or peanut butter, I might spend ten minutes trying to get a store clerk to reach the top shelves for me.

One day, I was asked to wait by a busy pharmacist, even though I just had to drop off a written prescription before I started shopping. The next woman to arrive began to nudge the footrests of my wheelchair with her ankle, trying to push me away from the register. She wouldn't stop with a look; I had to say, "Excuse me!"

"Oh. Are you in line?" she asked with a look of surprise I found difficult to fathom. I expected her to respect my place in line after that, but when the pharmacist came back, the woman placed her hand on me, leaned heavily on my shoulder and handed her prescription to the pharmacist right over my head. No one could have spun my world around faster. Used to a public that focused overtly on my androgyny, trying at various times to guess, assign or punish my gender, I was completely unprepared for how quickly that same public could turn me into an inconvenient object. And it was all because the rubber I was using to get around town was on a set of tires instead of a pair of Nikes.

For the next two years, I was alternately perceived as a visible freak and a background object, but less and less often. As my breasts grew and the sparse hair on my face diminished, strangers stopped perceiving me as male, or even androgynous, no matter my height. A tall woman, I might still stand out in a crowd, but I presented a gender paradox only infrequently.

As my breasts and face changed, my disabling pain spread into my shoulders, arms and hands. I set aside my cane in favor of bright purple crutches. Purple crutches are so rare—rarer still decorated with stickers and garlands—that they sparked conversation more often than dismissal.

For a time, with new friendships, lessening street harassment and renewed mobility through crutches, wheelchairs and drugs, life took on a deceptive normalcy. It became convenient, or perhaps just healthy, to forget that my body remained freakish because I identified as, looked like and was accepted as a woman, but hadn't had "the operation." The unnoticed truth was that my body had become *more* unusual, more directly challenging to American assumptions about gender, sex and anatomy. I spent as little thought on it as possible, but my body, in its cultural challenge, still wore a target. I never allowed my romantic partners to see me completely naked, and another episode of stalking and abuse on the way home from a bus stop left me shivering with the fear of "what if?" What if my stalker had attempted to rape me in my disabled, transsexual body? I thought of the many rapes and abuses of trans men and women, and of the haunting but unverifiable estimates of how likely I was to be murdered because of my body.

Still, as society's perceptions of me became more and more consistent, I lost some of the need to cling strongly to an anchoring self-identity. I became more free to imagine how others might see me, if they knew as much about me as I knew myself. Eventually, I realized, it was my *self*-perception that had begun to alternate more frequently between freakish and normal, or helpless and able.

Then came a summer conference, a radical women's gathering held in an empty, neglected building that had once been an athletic club. Several women had helped to build ramps to make some of the interior rooms accessible to me in the wheelchair I was using. But when I first used the bathroom I found that the stall with the space and handbars I needed had no door. Since the bathroom itself had no lock, I knew that for four days I would feel unsafe. Every time I transferred from my wheelchair to the toilet or back again, I would be naked to any woman walking in the door. I used the bathroom and tried to leave my fear there, but as I was falling asleep that night, my fear was still with me. It stayed with me in my dreams, and it was with me when I woke.

I hated that fear, and I hated the bathroom where my transsexuality and my disability conspired to make me vulnerable, to expose me, to put me at risk at a women's gathering, a place where I should have felt safe. If I could strip, I suddenly decided, then I wouldn't have to be afraid: There would be no new reactions to fear. Still, I felt like a freak, viscerally. Leaving the gathering seemed easier than exposing my secrets, exposing the breasts and the penis of my transsexual body, something I had never done—still have not done—for the woman who has become my romantic partner. If I hadn't believed so strongly that women's gatherings must be safe spaces for all women, I might have left, conceding to my fear and continuing to conceal my target-body. Instead, I announced to the gathering that I would teach a workshop on transsexual bodies and told my friends that I would strip, maybe . . . probably . . . at least a little.

I spent the morning worrying that the whole idea was crazy enough, and threatening enough, that no one would show up. To keep the workshop from becoming too personal, I felt I needed at least eight to ten women to attend. Instead, eighty to ninety women came. Nearly every woman who attended any part of the gathering, as well as the few men there, came to the room that had once been used for aerobics to hear me talk about transsexual bodies, and to see me strip.

I started with my socks, throwing them backwards over my head. For ten minutes or so, I spoke about my feet and about the appreciation for them I have gained through a friend who lost hers in a train-hopping accident. My necklace was next. It was my goddess image, which had its own symbolic significance for me, and I spoke about wearing it in the early days of my transition as a visible symbol of my core self. Then I took off my shirt and spoke of growing breasts, of second puberty, of the hormones I will take every day for the rest of my life. When I removed my pants, I looked at my legs. They seemed both weak and strong to me. I spoke of the days when my pain was less and I used a bicycle for transportation. I talked about how I would never lose the image of my legs swollen strong with blood after propelling me seven hundred miles in seven days. I spoke of the pain and how it changed from day to day. I spoke about what I still could accomplish using my legs and what was now out of reach.

And then I pulled my underwear past my knees, over my feet and off of my body. Using my wheelchair's arms, I stood. My testicles and penis, shrunken by estrogens, hung between my legs, while my breasts, firm and growing from the same hormones, stood out from my chest. I introduced the room to my transsexual body, my disabled body, my woman's body. I realized, as I stood naked, that I was the freak my onetime therapist wanted to keep me from becoming. I even told the gathering, "This is the body of a freak." And though I felt it, deeply, painfully and truly, that was not the description of myself or my body that was written in the eyes watching me.

I spent over an hour answering any and all questions, naked in body and soul, before it was time for the gathering to turn its attention to other workshops. Friends gathered my socks, thanked me briefly and left me alone to dress. It wasn't until then that I noticed the mirrors that had been behind me as I had been stripping and naked. It occurred to me that it might be years before I discovered exactly how naked I had been. I went to the bathroom, giddy and giggling with the twinges of insecurity I couldn't quite leave behind. In contrast to the intense fears that had been with me for a full day, I found the twinges more reassuring than frightening.

Coming home again, I moved through a city of hundreds of thousands with a different confidence. No matter which of those hundreds of thousands of different interpretations of the stereotypes of gender or ability I might have to confront, I had stripped naked. I had stripped naked, before women and men, and been seen not as a freak, not as an object, but as a woman, as a person, with a unique and human power.

lucy, i'm home
jill corral

MHF seeks . . . er, BiWF seeks companions of any gender for
friendship, salsa dancing, clubbing and forays to the border-
lands . . .

I love personal ads for their frankness. Gender, race and orientations
of all sorts are stripped down to the basics for optimal scanning.
Everything is black or white, so to speak, and there's not much room
for nuance or elaboration.

I've placed a few personals in my day and wrestled with the
available descriptors. I'm married and bisexual. I'm Cuban, and my
skin is white. *But, but, but . . . how many of the code letters can I*
use? Very few matters in life can be answered with a pure "yes" or
"no," or with the diligent circle-filling of a number two pencil. The
choices are confining, inadequate.

Instead, I've always been drawn to what author Gloria Anzaldúa
calls *la frontera.* Anzaldúa, a Chicana lesbian, describes "the border-

lands," where one inhabits two places, but is never entirely in either. *La frontera* is both a no-woman's land and a fertile middle ground on which to create something new. The lines in the sand can be literal, geographical, like those between countries. Or the boundaries can be fuzzier, like the personal politica of identity and community. I'm variously accounted for as Latina or Hispanic. I've been with women, and I've been with men; I could be described as bisexual, though I hate the word for myriad reasons. Body and identity politics are a bitch, mired in a morass of labels, line-drawing and in-fighting over authenticity. It's enough to make a girl strike out into a new frontier.

So I have.

My parents are Cuban-born U.S. citizens. As the daughter of immigrants, my self often feels split, part old country and part new. Spanish is my first language, but I speak English better and French just as well. I've never been to Cuba, though I've seen it once from a plane and another time from a cruise ship. It's illegal for Americans to go there as tourists. In the purest biological sense, the blood pumping through my heart is from Cuba. I am nostalgic for something I never lived. I am the first person in both my family lines born in this country, and the last to speak Spanish.

I was raised in the Midwest, near Detroit. For twenty years I didn't really know or interact with any Hispanic folk beyond my immediate family. I recently moved to San Francisco and am reeling from the Spanish radio, TV shows, billboards and neighborhoods with real live Hispanophones. I go down to the city's Mission District and load up on exotic "comfort" goodies—*malta, materva,* guava paste and huge green plantains for frying. This strange, far-away place was oddly homey to me from the moment I arrived. The ninety-mile distance between Cuba and Miami (the worlds-away migration my family made to the United States), though, still seems a much greater leap than the 2,500 miles I traveled here from Michigan. My mom likes to say her grandchildren will probably live on the moon.

My "Cubanity" is portable, not fixed to a geographical place, because for me there has been no dirt-or-sand homeland. It has been my family, their stories, my own off-center experiences and tropical imaginings that are the rocks and shells collected from my physical and spiritual lives—My Own Private Havana. I own this virtual nation, and its presence in me will always provide a vantage view from the edges of American culture. I have a bit of a traveler's gaze on the country in which I was born. My favorite video game as a child was "Atlantis," named for the mythical island civilization that sunk to the floor of the Atlantic. To say I feel I inhabit a ghost island wouldn't be inaccurate.

In the United States, I am Hispanic, but the technical boundaries blur with the winds of politics, when from one year to the next CubanAmerican falls from the dean's list of Hispanicity in terms of affirmative action, college admissions, the census or immigration laws. Mexicans "make a run for the border," and Cubans wash up on South Beach. Who's more "real," a brown or a beige Latino? Seeking hard-and-fast, outward "proof" of my inner landscape is futile. It is my soul, in fact, which often feels like the most definite clue to my Latin-ness. I often joke that my blood is imported, that I have a special kind of dancing gene, a Cuban spirit that comes through in the way I move, talk, gesture. It's the way I need to live near water, the way my eyes tear up at seeing U.S. and Cuban flags waving together. It's the way I laugh "too loud" and the way my ears understand Spanish guitar better than any other sound on earth. It's the way my Spanish voice sounds truest to me. The soul is not so easily hidden.

Growing up, the word *Castro* meant one thing only—Fidel, whose image my grandmother would burn out of newspapers with a cigarette. The cigar-chomping dictator was Satan on Earth, the man who had robbed my family of its homes and homeland in the 1960s Cuban Revolution. In the '70s in the United States, another sort of revolution took place, the "sexual" one, one that included gay liberation and the construct of what now stands as the gayest place in San Francisco and likely the world—a neighborhood called The Castro. I still have a visceral, negative reaction to the name—but in another way it also now means home.

I've inhabited three places in my life, all of them peninsulas—Florida, Michigan, San Francisco. The last of these lies on the edge of the continent, *in extremis*. From having a reputation as a fringe culture to being as far as you can go without falling into the ocean, California is where people have always come to reinvent themselves. It's *el Norte* to Mexicans, the far East to Asians and the far West Mecca to the gay world. More than any place, it's a near-borderless middle ground. At land's end. I could scarcely have imagined a more perfect outpost for someone like me.

In my favorite *Seinfeld* episode, the Elaine character can't figure out if the man she's dating is black or white, and spends most of the show testing him for clues—finally rejoicing when he refers to them as an interracial couple. In the end, however, it turns out that he thought she was Hispanic. Both are sorely disappointed to find themselves in an unexotic, plain white pairing. Then they go to The Gap.

I laughed my head off at the perfect similarity to my life. In 1993, I married my best friend, who is a Caucasian man. Technically, we constitute an interracial relationship. However, not everyone who sees us together notices that. My skin is pale, and with my black hair and small stature, I'm often taken for a Mediterranean import—variously interpreted as Italian, Arabic, Jewish or just Hispanic. My last name, Corral, is Spanish, but again not quite as obviously so as Garcia or Rodriguez. (*Hispanos* always know, though. Takes one to know one?) People tell me I don't look Cuban or Latina. I've had other more-Latina-than-thou types snub me for "passing," as if I had somehow chosen a deceptive skin color. Chalk it up to ignorance or insecurity. The truth is, it's interesting to travel *incognita,* to not be easily classifiable. And to emerge from obscurity when those around me think it's "safe" to make ethnic or homophobic slurs.

On paper, I'm legally straight. Although I'm married, I haven't stopped identifying as queer. I straddle the boundary delineating hetero- and homosexuality. The path of self-disclosure varies with the situation, if it is taken at all. On my resume, I list myself as a "native speaker of Spanish." Occasionally, it comes up in a job interview, and I will be interrogated on my ethnicity, although it's technically illegal to ask about it in that context. I once contributed to a magazine article on queer issues and found out later a manager had told my coworkers by way of introduction (prior to my arrival) that I worked on a bisexual magazine. Although her oversimplification could have caused me some undue problems on the job, I half wanted to thank her for saving me some work.

Mostly, I was bothered because I'm a very private person by nature. A very private person who nonetheless marched for miles waving a makeshift Bi Pride sign in San Francisco's annual parade and chanted *Hay maricones, en los balcones* ("there are fags in the balconies") with the marching throngs in the streets of Madrid. In the most literal way, those manifestations are a way to take up real space in the world, to let it know I exist. To make myself a nation. While hollering to the sky in public would seem to be a most visible way of identifying oneself, the mass of bodies and the nature of such gatherings make it one of the most anonymous, too.

With my long hair and generally feminine grooming, I'm not visibly queer. I'm no one's bite-size butch or androgyne (though I prefer the latter, myself). A lot of people, mainly straights, wonder out loud why lesbians "insist" on looking manly. Well, they don't, but those who don't fit an expectation tend to fly under people's "gaydar." And everyone is pretty much assumed hetero unless proven otherwise. The context of a queer bar, rally, bookstore, whatever, provides a way for queers to be able to make reasonable assumptions about those around them. Certain grooming styles or other physical clues can create this context or space in a more portable sense. Some are meant to be declarations to the world at large, like wearing an "I'm not lesbian, but my girlfriend is" T-shirt. Others are insider nods to peers, such as tiny black triangle earrings or a bandanna tied a certain way around the thigh. Mutual recognition of any of these traits creates a zone of familiarity, normality—it's a midpoint between living on the margins of society and living at one's center, a borderland.

So why do I hate the term bisexual? The words bisects, halves, divides. It describes a two-face, suggests a mathematical split. Are you *50/50, 60/40, 90/10?* It denies the possibility of being wholly two "opposites" at once. Some people—straight and gay—interpret bisexuality to mean indecision, cowardice or an anything-that-moves-style hypersexuality. Some bis like to draw a line between themselves and monosexuals—whether het or homo. What is bisexual space? It's the fluid middle ground. Dual citizenship is great, but you're also always a foreigner. The Lesbian Nation can cast out your pariah ass for sleeping with the enemy, but you're still a national of what's largely a homophobic world. It's a revolving closet door.

The scientific jury is still out on whether sexual orientation is biologically hard-wired into people or purely a social behavior. Regardless, it makes an undeniable claim to its existence in one's mind and one's bones. As the cliché goes, you just *know.* My skin covers a body that feels especially flexible and free. This instinct is as physical and certain a part of me as my wavy black hair.

jill corral   119

In my teens I compared myself to the luscious blond lovelies in *Seventeen* magazine. I am no more one of those than a strutting bull dyke. What can be painful about living in the margins is not harassment or even misrepresentation—it's the feeling of being nothing at all, invisible. You compare yourself to what you see and can come up wanting. Among my acquaintances, I'm often the most multicutural of the group. "You must feel really ethnic," a workmate recently commented. Get me in a group of Miami Cubans or recent arrivals, though, and I'm a sunny-side-up middle American. Context is everything. I adopt the dress of different territories and travel though them to see if and where I could live in them. In the end, though, it's usually a nice visit and a "thanks, just *passing* through."

I'm always on the hunt for other border dwellers, because it can get lonely in the borderlands. Never having lived in a Cuban community, I create a makeshift one from the occasional Puerto Rican, pinko Latin jazz musicians, and flamenco-loving Spanish fetishists. Some say, and I believe, that there is such a thing as a "gay gaze" of recognition. Well, according to my mother, you can also tell a Cuban by their eyes—the sad, deep eyes of an old soul. So I look for these in the crowds that pass me by.

It's important to me that I gather my flock, my tribe. To bring others who are like me, toward me—to be able to stake my claim to a share of the earth I can define and make my own. This seizing of personal territory, whether on the margins of a community or in the dead center of a nation, is political.

Why is it important to make something new, to think about this at all? Why not just go with the flow and land where you will? Because for me not to actively justify the elements of my being is to feel dead. When I was younger I had a lot of shame about my ethnicness. I'd call my mother "Mom" (rather than *Mami*) when friends were over. Around age seven I began to flat-out refuse to speak Spanish, unwavered by parental bribes to do so—I wanted to purge my difference. I lost a lot of the language in the many years that followed, which is a painful loss now. It's hard for me to remember when I tried to hide being, well, a spic. My father legally changed his name from a long, melodious one to a short, blunt one; my parents also made good and sure that my brother and I had English names, too. The older I get, the more I feel like everything—the history, the still-living first-generation folk, the language—is escaping me. And the older I get, the more I want to claim and own my birth culture and homeland—*Mi Tierra,* as Gloria Estefan would sing it. I cry when I hear that song. So I try very, very hard to rebuild it for myself.

The *frontera* can be in your imagination, but sometimes it can come alive before your eyes. I recently went to a USA versus Cuba soccer game, the first one played in forty-nine years. There were my inner demons, battling on the field. Like the Lesbian National Team and the United Straights of America duking it out, going for blood right there on the muddy grass. I was, predictably, cheering for both teams.

Weddings are much like sporting events, with their respective cheering sections, the promise of scoring. It's also a private space opened for public view and as such, a physical place of your own quite personal in making. I wrote a poem after mine called "Wedding Fiesta" that included the following:

> *I should've made a sign with Magic Markers that*
> *read*
> *Please note:*
> *The egalitarian nature of our deconstructed cer-*
> *emony.*
> *That no humans are being given away to other*
> *humans.*

And the lack of "binding" terminology.
Thank You.

We made every effort to create from the weighty institution a mini-world constructed from our beliefs. The minister was Unitarian Universalist, a denomination that honors same-sex commitments. We wrote vows exalting friendship, partnership, the joy we found in each other. We each entered the room on the arms of both our parents. It was our active public claim to a borderland. Construct your spiritual institution in the physical world. Build it and, well, they *will* come.

Marriage is a pretty conservative gesture. The way I can live with it, and this is partly why I chose it, is by helping to change the face and the nature of it—in many ways more powerful than ignoring it altogether. I try to live as an example, an example I wish I'd had. I can't own a cultural tradition. But I can take a crazy axe to its fences and make more room for me and others to sit.

There's irony in my wanting to be so out when, traditionally, as immigrants to a new country (or as gays in a straight world), people have tried to hide their differences for reasons of safety, security and social survival. In late '90s North America, while the straight, white blond is still queen, there's a lot of currency, amid the attention paid to multiculturalism, in being exotic. While I think the more color-ful face of public America is here to stay, at the time I write this the country's in a sort of hyperfocused phase, which brings identity issues to the forefront in private and public arenas, or at least gives people the vocabulary with which to discuss them.

We all size each other up based on appearance, placing people at some definite point on the sexual, cultural or political spectrum. People like me, who don't fit neatly, are often unfairly assumed to be weaker, watered-down versions of the real thing. Not Republican or Democrat? You're wishy-washy or soft middle. Not black enough for some or white enough for others? You're an Oreo. Bi-anything? You're undecided, confused, half of each and not enough of either.

But this fluidity is my strength. This middle I inhabit is richer than any extreme. I thrive in its duality and possibility. While I find some joy in subverting the paradigm, I don't live my life for the mere sake of subversion. I take Plato's observation to heart: "The unexamined life is not worth living." No one knows that more than those of us who build our castles in the borderlands.

the art of the ponytail
akkida mcdowell

My crowning glory is a war zone. Every day I wake up prepared to do battle, to fight both for and against the enemy that lies on top of my head.

For years, I clashed with my hair. I struggled to make it mind my fingers. I flip-flopped over the best direction to take with it. From outside sources, I got the message: If my hair didn't look good (to them), I wasn't any good. My hair dictated whether I went out or not. On days that my hair acted up, the TV kept me company. According to movies, my beloved television, my classmates and even my neighbors, a proper hairstyle not only completed the package, but defined and delivered it.

When my hairstyle differed from the elaborate norm, my classmates and peers viewed me as unacceptable. My search for simple hairstyles in the realm of celebrities, newscasters, billboards and family proved futile. Even perusing the aisles for hair care products bombarded me with the idea of change and improvement. To me, the presence of so many products equaled the vast amount of work I needed to do. I've since learned the mechanics of supply, demand and trickery, but at the time, I felt besieged. I became hard pressed to find products for women that stressed simple hair maintenance. Finally, I waved my flag and surrendered to a simpler style that has become my trademark: the basic ponytail.

The war is far from over, though. I may be perfectly content with my usual hairstyle (or lack thereof), but other folks are not. It seems like everybody has an opinion when it comes to my hair. You'd think they'd have more to worry about than the state of my tresses. Yet, I can hardly make it through the day without people offering unsolicited, Nike-esque advice: *Just do it.*

Still, I understand the fascination with hair—at least intellectually. African Americans have a rich "hair-story" that directly relates to our identity. Aside from my skin coloring, my hair tattletales that some "creeping" was done with a person of black African descent in my family. African Americans come in all shades, but those sporting my hair texture are clearly marked "black." This physical mark bears ancestral significance. In African societies, hair told your story. Hair transcended style: It conveyed status and condition. So depending on how your hair was braided, twisted or otherwise adorned, your hair could signify age, marital status, mood and community affiliation. That I choose not to decorate my head in braids or ornaments signals, perhaps, some form of disrespect to my heritage, an abandonment of my literal and figurative roots.

I'm not the only one obsessed with hair. Studies show that African Americans spend seven to ten times more money annually on hair care than any other racial or ethnic group. Throughout her various novels and essays, Zora Neale Hurston discussed our "will to adorn." Cultural critic Pearl Cleage states that "you can't be a black woman writer in America and not talk about hair." And, after all, hair is woven through much of modern African-American folklore and rites of passage.

For me, it wasn't so much the "good" hair vs. "bad" hair debate among African Americans (good hair being the silky tresses usually found on my fair-skinned compadres; bad hair meaning the kinky, tightly curled hair that I call mine). Left to nature, my hair is coarse and thick, but it's also wavy. I've even been told that I have a "good" grade of the "bad" stuff. I've spent time unlearning the implications of good and bad hair. I mean, it's silly—how can hair be good or bad? Plain and simple, if the characteristic of a whole group of people is devalued—be it facial features, body shape or whatever—that group is devalued. If I carry the image of "bad" hair with me, then I walk around believing that I was created wrong. Still, this self-defeating notion has scarred me, because it has shaped my understanding of my physical image, caused me pain and continues to color the lens in which the world views me.

During my childhood, Saturdays belonged to the beauty shop. When I was younger, my grandmother did my hair in her kitchen. I watched cartoons as she placed a hot comb through my locks and scolded me when I wiggled in my seat. I listened to her tell colorful stories as her fingers artfully twisted my hair. Later, I accompanied my mother to her favorite salon in the heart of Cleveland, where women lined the chairs to have their hair washed, pressed, curled, relaxed and braided. I saw women handling real business against a backdrop of music, gossip, steam and oil sheen. I encountered professional women, housewives, teachers and women from other walks of life. This world of hair belonged to us—young and old. I discovered the latest news, saw the recent fashion trends, ate delicious, home-cooked food and heard grown folks' talk. In that arena, I felt safe. I enjoyed this nurturing ritual and scarcely noted the tugging and twisting. I bonded with my grandmother and my mother and flourished in the company of the women in the shop. I had a standing appointment somewhere other than school and my house. At age ten, I had a life.

Today, the most compelling excuse I have for sticking with the simple ponytail is that I simply have no hair ability. I cannot do my hair. My vision of my hair (prior to any attempt) never lives up to the reality (the aftermath). I can play a pretty mean "Greensleeves" on the piano, hit a softball, hold my own with a calculus equation and write a thesis on the Japanese economy. However, the day after a hair appointment, I can't re-create the French rolls, the perfect curls or the shiny finger waves that adorned my head twenty-four hours before. Short of hiring a personal beautician on a daily basis or borrowing my brother's baseball caps, the ponytail is the only solution.

Now that I've dethroned myself from the beautician's chair, I admit that at times I feel left out of an important black woman's bonding ritual. As I got older and started trekking to the salon solo, I just stopped enjoying the process. Maybe it was the fear of a sizzling hot pressing comb conducting business less than an inch from my nervous neck. Or maybe it was when my head became a pawn in a game of tug of war called braiding. Or when I returned home sore and bruised from the battlefield, I mean, the beauty shop. Contrary to popular belief, I don't eagerly await the slap of no-lye (a big lie) relaxer to the beast sprouting on top. The smells and the waiting, the tugs and the pulls are really just unappealing. Reminiscent of an unfortunate trip to *the* clinic, the question "Are you burning?" plain scares me. Somehow, it seems perverse to apply the old adage "no pain, no gain" to hair care. Plus, it takes time to "do" my hair. Depending on the style, the process can take two days. That's a time

akkida mcdowell   127

commitment I can't always pledge my allegiance to, especially if the rewards last only until bedtime. So please forgive me if I don't rush to the nearest shop every month.

Maybe my ponytail comes off as a lack of self-expression or personal care. To many black women, hairstyles are a source of pride and beauty, evident by the intricate asymmetrical cuts, the vibrant colors and the crisp curls. I think that's wonderful, and in some ways, I feel the same about my hair. However, a mindless or excessive pursuit of vanity concerns me. Besides, keeping up with Patti, Janet and Brandy costs. Faced with other debts, *sans* the diva income, investing hard-earned cash into disappearing 'dos seems downright ridiculous. But many women gladly fork over their last fifty to look the part.

I'll admit that the pressure got to me once. I buckled for a while and tried to align myself with the cute ones. In the span of seven months, this poor, college-education-seeking soul witnessed the worst case of inflation this side of the Atlantic. The price of my mandated monthly visits jumped from $30 to $67.50 in the blink of my pretty brown eyes. I decided to retire from the salon circuit, convinced it was literally becoming too much for me. Yet, in the name of beauty, other sisters will scrimp and scrape to get their weaves in, their "kitchens" touched up and their hair braided while neglecting other, more pressing bills.

Aside from our underlying connection to hair, I can't comprehend what drives African-American women to be so heavily invested in our hair. After careful thought, I kicked around three plausible explanations.

First, black folks reject the Barbie image, and then end up buying into it anyhow. Only "Aunt Thomasinas" subscribe to the dictate of straight blond hair and blue eyes, right? Wrong. Let's face it, we've become accustomed to envisioning Eurocentric ideals. The prevalence of black people who espouse ideas about good and bad hair proves that the notion of inferiority still plagues African Americans. Though we know how to shake what our mamas gave us, we may find it difficult to shake what time and tradition have taught us.

Second, there's that strong black women thing. Black women are heralded as the strongholds in our families. We keep the faith—and the appearance of strength. I guess some of us use our looks to cover our pain. If I look like a million bucks (or like I paid a million bucks), then maybe I can fool the rest of the world (or myself) into thinking that my life is balanced and wonderful.

Third, those disappearing black men. I shudder to say it, but it's true. Many of us have bought into the idea that it's all about men—pleasing them, getting them, keeping them. I feel as if I've overdosed on the myth of the decent African-American male shortage. And the oft-cited lower marriage rates among black women can make the average heterosexual sister reach for the nearest curling iron. Deep down, we might even believe that we must be in a perpetual state of artificial fineness to attract men. Under this assumption, all women become competition. The prize (men) amounts to short-term rewards that must be continuously protected from our true states.

Allow me to get this straight. To get a man, I need to beautify myself by any means necessary—including starving and having my power/telephone/hot water shut off—in favor of phat hairstyles? To keep that man happy, I need to be overly beautiful at all times (read: in perpetual need of outside assistance)? To keep that man from straying, I must be more beautiful than the rest? It's all so disgustingly shallow. Whatever the reason for looking good at all costs, to me the end result is not worth it.

I suppose that the time and attention some devote to their hair is a form of pride, a product of their creativity. Art can be powerful. Hair used as a medium conducts power as well. Bill Gaskins, professor of African Studies at the University of Missouri and creator of the photobook *Good and Bad Hair,* calls hairstyling "one of the most dramatic and diverse expressions of black self-love and acceptance." Hairstyles convey messages alluding to class, identity, politics and mood. Hair directly reflects personality. I believe that my ponytail speaks of my casual nature: This particular pony belongs to a nonsuperficial individual. For some reason, others get a picture of carelessness or low self-esteem. Perhaps it suggests immaturity—unless of course, the tail flows down to your tail. After all, pigtails are often sighted on elementary school playgrounds. I'll concede that the pony supports my little girl look, but no more than my baby face, small size and high voice. My hair is unique and pretty regardless of the style. I am happy with the strands that adorn my crown. Yet, whether I like it or not, African-American hairstyles have complex implications.

Black women's hair care is on a cultural see-saw. It's not enough to have your hair nicely styled; the method of styling may be called into question. As I ride the pendulum between relaxed hair and its natural state, I consistently attempt to find the overlooked middle ground. The book *The Color Complex* describes how the political implications of our hair mirror the implications of skin color. On an intraracial level, we use hair to base judgments on class, consciousness and lifestyle. In her essay "Oppressed Hair Puts A Ceiling on the Brain," Alice Walker suggests that straightening one's hair is a sign of oppression. In subsequent works, she writes how natural hair releases "anger, hatred or self-condemnation." Tulani Kinard, author of *No Lye,* echoes Walker's sentiments. She contends that it is impossible for processed hair to be healthy. Thus, those sporting such unhealthiness limit their freedom and hinder their spirituality. Those who choose to relax, texturize or get jherried are accused of faking the funk. Scholar and writer Gloria Wade-Gayles sees an activist with straight hair as a "contradiction." Some harsher critics will even go so far as to claim that these folks are trying to be white. To them, people without their natural kinks trade in their African connection in exchange for American acceptance. These politically incorrect styles seem to cater to societal pressures.

Clearly, those making the choice to be "happy nappy" are in the minority. As a result, they probably receive teasing and harassment about their hair decisions. Many with natural hairstyles can recall shameful childhood memories as well as recent ones of feeling too nappy by nature. They often face criticisms of being unrefined, unhygienic, low class and ugly. Alternatively, they are accused of being militant, lesbian or out of touch with the times. Just as claims of uncleanliness and poverty are stereotypical and inaccurate, the concept of displaying sexual orientation or achieving righteousness with hairstyles is ignorance at its best. Granted, dreadlocks and braids often signify a spiritual undertaking and may indicate an enhanced cultural awareness. However, an overall indictment of Black Power indoctrination and holistic health practices are hardly applicable to all. I'm convinced that hearing constant reminders that the 1970s are over can be disheartening and insulting to my afro-wearing sisters.

As in the hair care industry, the decision to go straight can be all about the Benjamins—getting them. Tamed hair opens economic opportunities. In plain English, jobs are easier to get with straight hair. Of course, recent legislation outlaws hair discrimination. Nevertheless, a quick review of history shows that this holds little weight in the corporate world. Although I may have a legitimate case of hair discrimination, I'd have a snowball's chance to prove it before I got the job. In *Hair Raising,* Noliwe Rooks recounts her grandmother's politics of acceptance. Her grandmother understood America "as a place where power had to be finessed as well as met head on, in confrontations . . . straightening my hair would give me an advantage in the world." Her hair would be one less battle to fight.

Whatever the style or method, black women sport brilliant hair creations that are worthy of museum exhibits. As a collective, we are extremely innovative in the manner of our appearance. According to Gaskins, our hair expressions, regardless of the hairstyles chosen, "amount to an unconscious adaptation of traditional African hair adornment." By ancestral recall, Africa stamps all of those styles. Given the wide range of black people throughout the world, we need to expand our boundaries of acceptance. Blackness is not (and should not be) defined totally by a hairstyle. I believe there is room for all our expressions.

Gradually, my ponytail has evolved into a few variations, which are just as quick and easy. Sure, I engage in the fantasy of having naturally fine hair flowing down my back like my great-grandmother and grandmother. But when I look in the mirror, I automatically smile at the image reflected back. For now, I'm satisfied with my ponytail. It's an art that I've perfected, at least in my own eyes.

I'm not equating my ponytail with a political statement. Just a personal one. However, given the complicated nature of hair, I guess this, in itself, is political. I decided that there was no need to enter the ever-changing black beauty pageant. I'll forego making the choice between a fickle and false beauty standard and a showy display of fake consciousness. I choose to focus on the real. I don't feel the need to look outside myself for sources of affirmation. When you see me, recognize that a true image of beauty is standing in front of you. My image of beauty.

beauty
secrets

beauty secrets
lee damsky

At five, my femininity is at its peak, preserved in a family photo of me in a light blue tutu with a satin, sequined bodice. I cherish this tutu, a garment which to me embodies the essence of fairy-tale girlishness and glamour. In the tutu I can be a ballerina, a princess and a beauty queen all at the same time. My love for the magic tutu is pure and wearing it I feel complete. I'm sure that the tutu was made for me and will transform me in its own image.

I soon outgrow the tutu, but not my faith in its promise of perfect femininity. Through most of my childhood, I never doubt I'll grow up to be gorgeous. I'll look like the stars of *Charlie's Angels* (which I'm not allowed to watch). I'll wear lots of makeup and swish my long mane of feathered hair. I'll be thin, of course, with large bouncy breasts and I'll wear sexy designer clothes. To me, this is not so much a fantasy I indulge as a firm conviction that I hold for several years. It never occurs to me that as a grown woman, my body might not be "perfect." (Naturally, my transformation will be effortless.) True, most of the women around me don't look like the women on TV. I'm not sure why. I figure they must not want to and fortunately I know better. A small nagging part of me knows that this is "vain" and therefore bad and shallow. At the same time, I'm incapable of thinking about myself in any other way. Nothing seems as important or necessary as being beautiful, and I know that once I'm beautiful, I won't have to do anything else. I eagerly await puberty and scheme about how to get a curling iron without asking my parents.

The source of my misguided aspirations is unclear. My mother has a Ph.D. in biology and buys me kid science books as soon as they hit the shelves. When, horrorstricken, she overhears me saying only boys can be doctors, she buys me a stethoscope. I'm not allowed to watch TV or wear makeup. I'm told that girls are supposed to have careers and I can be anything I want. Secretly, I reject this. My fantasies of beauty are too compelling—there's no way my mother's work ethic can compete. I guard my fantasies carefully and keep them to myself, never risking parental disapproval.

I know better than to trust my mother, whose insecurities I know too well. With the hit-and-miss intuition of a child, I overlook the obvious ways she would make a strong role model for me and zero in on her own unspoken neuroses. I know that she doesn't think of herself as beautiful or attractive. I know that her body is a source of anxiety for her, not a source of power and joy. I'm puzzled by her insecurity. I wish she would snap out of it and teach me how to be a woman. I want a kind of power that my mother doesn't have.

By contrast, traditional beauty and femininity—as they appear in my furtive glimpses of TVs, movies, magazines and billboards, images all the more alluring because they are forbidden—seem to offer me absolute power rivaled only by a fascist dictatorship. Beautiful women have it all. Power is their birthright and they need not lift a finger. What higher power could there be than to simply *embody* perfection and wholeness? The question of who I will be when I grow up feels meaningless and irrelevant. If I'm beautiful, I won't need to be anyone.

So on the cusp of adolescence I am cruisin' for a bruisin'. Following on the heels of my girlhood expectations, puberty unfolds like a cruel, ten-year practical joke.

1983: I am twelve. This is the year I've been waiting for, but the only sign that puberty has started for me is acne. I have no breasts and no period. The war with my face begins with a visit to the dermatologist. He tells me to wash my face twice a day and gives me my first tube of benzoil peroxide. I resent having to follow a regimen. I know all this extra washing and medicating isn't really supposed to be part of my life, so at first I ignore the instructions and assume that the acne will just go away.

Soon I'm on a new regimen every few months. As my acne gets worse, taking care of my skin turns into a time-consuming and emotionally draining ritual. In a short period of time, I become completely alienated from my own reflection. Each morning I stare at myself in the mirror with a cold and critical eye trying to assess the state of my complexion. Everything I do to my skin is an exercise in powerlessness since my acne doesn't respond. My face is in constant flux as the acne flares up and down on different areas of my skin. I start to hate my reflection but become obsessed with looking the mirror, trying to figure out what I look like at any given time. The acne feels like a foreign element that's invaded my face but I can't even tell what my face would be like if my skin were clear.

The struggle to control my acne pits me against my own face in an ongoing, futile battle that hinders my identification with my own appearance. What part of this face is really me? The notion that I should love myself the way I am feels hopelessly ambiguous in relation to my skin, since the acne always feels like a disfigurement of the way I'm supposed to look "underneath." As time goes by I start to feel like the acne is an outer expression of my own inner unworthiness.

1985: My fifteenth birthday. I get my first period. At first, I'm surprised and happy. Then I start to cry because by this time I've convinced myself that my body isn't normal and I am never going to menstruate. I feel too old to tell anyone. Now that I'm in high school there's nothing special about periods anymore and I feel cheated and left behind. A few days later, I break down and tell my mother. She says, "Sweetie, I'm so happy for you . . . I was beginning to think, you know, that there might be something wrong with you." *I hate you. There is something wrong with me.*

1987: I am sixteen. My doctor finally prescribes antibiotics for my skin and my acne goes into remission temporarily. At first I can't stop staring at my face in awe. I touch my skin and am amazed at its smoothness. I'm the same person inside, but almost overnight, people look at me differently. I remind myself to look back at them. My acne always felt like a distortion of my real face, but after four years of bad skin I can't get over the feeling that my smooth skin is somehow fake.

Suddenly, I start paying attention to other aspects of my appearance that seemed insignificant before. I've gained some weight in my bored and sedentary suburban lifestyle and I decide to go on a diet. My intensive skin-care rituals, alienation from my reflection and adversarial relationship with my own face have already forged a mindset that is equally suited to an obsession with food and weight. The transfer of my critical energies from my face to my body is seamless.

1988: I am seventeen. My periods only come every three months, which I know can't be normal. My sex-ed books don't cover this. One book informs me reassuringly that every adolescent thinks he or she is abnormal, and like everything else, this too is normal. There's some faulty logic here and when I figure it out, I'm pissed. After all, not *everyone* can be normal. What about the people who aren't normal? Some of us who think we're abnormal must be right, and what are we supposed to do?

My mother takes me to a gynecologist and I'm diagnosed with polycystic ovarian condition, a hormone imbalance of unknown origin. The doctor tells me not to worry: My ovaries don't have cysts and cysts are not the cause of the disease. It's too late. I already have a mental image of my ovaries as two shriveled and lumpy balls. She explains that cysts can be formed over time by eggs that ripen but are never released: "Because of your hormone levels you probably aren't ovulating. Your organs are fine and you aren't infertile, but you may not be able to get pregnant without fertility drugs to trigger ovulation." She tells me I might want to have children young to make sure I don't have trouble getting pregnant. I can't imagine having sex, let alone having a baby.

The doctor puts me on the Pill to regulate my menstrual cycle and prevent cysts from developing in my ovaries. She says the Pill might even help my acne, which is also a symptom of my hormone imbalance. (My dermatologists, all men, never thought to suggest that I see a gynecologist.) She tries to reassure me by telling me that I have a mild case. "Some women with your condition are obese, have full beards and only menstruate once a year."

I feel like there's something deeply pathetic about being a non-ovulating virgin on the Pill.

lee damsky   **137**

1989: I am eighteen. As soon as I get to college I realize I'm in way over my head. All around me there's a race for self-expression. I get an A in Women's Studies 101, which doesn't prevent me from developing a full-fledged eating disorder alongside my interest in feminist history and theory. My politics change overnight but my feminist consciousness is no match for my own insecurities. Feminism gives me a vocabulary and an identity. It speaks directly to my body hatred and conflicts with my appearance. But on some level I can't quite believe that the feminist critique applies to me personally. I feel guilty knowing that my behavior feeds the system I'm supposedly fighting against, but my body seems too monstrous for me to possibly accept myself the way I am. My own flesh marks the limit of my sisterhood. Is it because deep down I don't believe I have a real woman's body that I have trouble identifying with "women's experience," that my body seems to fall outside the terms of feminist rhetoric?

1990: I am nineteen. I leave school and go into therapy for my eating disorder. Coming from a family that doesn't believe in therapy, the notion that talking to a therapist can actually help me with my problems is a revolutionary concept.

I reassure myself with the knowledge that a lot of people take a semester off—there's nothing wrong with it. I give myself six months to deal with my eating problems and my therapy is short and sweet. I return to school the next fall as planned with normal eating patterns, amazed at the shift in my own behavior from extreme dysfunctionality to normal activities and interactions. I've stopped using food to express my feelings, and I'm resigned now to the fact that my body cannot be changed. But I still cannot fathom what it would mean for me to change anything else.

1992: I am twenty-one. I find hair on my face and shave it off. Of all my physical attributes this is the most disturbing and shameful because it is such a blatant sign of androgyny. It takes me to a line that I don't want to cross. I'm haunted by the memory of my first gynecologist saying, *"Some women with your condition have full beards . . . ,"* eager as she was to reassure me that I still fit in, that I still met the minimum standards of femininity, that there were "other" women, not like her or me, who were different. I'm trapped between my fragile sense of femininity and the horror I feel when I look in the mirror or touch my chin. My mind goes in circles trying to come to terms with the sudden growth of a feature that is utterly shocking to me. I keep telling myself that it's just a mild physical symptom. But *of what?* Is it just my hormones? Just my appearance? Just my gender? Just my body? Just me?

I begin to wonder if my androgyny is a sign that I'm really a lesbian. Unfortunately, I can't detect any feelings of attraction to anyone, male or female. I do feel like I'm in a closet but I can't tell what kind. Something about who I am feels forced and unreal, but it seems to go beyond my sexuality. I try two new Pill prescriptions trying to make the hair go away. It doesn't.

Later that year, I got a tattoo of Medusa on the back of my neck in an attempt to find empowerment in ugliness. In Greek mythology, Medusa was a creature so ugly that anyone who looked at her was turned to stone. I thought that embracing this symbol of ugliness and inscribing it on my skin would be the first step in accepting my body and claiming it as my own. Determined to abandon the cult of beauty once and for all, I resolved to be ugly and proud.

But my tattoo soon created an unexpected aesthetic conundrum. I carefully researched archaic Greek representations of Medusa—all highly stylized, graphic images with bulging eyes, fangs, a mocking tongue and, of course, a head of curling snakes—and drew an authentic composite. Yet how could I not find my own drawing of this stark and ancient icon beautiful? Once I had the tattoo, people craned over to get a better look at my neck and said, "That's really beautiful." I discovered that when we revere something ugly, even what we believe to be the essence of ugliness, we transform it into an aspect of beauty.

In the end my empowerment didn't come from ugliness any more than from my fantasies of physical perfection. Instead, when I began to love my body as part of my whole self, sometime in 1995, the day finally dawned when I started feeling beautiful. This is the truth even though stories like this always pissed me off when I felt alienated and trapped in my body. At the time, "self-love" felt like one more thing I wasn't living up to. Hearing other people's self-esteem success stories was like having someone tell me my only problem was a bad attitude: *Why don't you adjust your attitude and feel good about yourself? Then everything will be fine.*

The stories I heard made it sound like teaching yourself to love your body was as easy as learning a mantra: *I love my body, my body is beautiful, I love my body, my body is beautiful . . .* For me, teaching myself to love my body was like teaching myself to love leftovers. At some point I gave up, stopped trying, surrendered. I had been trying to control my body and I surrendered, I had been trying to make myself feel better and I surrendered, I had been trying to achieve on a track that I thought would make me successful and I surrendered, I had been trying to make my life work out on paper and I surrendered. Finally, I admitted to myself that I didn't know who I was or what I wanted, and it dawned on me that if I kept living my life the same way, I would never find out.

After college I moved to Seattle and started over. My discomfort at falling into this east-coast-college-kid-seeks-grunge stereotype was erased when I discovered the advantages of being part of a demographic trend. Everyone I met in Seattle had come to start over. I went out drinking with ex-Mormons, explored the local music scene with grad-school dropouts and dropped acid with a Yale boy turned full-time raver. I started out in Seattle with very simple goals. Some of these goals, like finding a subsistence-level job, came easily to me. Others, like going out as many nights of the week as possible and flirting, took lots of practice. My family considered this "doing nothing," and a year earlier I probably would have agreed.

For me starting over was like stripping down. When I shed the trappings of my previous life, my defenses and disguises, what I was left with was my own body. My body traveled three thousand miles to walk the streets of Capitol Hill, the beach at Golden Gardens, the length of the ship canal and down Denny Way. My body channeled new power, experiences, emotions and soul. My body sniffed out friends, hangouts, risks and dates. Getting over my eating disorder, I had to relearn how it felt inside to be hungry or full. Now I learned to listen to feelings, intuitions and choices that also came from physical depths. For the first time in ten years, I lived in my body, and my body was what I fell back on.

The symbiosis between body, emotions, identity and appearance is still deeply mysterious to me. There is a delicate feedback loop here, which in a society hooked on images of perfection and technologies of control is easily corrupted, its pathways turned back against us. The notion that our bodies make us who we are is twisted into an equation between our appearance and our self-worth. Feeling bad about our physical selves puts us on a fast track to self-hatred. When we're growing up and get caught at the body's surface, we never reach the place where intuition, feeling and a sense of who we are live inside us, and our spirits never reach escape velocity.

Now feeling beautiful, to me, is a measure of how close I am to what feels right as a way to be and live. My beauty comes from having my own style, living my own way and knowing my own mind. No, I don't turn heads—but I do catch eyes. My beauty secrets are self-love and self-knowledge, my accessories are skepticism and ironic humor.

Skepticism is born of disillusionment, and shedding the fantasy of a perfect outer surface made me into a radical skeptic. I appreciate this now because I've found my skepticism to be one of my most attractive qualities. As a skeptic, I trust my own gut instincts over any other source of information. The skeptic in me shoots down anything—from fashion trends to well-meaning advice—that starts to undermine my own inner power, resources or core sense of self. In its suspicion of all surface images and motivations, skepticism is a powerful antidote to denial. I enjoy wearing dresses from time to time, but as a gender skeptic I never take femininity too seriously. While skepticism exposes contradictions in life, irony is a way of embracing them, twisting them and rising above them when they cannot be resolved. Irony plays with things that don't fit and frees us from pretending that they do.

Now that I truly feel beautiful, it's an ironic point of pride for me that, in a way, I've actually managed to realize my warped childhood dream. Although I've left my tutu behind, I know there's nothing wrong with wanting to feel beautiful, when feeling beautiful is an inevitable symptom of self-love. For me, the difference comes from knowing that no matter what I look like, there is no power to be had in a kind of beauty I have to put on or live up to, and the only kind of beauty worth having is always hard-won. Of course, I also don't feel like my looks really matter very much. After wasting years of my life feeling bad about my body, there is a deep strength for me in knowing that my power in the world isn't a product of my physical appearance. The power I embody is the power I create: How sorry can I be, then, that I'll never have the option of trading on my looks?

Six years later, my Medusa tattoo has a different meaning for me. In the myth of Medusa, the truly ugly is something at which we cannot bear to look. I once hated my face, skin, ovaries and body, but this never stopped me from examining myself under fluorescent lights, wanting to know the worst. At the same time, what I couldn't bear to explore and expose to this kind of scrutiny were things inside myself. The question of who I was and how I felt—abandoned when I decided beauty was the only answer I'd ever need—went unasked for over ten years. In the interim, part of me still believed that my appearance was a visible manifestation of my deeper internal ugliness—isn't this the logical extension of our entire culture's assumption that physical beauty symbolizes everything good and desirable? And so, glossing over my innermost feelings, I was trapped in an endless obsession with my body's surface. The poet Audre Lorde once wrote, "The woman's place of power within each of us is neither white, nor surface; it is dark, it is ancient and it is deep." Now I see Medusa as the guardian of this place inside myself that is also the source of my beauty.

lee damsky   143

mirror, mirror on the wall
leoneda inge-barry

We all have a favorite place. That quaint cafe on the east side of town, the last church pew on the right, any beach in July.

My favorite place, in case you were wondering, is the bathroom. It's the only place I've found that will let me be me. All two hundred plus pounds of me! No questions, no complaints.

In the confines of the lavatory, la toilette, or "The Jane," I am absolutely beautiful. My thick, scraggly hair shines like silk, and my sagging, brown breasts are sexy. Even when I didn't have breasts, my bathroom mirror showed me what I wanted to see: a "brick house."

These days, I spend even more time in my tiny haven of happiness. No, not popping zits like in the good old days, but actually cleaning that porcelain pot and washing out soiled diaper covers and T-shirts. That's what happens when you're amorously taken by the drooling smile of a four-month-old. You would do anything to make his life happy, even if it wears you out. So when I get a rare moment to myself, the time I used to spend gazing in the mirror is spent sitting comfortably on the toilet, reading a book and dreaming. I've learned to love my body, no matter how much society and fashion magazine editors have worked to convince me that I should stay in the bathroom obsessing over it.

I'm told I was a sweet baby and an agreeable child. Didn't talk much, but I was sweet. One reason I didn't babble on like the five- and six-year-olds who befriended me, I'm told, was because even though I was as big as they were, I was only two! My mother prayed my hair would grow so folks would stop making that "sweet little boy" comment. But what we both wanted to stop growing didn't—my legs. Oh, and my feet (since having my baby boy, Jean Christian, I'm close to an eleven medium). I don't remember any advantages to being the tallest girl in my class. When teachers would couple us off with the opposite sex for Christmas play routines and May Day dances, I always felt silly. The awkwardness of my body consumed every waking minute.

The self-consciousness I felt as a little girl would follow me through high school and beyond. As in the stories of so many other young girls, eating would make me feel better. Honey Buns were always my favorite. There was something special and secretive about gobbling up Little Debbie snack cakes and cookies while lying on my bed reading the latest Judy Blume novel. I could relate to the Deenies, the Margarets and, of course, the Lindas portrayed in the book *Blubber*.

I can't say I turned to food to get away from the reality of feeling and looking out of place because of my height. I ate, mostly sweets, because the taste and the quick fullness were rewarding. Every now and then, though, I would hear a relative whisper, "She's gaining a little weight there." Angrily, I'd wonder, Why doesn't she just print it in the paper? Tell the whole world! No one would talk to me about it, though—just *around* me. So I kept looking forward to the Sunday desserts my mother would bake.

My family and friends never came right out and broadcast it on the six o'clock news, but I know they wanted to. Someone's lips could be mouthing "Good afternoon," but their eyes seemed to be saying, "You're fat." Seventh grade was when I weighed in for the first time in public, during gym class. The clunky scale put me at 156 pounds. I haven't weighed myself since. Sure, there were more physicals and plenty of visits to doctors over the years, but I have never volunteered to ruin my day.

"That's why your clothes come out of the women's department!" Thyra McMillan yelled at me one day. All I could say to her skinny ass was, "And your clothes come out of the children's department!" Since most of my wardrobe did indeed come out of the same section my mother shopped in, I let her do all of my shopping. Being caught carrying a dress bag marked "Added Dimensions" was as humiliating as the day Lamar Douglas caught me in the grocery store with a box of sanitary napkins in my cart. "I know what those are for," he said with a devilish grin. I made my father purchase my pads from then on. My fat, like women's bleeding, was the unspoken secret that everyone knew.

Even though I had two sisters, dozens of neighborhood girlfriends and tons of cousins, I never "talked fat" with them. My fat was between me and the bathroom mirror. Whenever I felt alone and upset because I was forced to attend a Weight Watchers meeting or try the latest miracle diet, that's where I would end up—in the Jane, talking it over with my reflection.

My parents didn't know what to do about the situation. And, yes, it was a situation. My mother also had a "weight problem," but it wasn't the same, she would say. "I gained all my weight after having three children," she'd warn me. "You'd better cool it." The conversation never went any further. Whenever she would try to delve deeper, I would cry.

Once, on the advice of some co-workers, my mother drove me to an acupuncturist's office in a nearby town. He placed a small pin in my ear, which I was supposed to push whenever I got hungry. The subtle pinch would make my hunger pangs disappear. Right. Why wouldn't people just let me be? I cried, talked it over with my puffy-eyed reflection. The next day, I ripped the pin out of my ear and tossed it in the trash. All of a sudden, I felt twenty pounds lighter. Well I'll be darned, it worked!

By the time I turned seventeen, I was sick and tired of my subscription to *Seventeen* magazine. I was finally realizing that, no matter how long I gazed in my bathroom mirror, I wasn't going to suddenly look like the teen model Phoebe Cates. Oh, yes! Black girls in Tallahassee read *Seventeen* and dreamed just as much as the suburban girls who lived in Killearn, one of the pricey neighborhoods on the city's outskirts. The older I got, the more I realized how dangerous mass media can be. Being a triple minority—black, female and full-figured—can be tough.

Seeing daily reflections of who you are or who you could be is imperative for young girls of color. Without that, it's easy to lose perspective, to lose your place in the world and your sense of reality. Good or bad, I daydreamed constantly, just like I did as a preteen. Pretending I was somebody I wasn't was as easy and rewarding as eating a Honey Bun.

One of my favorite television shows while growing up was *Bewitched*. I was fascinated by how Samantha and Tabitha could wiggle their little noses and make the biggest problems disappear. Oh, how I dreamed that was me. "Wiggle, wiggle, wiggle—goodbye, fat-farm girl Leoneda. Hello, lean, long-haired Leoneda!" Who didn't want to look like all the girls and women who were portrayed on television as goddesses? *Gimme a Break!* As much as I watched that program on the tube, I never wanted to look like Nell Carter. She was a talented black woman, but because of her size and skin color, they made her a loud-mouthed, nosy maid.

In helping to mold a more positive self-image, I credit my attending an historically black university. There's nothing like seeing people just like you, who are happy and smart, as you walk across campus. Conversations in front of my bathroom mirror, now in my college apartment, became shorter and happier. There was less of a need to convince myself that I was beautiful. I could now use the mirror to comb and curl my thick hair and to color my eyes, lips and cheeks.

My first week at Florida A&M University, I sat on the hill with new friends and listened to the marching band practice. I knew I was in the right place. No longer too tall or too fat. In fact, there were hundreds of me walking around. If I had attended a predominantly white university right out of high school, I don't think I would be the woman I am today, able to walk and talk freely among all people without feeling out of place.

As wonderful as it felt to bask in the Florida sunshine with my sun-kissed brothers and sisters, I could sense those bewildering junior and senior high days were about to creep back into my life, when, after several college internships, I dove into my career of choice, broadcast journalism.

I was and still am a "big girl," but I had been told that I was a very good broadcaster. I was also told that I was attractive and could make it on TV. But down south, no one was ready to hire an Oprah Winfrey type just yet. I decided to go the radio news route, and I've been there ever since. Back then, I thought I was "settling." Today, I know I made the right choice. Radio has taken me to heights by my present age I don't think I would have reached in television. Like radio, television news anchors are voices of authority. But our world is not yet ready to receive the day's news via the tube from an intelligent, attractive, full-sized woman of color. Our success is still confined to the role of the maid, the mammy or maybe even the Oprah—the one who takes care of everyone's problems. But like many young journalists, I still had dreams. I wanted to be the first black woman correspondent on CBS's *60 Minutes.* Yep, dreams. But I don't have to toss this dream into the circular file just yet. Have you seen *60 Minutes* lately? I may still have a shot.

After years of trying to keep my weight down and learning to appreciate the woman I've become, my big belly finally became an attractive sight for me. And my mirror agreed. Being pregnant was a wonderful time. At last, it was okay to have rounded hips and a chubby face! I cherished my private moments in front of the hall mirror this time. Rubbing my stomach, breasts and arms with cocoa butter and vitamin E was a pleasurable ritual, for both me and my husband. I would just stand there in the nude and look in amazement. How beautiful.

Because I wanted to do everything right, I actually lost weight during my pregnancy. Doctors say that when you're with child, it's the wrong time to diet. But I wasn't dieting. I was eating and drinking the right amounts of fruits, grains, breads, vegetables, dairy, poultry and water each day. I loved my body, and it loved me back. Sweets? I craved chocolate cake for a while. But my biggest craving was for watermelon.

No morning sickness for me. I just woke up every morning happy to be carrying my gift from God. And because of my height, I carried him well. I was so comfortable being big and pregnant that I bought a fuschia swimsuit and floated in the most public of pools. A little black girl waded up to me one day and said, "You're about to have a baby, aren't you! Can I touch it?" Since I loved touching my tummy, I didn't mind others doing the same and granted her wish.

Funny, the bigger I got while pregnant, the more people smiled at me. Pregnancy is so universal. No matter what your color or culture, you're treated special because you're carrying a living, breathing thing. The only downside was that I retained a lot of fluid and my fingers grew too big for me to wear my beautiful wedding ring. And even though I knew I was married, there were days when I felt the world was judging me. I loved what I saw in one mirror, but I still had to face stereotypes. Remember, I report the news on a daily basis. I hear the backlash against unwed black mothers who need welfare to get by.

I support the rights of those women and will always do so, but I wanted to shatter the stereotypes as well. While pregnant and ringless, I found myself explaining my situation to people, sometimes to complete strangers. You see, my husband didn't live with me for the first half of my pregnancy. He was working in Wisconsin and I was in graduate school in Michigan. So not only was I a black woman with no wedding band, I didn't have the man who put me in this predicament to show either. "I hope my husband likes this," I would say while shopping for maternity wear. "Do you have the time? Boy, it feels so funny not being able to wear my watch, wedding rings or any jewelry these days." I just wanted to make sure that the image I had of myself wasn't being chipped away by others. You can't control how others think, but you can darn well shape it. My mother told me that, way back when, she and her friends would buy pieces of metal and mold them around their ring fingers when pregnancy took its toll. Sisters were made to feel self-conscious back then, too.

While Martin Luther King, Jr., waits in his grave for little black and white children to join hands and travel through a color-blind society, I can't wait until the day comes when I can walk down the street and not think I'm being judged by the color of my skin or the size of my dress. But if that day never comes, I won't lose any sleep. I've decided to stop waiting anyway. Three decades have passed, and I want the next three decades to center on loving myself so it rubs off on my child. The image that reflects back to me today is an image of confidence and love. When I tote Jean Christian around the house, we stop and look in every mirror we pass. You know babies and mirrors. I smile hard and happy, and he does the same, drool dribbling down his chin. It's the most beautiful image of all.

intimate enemies
jennifer berger

My body is long, white, marked. It has blue-green eyes and red hair. It smiles, moves, sleeps. Once flying and free. Inwardly crazy, longing. Sometimes my natural sense of spontaneity is too much for it, and I want to escape, crawl into another, healthier body and become reckless.

But my body has disciplined itself, and it disciplines me. It is a body straining to breathe, often unable to eat. It punishes me when I give it the wrong air, the wrong food or not enough of either. My body has a mind of its own, and it rules me. It tells me, "You can't sleep here, I won't be able to breathe in the morning," and "You can't eat that, or I'll be in some serious pain."

I was born with a food allergy so severe I would vomit certain foods as soon as I swallowed them. I couldn't eat eggs, nuts or anything containing them. The list of foods I was allergic to grew over time, and now includes anything that once had feathers and wings, some fish and all nuts. Sauces with mayonnaise (more common than one might think) and soups made with chicken broth are out. Even two bites of bread or pasta that contains egg whites can put me in agony for hours with cold sweats, vomiting, diarrhea and stomach cramps that leave me in the fetal position. More than two bites, and I get skin rashes, and breathing becomes difficult.

As a child, I was outgoing, a Sagittarian clown and a singer. At three, I was swinging on the swings sideways, upside down and, according to my dad, "any way but the way all the other kids were doing it." At age seven, I was running around the playground teasing the boys and playing on the monkey bars with the girls. Stopping to use my inhaler was a pain in the butt but became a pattern in my life. Although inhalers became more plentiful by the year, the only thing my allergies stopped me from doing was eating what most other people ate.

It was at age seven, around the same time I was shaking empty inhaler canisters like some kind of fiend trying to get the last hit that I first heard women tell me, "Oh, you're so skinny!" At that age, *skinny* sounded like an insult to me. I was angry they were talking about my body when I just wanted to shine, to be confident in the world. Their words precipitated my first sense of self-consciousness.

I wanted to do so many things. Soccer and a run longer than ten minutes were nixed from my plan—but not from lack of trying. In P.E. class, I was always the kid who brought up the rear when we had to run laps. I was still doing laps when everyone else had moved on to basketball. I lost the joy of competing with the boys in sports, something I desperately wish I could have done. And, God, was I mad. Who was sitting up there during my conception and mixing up the genes to make me?

When my period came, things got weirder. The hormones surged, and I was stuck on steroids and too many inhalers and still unable to eat all those good things my friends had at their birthday parties—chocolate cake, pancakes after the sleepover. Because I couldn't eat anything with eggs in it (mayonnaise, most pastas, many breads, cake, cookies, crepes, on and on), I continued to be thinner than other teenage girls I knew. Not only was I a novelty at the dinner table, but, ironically, I became the object of envy.

Yes, my food allergies kept me thin. But what price would some women pay for thinness? Would they pay my price? When women—of all ages—tell me, "I sure wish I had your problem," it only shows how our culture screws us every day. We're taught that fat is bad, so thin is best, regardless of the sacrifice. Women who are probably otherwise pleasant sneer at me in fitting rooms. They envy my thinness but don't realize it's a product of trying to survive. Our culture still teaches us that thin equals healthy. Most women refuse food because they're scared to death of getting fat; I refuse it because I'm scared to death I'll kill myself by eating it. When you can't eat, eating well becomes a luxury.

I've considered what would happen if my asthma and allergies had made me overweight instead of the so-called thin ideal. I have no doubts that, in our culture, larger people encounter more biases and more negative stereotypes than thin people do. I've even excused myself for being thin and therefore offensive to some by explaining that I have food allergies. But if I had gained weight instead, would I make those same explanations? More important, would anyone believe me?

As it is, I am not immune to body image pressures, although many women assume that thin women have no problems with body insecurity. Last year, I was finally feeling content with my body (ig-noring that my face had swelled like a chipmunk's, as do the faces of people who must use high levels of steroids), thinking that I had "filled out." However, when I went off the steroids, I discovered the "filling" was just water retention. Weird body image problems, I tell you, thinking you're too thin.

As I write this on my twenty-second birthday, all that steroid use has suppressed my adrenal glands so that my body does not make cortisol (our bodies' natural steroids), the swelling in my face is just going down and I was recently diagnosed with an early form of osteoporosis. So now I am walking every day with two-pound weights on each ankle and wrist, taking my Tums for calcium after every meal, puffing morning and night, telling waiter after waiter "I have a severe allergy to eggs," and I'm still trying to figure out where the freedom and joy went.

Once I was spontaneous, in love with my life; I felt as if I was flying. Now I take care of my body so well that my life seems boring: Colder than twenty degrees and I have to wear a scarf over my nose and mouth that quickly gets sweaty and soggy; more than forty-five minutes in a smoky bar and I awaken the next morning gasping for breath; seven puffs of three different inhalers twice a day, two tablets of asthma medication—all or any of these forgotten, and that's another three hours sucking vaporized medicine in the emergency room, another eight hundred dollars down the drain for the visit and many more hours trying to recover emotionally. As an adult, I blame myself when I forget or rebel against the routine. So I live very carefully; I take nothing for granted.

How does it happen that such a creative and free spirit becomes stifled by its own body? I am angered—and yet blessed. Perhaps my wildness would have killed my intellect. Perhaps my wildness would have killed *me*. Maybe I was saved by my body's own weaknesses.

I can't simply be furious with my destiny. What hasn't killed me has made me stronger—much stronger. I pick my fights well and often: I fight for women's rights, I fight to be informed about my health, I fight for other people to be comfortable in their bodies. I have learned that my time is limited, and that I will do nothing for this world if I don't do it fast. On a number of occasions, I have thought I might die. Any one of my asthma attacks, any time I eat eggs by accident, could be the end. Our time is not endless—and my illnesses have taught me that much.

I release the anger in any and every way I can. It's still an inefficient process. Sometimes I internalize the stress and depression from the asthma and food allergies so much that I have moments of self-pity. But I have become myself in a way I never imagined I could. I talk about the things I care about with great fervor. My life is absolutely sacred to me in a way it wouldn't be without my health problems. I decided at age seventeen, when I went to the emergency room for the first time, that I would "live juicy" as the author and artist SARK advises, doing everything I've ever wanted to do before I die. I'm packing those plans into my life right now.

Because of my asthma, I have been in contact with doctors who pumped me full of steroids "just in case," despite the health consequences, and doctors who didn't listen when I told them, "My asthma attacks only happen three days before my period starts, so I think it has to do with my menstrual cycle." Emergency room doctors have routinely ignored me when I told them I was fine to leave the clinic. While I have a wonderful allergist now, others have said, "You will be dependent on steroid inhalers for the rest of your life." I refuse to believe them, and it pisses me off more than anything else I've been told.

I know this happens to many women in many doctors' offices, for many diseases. We have been under the thumb of doctors who "know best" for far too long, and we've looked upon them as gods. We've been told we're helpless without their services, and we sometimes end up believing it because we're desperate for a treatment that works. Well, I've decided I'm not helpless anymore. My strength on this issue comes from my illnesses, which I someday hope to cure *by myself.* After all, who knows women's bodies best? The answer is clear to me.

My body and my spirit continuously struggle. It seems one must lose for the other to win: It's either the freedom to go to that late, smoky party or the freedom to expand my lungs in the morning. It's a weird life, but it's life and I'm still thankful for it.

Besides, there's so much more than those parties, those bars, that smoke and dust. There are friends who make me special egg-free chocolate chip cookies, who try their best to understand why I can't stay overnight, who vacuum often because they know I can't handle dust, who put their cats in a separate room when I come over. There are waiters who understand when I explain I can't have the linguine or the bread on a sandwich, and who check the rest of my order with the chef, too. And roommates who scrub the frying pan thoroughly after they make an omelette.

In the war with my body, we have become intimate enemies. My body is my own, although it betrays me without mercy. I live with it and take care of it. My body talks to me. I have a talent in knowing exactly when I need to sleep, when I need to eat, when to stop the stress of research papers and exams. I'm so in touch with my body that I sleep when I should be writing those papers. I don't have less energy than others; I'm simply more aware that I'm running down before I actually run myself down. I have been given the gift of self-awareness, an awareness that other people I know haven't developed as much.

Most people say they don't even think about breathing, which is a totally alien concept to me. I am constantly aware of what my lungs are doing and what my breathing sounds like. My body keeps me in check by making it more difficult for me to breathe when I'm not giving it what it needs. It keeps me responsible for it. American culture teaches both women and men to cover our ears when we hear our bodies talking to us. By silencing our bodies, we end up with health problems, because we've driven ourselves hard, ignoring the instinct to take a nap *before* starting on the bills, the big report or all those errands.

Most days I try to revel in the things I *can* do. It's the stuff of which self-help and motivational tapes are made. I am "able" in so many ways. I can be joyful and still take care of my body. I can fight for a woman's right to fabulous medical care. I can rally for the elimination of that despicable female body "ideal" that results in eating disorders. When I go somewhere, I just happen to be the woman who brings her inhaler, her Medic Alert bracelet and her insurance card with her. I strike bargains with my body constantly: "If you let me have a good soul, I will take care of you as its home." Somehow, the two end up reciprocating, and I remain strong.

appraising god's property
keesa schreane

There were no curfews set for me in high school. My parents didn't
bother. My friends usually had parents like mine who told them, "You
know better than to come back in this house at all times of night."
But people with less strict homes were generally so afraid of my
six-foot-one, 250-pound daddy that they never fixed their mouths to
suggest a post-midnight rendezvous.

My first year of college delivered me from my southern, old-
fashioned Baptist upbringing right into the land of temptation. And,
oh, did temptation look ripe for the picking! Sometimes it was a sexy
six-foot-plus, caramel coated, muscled mass of iron. Other times,
temptation emerged while I listened to my girlfriends recount their
steamy weekend experiences, wondering what it would be like to get
a little "groove" of my own. Scariest of all, I found temptation writh-
ing in my head, tainting the thoughts that I tried to keep innocent.

At the time, I saw sexuality as pure evil, whether it material-

159

ized in my thoughts, the way I moved or the looks I saw in my male companions' eyes. After a beautiful night of dinner, conversation and occasional hand-holding, I dreaded the moment when young men poised themselves for the infamous good-night kiss. My firm-but-polite *no* resounded in the still darkness of my doorway, sending them scrambling for their egos. I was lucky to be left with a light peck on the forehead and a "Well, I'll call you tomorrow, Keesa," before they fled the premises in shock and embarrassment.

In high school, I belonged to a youth group that traveled around Tennessee promoting abstinence and the use of contraception. Group members, who ranged from abstinents to teen parents, were required to understand and discuss condoms, birth control pills and diaphragms. This early knowledge of such a taboo subject gave me a tinge of maturity I would have otherwise lacked. Although I had the giggling, timid reactions during my first lessons, I later grew to understand the need for sex education. If I was going to be a virgin, at least I could be an enlightened one.

My role as abstinent teen had plenty of challenges. Inmates in the various detention centers we visited thought they had the tools to crank my engine. I would deliver my panel speech on why I didn't have sex. Then the lewd, crude comments began: "Can I get with you?" or "What's wrong, nobody wants you or something?"

Frankly, I didn't understand the preoccupation with sex and why it was so difficult to resist. At the time, I wanted to pursue a career as a journalist and actress. I had no intentions of giving this up for one night of ecstasy. Waiting for the development of my career, and the development of a husband, seemed to be a wise choice for me.

My church, and the warm support of its members, encouraged this resolve. Growing up as the youth secretary, usher, choir member and all-around good girl rooted me in the religious reasons to hold onto my virginity for dear life. I got constant reassurance from the church folk. From the well-intentioned deaconess who delivered the "Don't let the boys fool you" tirade to my pastor's stern "Are you sticking to your church teachings?" lecture, I was more than a little bit scared to stray. Once I left the security of those church walls, I ventured on my own to study God's rules and why they are what they are. I came to a deeper spiritual understanding of my abstinence at a time when I seemed to be the last lone soldier.

In my undergraduate career, I was thrust into a land where booty calls were "in" and waiting until the third date to hold hands was "out." And all four years, I was definitely out.

I experimented with the dating game, but the rules were too confusing: Meet a guy, become attached at the hip, fall in love, try to make him love you back. And somehow, the same disastrous results followed. A mysterious phenomenon would occur, leaving my girlfriends red-eyed and teary or swept into a tempestuous rage, cursing the day they ever laid eyes on their former loves.

I quickly concluded that having a serious relationship during college was not tops on my agenda. Instead, I dated a few select men who met my strict standards. For several months, I enjoyed the company of a young, respectable businessman who thought my innocence was cute. His handsome looks, three-piece suits, sensuous fragrances and shiny Lexus always elicited stares and looks of admiration from my dormmates. After a few weeks of holding his hand in shows and restaurants, I allowed the cheek kissing on the doorstep. I let him know upfront that the horizontal touchy-feely stuff was not my cup of tea. After a few failed attempts to change my mind, he finally gave up.

Then, I found friendship with a sweet undergrad who didn't expect sex, seemingly for the same reasons I didn't. I felt completely at ease with his cheek kissing and light embraces after dates. I saw no need to settle down with one man. I was flying high! Among my peers, I was an anomaly—a sexually inactive fox of sorts—because

I gathered a whole harem of admirers who wanted to be around me even though I wasn't giving it up.

Then, it happened. After dating what I took to be the most sophisticated, funny, intelligent man in the universe, I thought, *maybe it's time for a real relationship . . . a real (and, of course) sex-free relationship.* Why not? As a graduate student, I was immersing myself in my profession and developing into a healthy, emotionally stable woman. He was an MBA candidate with a burgeoning career. He complimented me, cooked for me and adored me.

After several weeks of dating, he finally cut to the chase and asked for an exclusive relationship. Along with my request for time to consider his proposition, I blithely delivered my "no sex" spiel. Here are highlights from the remainder of our conversation:

He: Can we make love, sweetheart?

She: No!

He: Why not, sweetheart?

She: Because I want to wait.

He: How long, sweetheart?

She: Until I'm married.

He: Later, baby!

I was hot! I was hurt! How dare he ditch me because I wouldn't share myself in that way? Why would he reject my mind, heart and spirit because I wouldn't share my body? It took a few conversations with God and my parents to show me that he obviously wasn't worth my time.

It took courage, but I had to admit to the painful reality that this man wasn't the only one out there who felt this way. I have come across many people who have ridiculed, denounced or misunderstood my reasons for abstinence. These reactions led me to ask myself some hard-hitting questions. Are sexually active people ignorant to the fact that I can be a sexy siren without having sex? Yes!

My girlfriends are always confident that they can cast spells on men with erotic gestures and suggestive looks. But when they see me dating a classy *GQ* type or stepping into a formal event with the hottest date in the room, I'm always questioned on how I managed it.

I can feel attractive in my body—and project this—without having to allow men to act on their attraction. Have I set the feminist movement back a couple centuries with my loyalty to virginity? I do think of myself as a modern woman. I disagree with the notion that I'm enslaving myself by abstaining. Just the contrary—it's empowering for me. The feminist movement has stressed the importance of women "owning" their bodies—and I am nothing if not in control of what happens to and within my body.

Should I feel relief knowing that I debunk and add humor to the myth of black women as sexually insatiable creatures who live only to fulfill those desires? It gives me great pleasure to know that I have a *choice* in my sexual behavior. I wear the gifts of my beauty and intelligence with pride.

These questions are burdensome, but because my choice of abstinence is based on a higher authority, the answers are a source of strength. My faith in God keeps me steady. My relationship with God is spiritual, but my body reflects the strength our relationship gives me.

I am a structured person because I have goals I plan to reach. Treating my body as sacred is the foundation for that. Physical health is important to me. No matter what the temperature or weather condition, I usually spend my mornings in the company of other dedicated walkers and joggers. Friends believe that I border on obsession with my habit of drinking two glasses of water with each meal. I believe that what I put on the inside shows up on the outside. Mentally, I challenge myself to read one book a month, no matter what my school workload is like. I find that reading and attending arts performances and lectures add a dimension of culture to my life. Emotionally, I use my personal time to reaffirm my self-love and to clear away negativity.

God lives within me, which makes my body a special place. I think of it as a temple. When I share my temple with someone, I must be a complete person—the person God wants me to be. Then I'll be able to share myself with my partner, body and soul.

dancing toward redemption
meredith mcghan

*When I remove my top during the second song, the audience claps
and cheers. I look at them now, not really afraid anymore, just a
little nervous. I recognize genuine lust in some of the men's eyes.
I can hardly believe it—they think I'm sexy, me. These men are
strangers—strangers who typify The American Male and what
he wants. These are the men who hide* Playboy *under their beds.
They're clapping, cheering and coming up to the stage to tuck
bills into my thong. Exhilarated, I walk offstage, wanting more
of their attention, more of their money. I count the bills in my
waistband—ten dollars for a ten-minute routine. I had done it!
I had guts. I had nerve. I had power.*

And so began my career as a topless dancer.

When I tell people that I used to strip for a living, they're always
surprised. "What? You, a feminist?" There's an immediate, visceral
association. Exotic dancers are supposed to be hard, jaded and, well,

not exactly bright. Aside from supporting our various drug addictions, we dance because we're so economically oppressed we can't recognize our own exploitation. We're tall, bleached-blond bimbos with breast implants, who occasionally appear on *Jerry Springer* to reveal our "secret" occupations to shocked parents and boyfriends, followed by a gratis studio performance.

I don't fit the expectation. I've never had a guy beg me to "quit the profession" on national TV. I'm also a middle-class white chick with a master's degree in women's studies, a woman who's far shorter and heavier than the buff Demi Moore in *Striptease* or the lean, leggy Elizabeth Berkley of *Showgirls.* And I'm neither blonde nor tan. But I often think that my not being a Demi or an Elizabeth propelled me into the sex industry, where, ironically or not, I pieced together a new self-image.

The women's movement has always faltered when feminist sex workers bring their voices to the discourse. There's a hesitation to support the premise that women can *choose* to do this work, that feminism should advocate for women's rights to use sexual power in a professional way. Many feminists strongly disagree that sex work offers women an element of choice at all—and to an extent that may be true. After all, we live in a system that makes it difficult for women to earn as much money in jobs that don't involve their beauty or their sexuality.

Still, I never got the impression that any of my co-workers felt trapped in their jobs, unable to leave or forced into dancing—at least not anymore than anyone else working in the blue or white-collar worlds. The dancers I met came from a variety of situations. Some, like me, were artists or students looking for a part-time job that paid a lot and left them with time to pursue their interests. Others were single mothers who needed the free time to look after their children. For the most part, they enjoyed or tolerated their jobs like anyone.

Besides the money, why did I choose the sex industry? To answer that, I have to go back to the stash of soft-core porn magazines I discovered in my father's study when I was nine years old. *Playboy, Penthouse, Oui* and the occasional *Hustler* were my first exposure to what adult women supposedly looked like naked. I didn't know that photographers used tricks to make models look like fantasy women— airbrushing, soft focus, strategic posing (any woman's breasts look perky when her arms are raised and her chest is pushed out like a pigeon's). And it didn't occur to me that I wouldn't resemble those images when I grew up.

Not long after finding the magazines, my breasts started to develop. In fourth grade, my mother was urging me to wear a bra. I was terrified. It was too early. No one else in my class wore one yet, and I felt like a freak—I couldn't even bring myself to say the word *bra.* I wore layers of clothing to hide my chest, but my breasts grew rapidly. By the end of the school year, I was getting different looks from men on the street, and it frightened me. At school, boys would tease me and try to grab my breasts or snap my bra strap, and other girls would remark, "Wow, you have big boobs." By fifth grade, I was wearing a 34B and had reached my full height of five feet nothing. I thought there was something wrong with me. Why did I have to be short and curvy, when it was obvious even to a fifth grader that only the tall and willowy were considered beautiful? And if you weren't beautiful, you weren't anything, right?

I begged my mother to take me to the doctor to find out if, indeed, something was wrong with me. My mother didn't have much time or patience for this. She told me that early development ran in the family and I should just deal with it. The doctor agreed. So I dealt with it. I dealt with it by deciding that my body was a traitor and I hated it. I dealt with it by ignoring most of the other kids at school (who needed friends? I could always read a book instead of play). And I dealt with it by deciding that I had better start overcompensating for being a freak by being perfect in every other way.

So when my father suggested I stop eating desserts and take smaller portions, I began dieting in earnest, turning my precocious reading skills to weight-loss books. The books told me that a five-foot-tall woman should weigh a hundred pounds, and for each inch over five feet, five more pounds were permissible. My overcompensation kicked in, and I decided to beat the hundred-pound standard and try for ninety-five. I drank a lot of diet soda to fill my empty stomach, ignoring the head rushes and tremors. But even as I hovered just below a hundred pounds, my curves were still obvious. By the time I was twelve, my war against my body was firmly entrenched. I was convinced I was a fat, ugly freak, and I was miserable.

Imagine my surprise when I turned eighteen and met a guy who was genuinely attracted to me. Though I still saw a disproportionate dwarf in the mirror, I began to hold male opinion as an article of faith. I told myself that as long as I was attractive to men, the ugliness I saw in the mirror must be a delusion. That was as close as I could get to feeling good about my body.

The topless dancing seed was planted when I noticed that a few women from my hometown were driving across the border to strip in Canada three nights a week—and raking in the money. I was intrigued but disdainful. Why would they want to exploit themselves that way? Wasn't it dangerous and humiliating?

The idea crept closer to home, though, when my friend Jen began dancing at the local Déjà Vu strip club. One night, a couple of guys I knew convinced me to go to a show—just to see what it was like. Jen wasn't working that night, but we stayed for a couple hours anyway. To my surprise, I wasn't really offended. As I watched the dancers grind their hips and gyrate in men's laps, I was captivated. Their bodies were vastly different from what I had expected—and far from perfect. They had sagging breasts, stretch marks, cellulite on their thighs. Some were unabashedly plump. And they were all getting money—and compliments—from men.

I turned to my friend and whispered, "I thought you had to be a super-skinny model type to do this kind of work."

"Some clubs you do, but not here," he answered; then he teasingly nudged my shoulder. "Why—you thinking of doing it?"

"No way," I said. "I'd feel exploited."

"The men are the ones getting exploited," he argued deftly. "The women are in control. I mean, they're making all the money."

I wasn't sure I agreed, but the idea stayed in my mind.

A few years later, I met a woman named Katie at a party. We got to talking, and she told me she danced at a local club that was owned and operated by women. "I make about $300 a week for twenty hours of work," she told me. "The rest of the time I spend writing and going to college. It's great."

What a luxury, I mused, reflecting on the gamut of dull, low-wage temp jobs I'd worked since graduation. After forty hours a week, I was usually too tired to find much inspiration for my writing. I confessed to Katie I was looking for an easy, part-time gig that would pay my bills without draining my creativity.

"Oh, it's a *per*fect job for a writer," Katie gushed. "You should totally try it."

"Yeah, well, there's one problem," I said, waving a dispassionate hand at myself. "I hardly have the body for it."

meredith mcghan   **169**

"Are you kidding?" she laughed, patting my arm. "Just come to my club sometime and see what you think. If you want a job, I'll get you in."

A week later, I gathered up my courage and asked a male friend to drive me to Katie's club. We parked on a rundown street, below a painted sign of a dancing, bikini-clad woman. "I don't know," my friend looked at me. "It looks like a dive." I pulled him through the doorway.

The club made no pretense at classiness. Its squat, shabby tables and chairs were mostly empty that afternoon, and a woman danced on stage to an audience of one disheveled, hooting old man. The place reeked of the cigarette smoke hanging visibly in the air and an undertone of sweat. A sweetness touched the air, too, the scent of the dancers' many mingled perfumes and lotions and shampoos.

My friend, uncomfortable with the scene, averted his eyes. I watched avidly, taking stock of the scene, measuring out a place for myself in this foreign terrain. I spied Katie across the room, doing a table dance. She picked up her breasts, leaned toward a guy and shook them in his face. Another dancer rubbed her small breasts surreptitiously against a man's cheek. "Oh, baby," he groaned, and tucked a twenty-dollar bill into the elastic of her fuschia thong.

Katie finished her table dance and headed my way. I covertly checked out her body as she walked. She was a little taller than I was, with large breasts and a thick waist. We were shaped differently, but neither of us fit my image of topless dancers. A glance around the room showed me that the other dancers didn't either. A few were what some might call fat. Some were bone-thin. Only a couple were, by society's standards, drop-dead gorgeous. And their work didn't look that difficult. Since there were hardly any customers, most of the dancers were sitting at a table near the DJ booth, talking and sipping water. No one had any fancy moves. No one was sweating. The atmosphere was almost comfortable. It certainly wasn't intimidating.

"What do you think?" Katie asked, plopping down next to me.

"It looks pretty easy," I said, trying not to stare at her breasts. "But do I have to touch the customers?"

"You're not supposed to," she answered, twisting her hair into a ponytail. "And they're not supposed to touch you. I've smacked people before for trying stuff."

The small-breasted dancer had obviously been playing against the rules. Katie didn't, though, and she made just as much money.

"So when are you going to audition?" she asked.

"I don't know. I have to think it over," I said. But I already knew I would. I had spent over half my life hating my body. I wanted redemption. I wanted to be someone's fantasy for once. Just long enough to prove that I could be. If it was too hard to reconcile with my feminist principles, I could always quit. But I'd never know unless I tried.

The next morning, I called Katie. "I want to audition," I said. She volunteered to come over and help me practice. In my basement, Katie demonstrated a few moves on the thick, floor-to-ceiling pipes, showing me how to remove skimpy clothing as part of the dance. I mimicked her, feeling self-conscious as she adjusted my hips and stepped back to appraise my performance. But after a while, she said I had gotten the gist, so we drove to Woolworth's to shop for cheap lingerie. "You're going to need a few thongs," she directed, dumping a handful of them into our shopping basket. "Get some matching bras, too, and a couple of lacy tops."

The next day I went to the club, already dressed and made up "for the stage," as Katie had advised. I introduced myself to the other dancers, who were friendly and encouraging. One even rushed off to get me a shot of liquor. "Drink this," she patted my shoulder. "Then just get up there and dance. Pretend you're all alone in the room. Don't look at anyone. The men don't care, and they're going to hire you anyway."

When the DJ called my name, my walk was surprisingly steady in my three-inch heels. I felt as if someone else was taking over—someone on the brink of tasting a new kind of power. A glance in the mirror behind the *barre* showed me that the heels slowed me down, made me sway my hips, elongated my legs. I held the *barre* for balance, gyrating and bending as I had seen the other dancers do. I didn't dare look at the audience during the first song, but I could hear their primal hoots and inarticulate pleas. As I continued to dance, I grew more comfortable under their gaze. It was all context. I began to relax and enjoy the music and the movement. And when the manager told me that I could start tomorrow, I felt good about my body for the first time in my life.

During my six-month stay at the club, at least two men would tell me I was beautiful every day. I was surrounded by women of different shapes, sizes, ages and ethnicities, all of whom had their particular admirers, as did I. Some men would come into the club, ignore the tall, thin, blond dancers and be all over me. I can't count the compliments I got. "Your legs look so strong," one guy told me. "You must work out." My friend Kitty, considered among the dancers as the most attractive with her waist-length blonde hair and willowy figure, said she envied my legs and wished her own "weren't so damn skinny." Twenty hours a week for six months, I got positive reinforcement for my body—and a paycheck to boot. I had put myself in an environment where I was saturated with praise for my looks, and my old self-image was eroded there, little by little, until I became proud of my appearance. Even my severely distorted perception could not withstand the power of the relentless compliments—and the money I made responding to them.

At the time, I didn't analyze the drastic way my self-confidence rose when I stepped on the platform. I was drunk with the validation, the thrill that I had faced my inner demons and walked away victorious. There were no disparaging "fat" remarks, no eyes scanning me with disapproval. The men there were as delighted by my body as I was with their attention. I made them weak with desire, like the pictures in my father's magazines. The mere sight of me flipped on a primal switch in these men, as though I held some mysterious power.

And all it took was a simple dance number. Reveling in the movements of my body, the sight of my own skin, freed me from a lifetime of self-hatred. Never had I imagined that my body—my despicable body—could grant me so much control. Once I discovered it, I was willing to go to extremes, to put politics aside, to keep that feeling alive.

Yes, there were things I wanted to be other than just a body—a poet, an editor, a student. But more than anything, I wanted to be beautiful. My body hatred had superseded all I wanted for myself spiritually, intellectually and ethically. I had friends in the fat acceptance movement, but my own body obsession drove a wedge between us. I felt terrible about my own hypocrisy, but I felt even worse when I looked in the mirror and didn't see what the men at the club did, a body that could command the power of lust and desire.

When the initial glow of realizing that I was as attractive as anyone else wore off, the men at the club became annoying. I started to feel cheapened and objectified, and I became increasingly aware of the inherent danger tingeing my new position. The fantasy realm began to spill into the safety of my outside reality. Customers began asking me for my phone number and wanting to see me off the job. A couple of the other dancers had stalkers. I was worried; the place was in a rough neighborhood, and I couldn't even walk to my car alone.

I finally quit when the bar made lap dances legitimate. Once the owners relaxed the rules, the dancers who didn't allow a little feel-copping wouldn't get tipped. My earnings fell off, and the customers' out-of-line behavior got worse. Work became a dangerous place.

For the first time in my life, I felt that being attractive could make one vulnerable. When I had believed I was ugly, I imagined that beauty would make me safe—acceptable, not a reject. I hadn't bargained that beauty would make me into an object, an object that some men believed belonged to them. I knew I had truly crossed the line then—when I was so sure that I was attractive that I could afford to wish, sometimes, that I wasn't.

Dancing convinced me that I'm physically attractive to many men. To a degree, that will always matter to me. Feel like your body is unattractive—even unacceptable? Take it all off onstage, and you'll hear a different story.

Yet, I realize the irony of my experience. My original body hatred was the result of our society's appropriation of the female body as an object of consumerism. Had there been no *Playboy* standard with which to compare my developing figure, no father who told me I was gaining weight, there would have been no obsession with looking perfect. I conquered much of that body hatred by proving to myself that my body was an adequate object of consumerism, that it wasn't too much worse than the standard. What if I had not been able to do that? What if, instead of a bad body *image,* I had a body that truly could not, in our society, conform to the norm? I like to think I would have somehow been able to love my body anyway. I like to think I would have found a way.

There are so many contradictions in the sex industry. My sense of empowerment from dancing was bound on all sides by not only the glass ceiling, but the glass floor and walls, which keep women from having easy access to well-paying jobs. And I wonder how my self-image would change if I suddenly no longer fit the norms of attractiveness. My body image, though now fairly good, is still dependent upon outside forces.

I can't deny that I feel better after dancing, but I also can't deny the irony. I haven't become a person who can accept her body unconditionally—not yet. I have become a person who is tremendously relieved to discover that she really does look okay to her oppressors. Thus, I tacitly admit that my oppressors have the right to define who I am, and I tacitly betray my sisters who are crusading for a new standard of beauty. How do I live with this? I want to resolve these contradictions. But perhaps they can never be resolved in our culture. However, by owning my struggle with them, I can begin.

conquering the fear of a fat body:
the journey toward myself
regina d. williams

Twenty minutes before showtime. I must confess, there's something about modeling that brings out the exhibitionist in me. I love the attention, the excitement and, most of all, knowing I look *good!* I see him from backstage. He cuts through the audience like a jungle cat, sleek, powerful, confident. *Um, um, um,* good Lord, is he *fine!* Big, strong and sexy, just the way I like them. It's been a long time since I've been this attracted to anyone. As I give myself the final once-over, I wonder if he'll be interested in me. Will he see what I see right now in the mirror? Glistening, milk chocolate skin. Full, sensual lips. Large, inviting eyes. I look really good in this green swimsuit. In fact, I look so good, I know the other guys in the audience are gonna go wild as soon as I hit the stage. But will he? Will he like this fat body?

Six or seven years ago, I wouldn't have asked that question. The notion of myself as attractive would have never entered my mind.

See, for my whole life, I have been fat. Not "fat" as in I can't fit into my jeans after Thanksgiving dinner. "Fat" as in I can't fit through doorways or into movie theater seats or restaurant chairs. When you weigh around three hundred pounds, like me, you can easily spend your life trying to fit your fat body into a world designed for people of so-called normal size.

Growing up, I was constantly admonished about what I ate and how I looked. "Regina, why don't you lose weight? You'll never get a man." "You know, you really shouldn't be eating that." Or, "Come on, let's go on a diet and get skinny together." No one ever seemed to notice that I was intelligent, loving, talented and creative—or even that I had a pretty face. At times, I tried to assert myself and point out those qualities, hoping to draw the focus off my body. But I was never allowed to forget that no amount of brains or talent could cover up that I was fat, and, therefore, unacceptable, undesirable and essentially good for nothing.

Oh, I was useful for babysitting on Friday nights because I would never have a date—who would want to take out the fat chick? I could offer advice on which clothes looked good on my friends, but I could never be fashionable myself because the only clothes for us tubbos were tents, polyester pants with "speed bumps" down the middle and those lovely, floral-print drawstring blouses. I was the greatest friend when no one else was around, but always the subject of surreptitious jokes and laughter in a crowd. I knew that my friends and family made fun of me, but I never had the courage to stand up to them. I just worked harder to try to please everyone, to show them that I was more than just a fat body.

My dieting cycle began in early grade school. Each time, I prayed that this one would magically, permanently transform me into a girl people wouldn't laugh at anymore. Sure, I lost a little weight, got the attention and the compliments. *Woo-hoo,* I was on my way to the

regina d. williams   177

world of acceptability! I started dreaming about wearing all the cute outfits that the other girls wore. I'd have friends that really liked me, I'd go out on dates and, best of all, no one would laugh at my fat and ugly body.

But, alas, it was not meant to be. My prayers went unanswered. Every diet worked for a while, but in spite of my resolve to keep the weight off and maintain my new status, my body always betrayed me. Time after time, I gained that "disgusting" fat back and then some. I learned at a very early age to hate the treacherous body that kept me from living a life like everyone else's.

Growing up as a fat teenager intensified my self-hatred. On the outside, I was a lot of fun to be around—still the great friend. In fact, I was quite popular in high school. I never dated, though, which was partly my fault. A couple of guys genuinely liked me, but I could never accept that someone actually found me attractive. I dismissed them as potential boyfriends, thinking they were playing some kind of cruel joke with me as the punch line. I even missed my senior prom, because I could not, would not, believe that the guy who asked me was serious. I even laughed at him when he invited me. No way was he getting the last laugh on me.

Besides, I was secretly in love with another boy. This boy and I spent a lot of time together platonically, and while I wished it could be more, I knew it never would. In class one day, my best friend whispered furtively that she had something important to tell me. Thinking she was going to reveal that she had a fatal disease, I braced myself to hear the worst. Instead, she told me that the boy I loved really liked me and wanted me to be his girlfriend. But, she added, he couldn't go through with it because he didn't want his friends to laugh at him.

Let me tell you, if a man said that to me today, I'd give him a hand-engraved invitation to kiss my hind parts. But to a sixteen-year-old who only wanted love and acceptance, the boy's cowardly attitude cut my heart into ribbons. Oh, I understood why he felt that way. I even accepted it. I guess I hoped that just this once someone would think I was worth loving in spite of my body.

I never let the boy know what I had heard. I continued to be his friend (when you're fat, you learn early to become a good actor) even though every moment I spent with him caused me pain beyond compare. I went on yet another failed diet, praying again that this time I'd become a girl he wouldn't have to hide.

Eventually, my craving for attention superseded my questioning of men's motives. When attention came knocking, I was already standing at the door. Adulthood launched me into uncharted waters . . . I discovered sex! I'm not saying at the time I always liked it, but it was contact with the opposite sex. It was attention. Sure, I knew the guys I dealt with didn't want to be associated with me publicly as a girlfriend, but I needed to fill a void, to ease the pain of loneliness. Something was better than nothing, so I did what I had to do. I figured that a piece of man is better than no man, right?

Some time ago, I wondered what it was about crack cocaine that made its users sell their very souls for another hit. Supposedly, the first time you try it, the high is intensely fantastic—but it only lasts a moment. You then spend the rest of your life chasing that same high in vain.

I can honestly say that I can relate. As a fat girl who's never been paid much attention, I was good to go at the first inkling, if you know what I mean. I felt like the horse with the proverbial carrot dangling in front of it. That first show of positive attention toward my body kept me chasing the experience for most of my life.

Tragically, I wasn't very selective in my choice of lovers. The man *du jour* didn't have to have a job or a car—heck, he didn't even have to be well groomed. I was once involved with a crack addict who didn't have any front teeth! In fact, I accepted just about anything from a guy short of physical abuse. Thinking back, I was so desperate for love and acceptance, I probably would have tolerated that as well. After years of conditioning, I truly believed that I didn't deserve better than what I was given. It didn't matter that I degraded myself over and over again, or accepted substandard behavior from men and everyone else in my life. I endured it because I kept hoping these people would realize that in spite of my fat body, I was a human being and should be treated with respect.

Well, it's a good thing I didn't hold my breath waiting for the people in my life to get a clue, or I wouldn't be here today to tell the story. One day, however, the clue bus did stop at my house. After years of banging my head against a brick wall, I realized that it hurt! No amount of painkillers and Band-Aids would take away the pain I felt at being treated badly solely because I was fat. Those were only temporary fixes. I needed to find a cure for this malignancy called self-hatred before it completely destroyed my life. I realized that for the healing to begin I first had to accept that no one would ever love and respect me unless I learned to love and respect myself.

You know, that sounded really good—on paper. But to a person who had spent her entire life loving others more than she loved herself, I admit that I just didn't know how to do it. I remember telling one guy that I loved him so much that if someone tried to shoot him, I'd get in front of the bullet! Pretty sick, huh? I didn't know how to make myself believe that I mattered, that I deserved respect. How was I supposed to love someone who's unlovable?

I figured a good place to start was by getting rid of the current loser in my life. I still wanted to be in a loving, accepting relationship with someone, but before that could happen, I realized I had to develop a loving, accepting relationship with myself. I had to become intimate with myself. I had to learn who I was and love that person. I stopped everything and confronted what was keeping me from my goal: my fat body. Then I began the difficult road in search of peace—with every pound, roll and inch of myself. I had to rethink all I had learned by educating myself about being fat, by educating myself about size discrimination and its impact on my emotional and physical health.

I gathered all the information I could and read every article about being fat in this country. I was amazed at what I found. Did you know that the National Institutes for Health report that 98 percent of people who lose weight gain it back within five years? And that about 90 percent of those people gain back more weight than they lost?

I don't know about you, but if I had a serious illness and the doctor gave the proposed but risky treatment only a two percent chance of success, I definitely wouldn't subject myself to the frustration of its probable failure. The medical profession has been so narrow-minded in regard to fat people that the only means of "treatment" is to try and make us thin. Doctors ignore evidence that shows that the physical damages of frequent dieting can be permanent. It's a common misconception that we're losing fat when we diet. Study after study shows that dieting destroys muscle, bone, organs and even brain tissue.

The muscle that's most affected by dieting is the heart. The Framingham Study, published in the *New England Journal of Medicine* in 1991, found that the risk of death from heart disease is seventy percent higher in people with fluctuating weights than in those whose weight remains stable, regardless of initial weight, blood pressure and level of physical activity. Studies show that high blood pressure is another side effect of the mental and physical stress of dieting. The nutritional stress can also result in electrolyte imbalance (excessively low levels of potassium in the blood), which can cause heart attacks. The list of illnesses now associated with dieting—anxiety, depression, heart disease, eating disorders, reduced resistance to infection, osteoporosis—grows longer every day, as new studies find that the "cures" for obesity are killing us.

Surprised? I sure was. Especially when I found out that fat is hereditary. Eighty percent of fat children (even those who weren't raised by their genetic parents) have fat parents. And here I grew up thinking I was fat because I ate too much. More than twenty studies have tried to prove that fat people eat more and are less healthy than thinner people. Nineteen of those studies concluded that fat people eat the same or less than thinner people. Only one found a higher rate of consumption among fat participants.

I was amazed by how little of this information was even readily available to the general public. Millions of people in the United States alone embrace dieting as the end-all-be-all cure for fatness, spending billions of dollars in their attempts to achieve it. Yet, two-thirds of Americans are overweight.

But over whose weight? You might be surprised to know that those height-weight tables used by the diet commandos to terrorize us all into thinness were created by Metropolitan Life Insurance Company in 1959. The statistics (which were revised just slightly in 1979 by the U.S. Department of Agriculture) are based on a sample population of rich, white males—not on medical studies. They didn't even bother to include women or people of color. I wasted years believing that my fatness was somehow my fault, feeling like a loser because I couldn't maintain or achieve thinness. I was overwhelmed and angry that I had been lied to all my life and denied information that should have been available to me and everyone else who has struggled with their weight, information that was suppressed by an industry that has a vested interest in keeping us unhappy with our bodies—to the tune of sixty billion dollars per year.

Lately, I've heard talk that being heavier is supposedly more ac-cepted in the African-American community. Well, if that's the case, then why did I grow up so miserable? Why was I always teased about my weight? Where were all the black men who supposedly loved big women when I wanted someone to love me for me? As far as I see it, the whole thing is a myth. Sisters are more accepted if they have big boobs or a big butt, but don't let us get *too* big or we're classified as undesirable.

In my experience, most African Americans define a full-figured woman as somewhere between a size sixteen and a size twenty-two. Anything larger than that is considered fat and is not readily embraced. I'm always hearing from my white sisters that African-American women are more comfortable with our bodies. What I see, however, is that the more we as a people try to assimilate into the mainstream society, the more we embrace the Eurocentric standard of beauty as it's depicted in the media. African Americans are now ridiculing what was once accepted, loved and respected within our communities. Our "Big Mamas"—mothers, sisters and aunts—were once considered women of beauty and strength. Today, they're a source of embarrassment, the object of cruel remarks and constant harassment about their weight.

My search for complete love and acceptance took me to NAA-FA, the National Association to Advance Fat Acceptance. I heard that there were men there who loved fat women—found us sexy, in fact. Jackpot! Hot dog, I was going to finally meet the man who would love me for me, and we'd ride off into the sunset forever and ever, amen.

As I quickly became active in the size acceptance movement—and in its missions of enriching the lives of fat people through activism, education and support—my priorities shifted. Finding a mate no longer became important. What mattered were the millions of people in this country who hated their bodies because they didn't measure up to a standard constantly portrayed in the media. Out there were intelligent, talented people who, like me, believed their dreams, goals and aspirations were unattainable because they were fat. Even worse, there were people waiting for that "miracle" diet that would allow them to start living their lives. There were people in emotionally and physically abusive relationships because they truly believed they deserved that abuse, or that no one else would want fat and ugly slobs like them.

Somewhere, someone was starting another diet or beating herself up about another failed diet. A child was dreading going to school because she didn't want to be called "fatty fatty two-by-four" (yeah, I know I'm dating myself). Worthwhile, intelligent, creative people were being denied well-paying jobs because they happened to be fat. Even as I write this, someone is at her doctor's office hoping to be treated for something as minor as a common cold, yet she is being berated for her weight and lack of self-control.

I admit, I joined NAAFA to meet Mr. Wonderful (hasn't happened yet). But I stayed to join the fight against the rampant discrimination against fat people in this country. NAAFA provides a network of support within the size community by offering its members resources for shopping and fat-friendly social events. There are opportunities to collectively speak out against fat discrimination. Most importantly, NAAFA provides the opportunity to learn to love yourself just as you are, not for what you could be or for what someone thinks you should be.

Joining NAAFA and the size acceptance movement opened my eyes to many things. It taught me that in spite of society's sick obsession with looks, I don't have to buy into it. I've discovered that our culture is uncomfortable with anything and anyone "different" from the standard image of beauty. That same discomfort with my body caused some unpleasant things to happen to me.

If I allowed it, I'm sure I could be quite bitter about it. I was definitely angry at first about my past, but I learned that, to some extent, people will only treat you as badly as you permit. As a child, I didn't have the tools to stand up for myself. As an adult, however, I have all the power I need, and no one takes that unless I surrender it.

I've also discovered body hatred is not the exclusive domain of genuinely fat people. I know so many women who, for all intents and purposes, fit the current beauty standard and *still* hate their bodies. They never feel thin or beautiful enough.

I've learned that beauty is an evolving concept and that the norms have changed over time. At the turn of the century, the leading sex symbol, Lillian Russell, weighed over two hundred pounds. If Marilyn Monroe, the object of men's fantasies in the '50s and '60s, were alive today, her (size sixteen) voluptuousness would be considered "too fat."

What can I say? Society is fickle. One minute, you have to be curvy and voluptuous to be considered attractive, the next minute your hip bones and rib cage have to be showing to be one of the beautiful people. I made a conscious decision nearly seven years ago not to make someone else's opinion my reality. That decision gave birth to another decision: to give up dieting. That didn't give me a license to eat all the cookies, cakes and pies I could lay my hands on. Instead, it showed me that I now had choices about what I could eat. It set me free from obsessing about calories and fat grams, and left me with time to ponder more important things.

Yes, I still have those moments of insecurity, the feelings of inadequacy, the loneliness. But I will never go back to those desperate days of feeling as if I had to step down from my standards just to gain someone's approval or acceptance. I refuse to look up to anyone who looks down on me.

I'm still fat—and probably always will be—but I finally know who I am. I'm a fat black woman. I'm all of the things that society dumps on. And I will no longer apologize for my weight, my race or my gender. I will never feel guilty about what I put in my mouth, except maybe White Castle. I wear cool clothes—including mini-skirts, lingerie and two-piece swimsuits. If anyone doesn't like it, they don't have to look! Never again will I allow anyone to put me down or mistreat me because of my weight. I love me, all of me, right now, just the way I am. If I happen to lose or gain weight tomorrow, I will still love myself. And if anyone has a problem handling that, it's their issue, not mine. Life's too short to expend energy on people who can't deal with who I am. Quite frankly, I no longer have room for such people in my life.

Oh yeah, I almost forgot that sexy guy. Well, I took him back to my room, and now he's my love slave. Just kidding! No, we didn't ride off into the sunset or profess our undying love to one another. After the show, we talked, we danced (I looked stunning, of course), I got a foot massage.

Then I did something my friends will tell you I never do. You see, in spite of my newfound confidence, I'm still a little shy around men I find attractive. But I figured, what the heck? I let this man know I was attracted to him and would like to get to know him better. I mean, I felt *something* could be there—the man massaged my feet, for heaven's sake! In the end, he was such a craven coward, he didn't have the integrity to tell me that he was interested in someone else, or just not interested in me. Instead, when we exchanged numbers, he gave me back my own number. I didn't realize until I checked the slip of paper a couple days later, and, I admit, it threw me for a loop.

There was a valuable lesson in that experience, though. Just because I'm secure with myself doesn't mean that people I encounter will be secure enough to handle involvement with me. Chances are, many men and women alike will be intimidated by a show of confidence from someone they feel shouldn't have any confidence at all. Out of that intimidation, I've faced rejection or, at the very least, a change in my existing relationships. Although it hurts, I now realize it has nothing to do with me, and everything to do with those people's inability to deal with my enhanced self-esteem.

I'm not suggesting that I immediately write those people off. I give them the opportunity to accept me and treat me with respect. But if they don't . . . well, I believe they sell those hand-engraved invitations in bulk.

breaking the model
graciela (chely) h. rodriguez

"Are you a model?"

I had been walking through the metal detector at the Los Angeles airport last month when one of the attendants addressed me.

"Would a model be eating these?" I replied, pulling a huge bag of Doritos out of my purse.

I know the question was meant as a compliment, but it brought back a lot of painful memories. You see, I spent the best part of my teenage years "train[ing] to be a model . . . or just look like one." I didn't end up on the catwalk, but rather, in the hospital, recovering from anorexia and bulimia.

That's right, me—an eighteen-year-old Latina who's supposed to be immune to such things. Or so I'm told. Everyone from magazine publishers to television producers has suggested that Latina and African-American girls aren't likely to develop eating disorders, that we're less influenced by the skinny-girl images than our white peers.

But how do they explain me? I come from a traditional, hard-working Mexican family. We celebrate all the Mexican holidays, practice the Catholic religion, and, by nature, our appearance resembles that of our ancestors—prominent facial features, thick bodies and brown skin. I learned Spanish at an early age, as my parents had emigrated to California from Mazatlán, Sinaloa, when they were nineteen.

I've lived in the small town of Carpinteria, California, for my whole life. It's one of the few towns I know to be truly multicultural. My schools have always been filled with kids from all backgrounds—different ethnicities, races, religions. My own Latina identity has been just one among many—and it's never held me back. I've worked hard to fit in and be accepted.

As a young teen, I shared the dream of many girls: I wanted to be a model and an actress. Like most girls, I wanted to be popular, and more than anything that meant I had to be attractive. When I was thirteen, I was scanning a fashion magazine and saw an ad for a model search contest that was coming to Beverly Hills. I jumped at the chance and begged my parents to take me.

At first, my father was against the idea. But with a lot of pleading, I convinced my parents to make the two-hour drive one Saturday afternoon. I entered the contest with more than two thousand little girls, boys, teens and adults. There was no cost to enter, and it seemed like the chance of a lifetime. And it was easy. I just had to parade down a runway and introduce myself to a panel of judges by stating my name, my age and my interests.

Three weeks later, I got a phone call from one of the representatives, saying that I was a finalist. I wasn't one of the top *five* finalists, who were awarded money and free modeling classes. I was, however, a runner-up, which made me eligible for a partial scholarship to help cover modeling and acting lessons. My parents would only have to pay two thousand dollars, the rep told me. To this day, I'm not sure why they did it, but my parents withdrew the money from their savings. Every Saturday, we made the two-hour drive to Beverly Hills, and they waited for eight hours while I learned how to strut, pose and walk with a supermodel sashay.

On my first day, an agent named Pat took my measurements. He frowned and clucked his tongue as he scribbled my dimensions onto a clipboard—five-foot-three, 130 pounds, size seven. Then, he told me that the average model wore a size three and recommended that I drop down to that as quickly as possible.

For motivation, Pat handed me a stack of fashion magazines. He suggested I study the models in *Teen* and *Seventeen* and watch *Beverly Hills 90210* to "get an idea of what real models look like." It didn't matter that I was only thirteen years old and not even fully developed. I was expected either to lose the weight or to get lost.

I left depressed, thinking I would never look like a model because I came from a line of full-figured Mexican women. Even if I lost the weight, I would still never look like most of the girls in the magazines. I remember wishing I'd been born with blond hair, blue eyes and a small waist. I also started to think that if I got a nose job to create that perfect "button" nose, then maybe this career I really wanted could happen. Though I still had doubts whether my genetically given body could be shaped into model material, I believed that if I worked hard enough, I could succeed. As I entered junior high, my goal was not just to *look* like the characters on *90210,* but to *live* like them. I wanted to be popular, like the typical girl on TV. I wanted to be thin—to fit in.

I've been told that sometimes the desire for thinness is learned or reinforced at home. For me, that was true to a degree. My mother is a full-figured woman who's always been concerned about her weight. When I was younger, she used to exercise and limit her portions at mealtime. In fact, she even did some small-scale runway modeling for friends who had boutiques or clothing lines.

But my mother's example didn't spark my desire to model, even though she supported my decision. I feel the media's and society's images of women were more responsible. Like they do for so many girls, these images promised acceptance and happiness if I could only look like them.

However, my mother's habits and shaky self-image did make it easier when I began to diet and exercise obsessively at age thirteen. Early on, I discovered her diet pills and began taking them secretly. When she caught on that some were missing, she confronted me and I denied it. She didn't believe me, though, and even had the principal search my school locker. I remember thinking, "God, now people are going to know why I'm losing weight." I wanted everyone to think it was natural, and I felt like my secret had been revealed. In reality, no one else knew except for a friend (also Latina), who'd given me the idea in the first place. Soon after, I started to buy my own appetite suppressants, which I hid in my change purse.

I was eager to lose weight, and the modeling agency was happy to help. They gave me a list of "forbidden" foods, which was basically anything that didn't taste like sawdust or water. Every day, I had a salad with lemon juice or a plain baked potato, and that was it. I ate only once a day, limiting my intake to a 250-calorie maximum. After a year, my body submitted to this starvation regimen, and my appetite nearly disappeared. Although my stomach would rumble loudly in class, I learned to drink lots of water to fill it for long enough to spare me the embarrassment.

My parents noticed the dramatic change in my appearance, but they mistakenly trusted that the agency had put me on a healthy diet. Since they both worked long hours, and I was busy with extracurricular activities, they didn't have time to monitor my eating habits

graciela h. rodriguez   191

anyway. On the rare occasions that the family ate together, I would eat enough to escape their scrutiny, and then secretly throw it up later.

Bingeing and purging became a ritual. The same friend who introduced me to diet pills taught me that I could eat whatever I wanted and then force it back up so I wouldn't gain any weight. After a while, I didn't even have to stick my finger down my throat; I could throw up just by eating a chip. I also exercised for at least two hours a day at a local gym and at the park near my house. I was so obsessed with losing weight that I would wake up as early as 3 o'clock in the morning to run, and then jog again in the afternoon. I also enrolled in aerobics classes, and in eighth grade, I became captain of the cheerleading squad and president of the student body.

People ask me how I found the energy to do all this, especially with no food in my stomach. I can only answer that I was so driven to achieve "perfection" that it wiped out any concern I might have had for my body or my health. I would come home from school exhausted some days and flop down on my bed. But I was surrounded by pictures of teen models that I'd ripped from magazines and taped to my walls. My response was instant—one look at the wall and I'd be lacing up my Nikes and heading for the track.

But by eight o'clock, I was exhausted. Some nights, I was too tired to finish my homework, and I usually declined invitations from friends so I could stay home and work out. I wasn't the only one, though. Many of my friends—who were mostly Latina and African-American—were going through the same thing. Although there were few models who looked like us in *Teen* and *Seventeen,* we read those magazines anyway and bought into their messages. At the very least, all the girls at my junior high cared about their weight. Most of us worked out, and a lot of our conversations centered around how little we'd eaten that day. There was an unspoken competition, or at least a comparison, to see who had the most "willpower." Somehow, the quest for that power made us overlook the throbbing headaches and the gnawing hunger pangs that came with the territory of thinness.

At the modeling agency, most of the girls were also on strict diets and concerned about their bodies. In the end, going to extremes never paid off. None of us ever got any real modeling jobs. I did a couple of department store fashion shows, but that was it. It never amounted to the money my parents shelled out for my lessons.

But I did lose weight. After three years of hard work, the scales put me at one hundred pounds. In fact, I outdid myself—I dropped down to a size one. Finally, I felt okay wearing a bathing suit in public. I wore cropped tank tops and shorts all the time. There was no lack of attention or praise. People commented on how great and "healthy" I looked, and my self-esteem soared. I might not have been as "beautiful" as some models—after all, none of the models I saw on TV were Latina—but at least I was as skinny as they were.

Still, like most girls with eating disorders, I was never satisfied. In fact, I was unaware that I even had an eating disorder. All I knew was that I didn't feel "perfect" yet. My quest for the perfect body ended when a family member caught me throwing up in a restaurant bathroom. She told my parents, who took me to the hospital immediately, where I was diagnosed with anorexia and bulimia.

My family was as surprised as I was. Fortunately, I began counseling immediately. My counselor helped me to recover from my insecurity and to rebuild my self-esteem. I began to recognize that my worth was not based solely on my looks. It took me about a year to recover. I started to eat more and more and turned to healthier sources to stay in shape. I still exercised, but not nearly as much.

To this day, weight is a big issue in my life and may always be. Last night, I was watching an interview with Janet Jackson, and the thought of looking like her crept into my mind. I started to think, *God, I wish I had abs and a firm butt like hers.* I caught myself falling into

graciela h. rodriguez   193

an old trap. But I was able to stop myself by refocusing my thoughts on all of my good qualities and reminding myself that this was only an image.

One of the most influential things my counselor said to me was, "Chely, you are beautiful inside and out." It seems basic, yet somewhere in my quest for the perfect body, I had forgotten this. I decided never to change for anyone or try so hard to fit in. If I had had real role models—girls with round stomachs and pimples—I would probably have felt more acceptable. After all, that's what most teenage girls look like. Of course, that kind of beauty doesn't sell the way the fantasy kind does. There's a reason we're given an image that's so hard to achieve. As long as we're chasing an impossible weight, we'll always have a reason to buy more diet products, to watch *90210* and to read *Seventeen.*

I now weigh 130 pounds again, and I'm proud of my body. But I need a lot of support to maintain that. Whenever I feel bad, I remind myself, "If people don't accept me the way I am, it's their problem." I also continue to heal myself by helping others. I'm actively involved as a peer advocate, countering unrealistic images in magazines, TV shows, websites and other media that can damage girls' body image. I promote healthy eating habits and exercise and encourage girls to get involved in sports. I'm now a high school senior, and I'm still involved in cheerleading and soccer (I often find myself "counseling" younger teammates about body acceptance). I'm also active in a number of girls clubs that help me maintain my self-esteem in the face of negative body image messages.

After recovering from my eating disorder, I participated in an organization called Girls Incorporated, which helps nurture young girls to become strong, self-confident women. Girls Inc. recently awarded me ten thousand dollars toward my college tuition. I've never been prouder. It felt incredible to receive a scholarship that was based on my achievements, rather than on the way I looked.

When I talk to girls, I tell them what I've learned—that it can be okay to want to look attractive and to be concerned about body weight, but we have to understand how far to take it. Finding that balance is tricky. The influence of the media is extremely powerful. I tell my story at conferences where big-time media executives are in attendance. I challenge them to provide young people with better role models and to stop portraying girls as victims and sex objects.

Eating disorders affect girls of color, too. I'm a perfect example of a Latina who developed an eating disorder because I so badly wanted to look and be like the thin, popular girls I saw in the media. I saw very few Latina role models on TV, and if I did see any, they were in gangs, wearing bikinis or cleaning houses. I have rarely seen a Latina get acknowledged for her accomplishments rather than her large breasts. If I'd had positive Latina role models, I might never have felt ashamed to come from a full-figured line of women. I would have felt proud.

In the meantime, I've decided to become my own role model by reminding myself who I am every day. I am an eighteen-year-old Latina, a full-figured former model. I have survived an eating disorder. And I'm learning to love my body.

body image:

third wave feminism's issue?

amelia (amy) richards

In the United States, each wave of feminism has fought its own battles with body image. The suffragists of the late nineteenth and early twentieth centuries rebelled against corsets and fought the characterization of women's-righters as unfeminine, homely and pretentious "blue-stockings." In the 1960s and '70s, the second wave of feminists fought stereotyping that pegged them as humorless, ugly and anti-sex. Women struggled to be taken seriously, to be more than just pretty faces and pin-up girls. They wanted to be defined by their minds rather than their bodies.

In the late 1990s, among the rising third wave of feminists, image and body are at the center of feminist analysis. For many women, our bodies have become the canvasses upon which our struggles paint themselves. Body image, in fact, may be the pivotal third wave issue—the common struggle that mobilizes the current feminist generation.

The first two waves of feminism were organized movements, with clearly defined goals. The first wave fought to establish women's right to be citizens—to vote, own property, divorce and inherit money. The second wave's agenda was to elevate women's status to that of men.

In the third wave, we've expanded the fight for equal status. We are aware of the need to express our various identities—racial, ethnic, sexual, political, religious and class—as well as our feminist identity. This individuality is necessary, but it also poses a challenge. Because we now have many different paths to—and definitions of—empowerment, it's become difficult to organize a unified movement. In this wave of feminism, you're as likely to run into women who defend, enjoy and create pornography as you are to come across feminists who see pornography as the ultimate oppressor. You are also likely to find women who are tired of the pressure to act and look "perfect." Others pack their feminist toolkits with lipstick and nail polish, forgetting that while lipstick and nail polish aren't feminist concerns, the right to choose—or not choose—them is.

It's also difficult to unite everyone under an umbrella term like feminism when the third wave feminist vocabulary has been co-opted by the media. For example, "girl power" has been transformed from an expression of individuality and empowerment to a slick marketing slogan. And many women have taken the bait, assuming that the "girl power" label comes complete with feminist securities such as reproductive freedom, freedom from violence and other issues played out on women's bodies.

To unite today's young women, we need to focus on a particular issue and then bring together the diverse feminist opinions on the matter to create a rich, complex dialogue. Better to disagree than to be silent, to fill out feminism rather than trim it down.

Second wave feminists named our struggles—domestic violence, sexual harassment, equal pay for work of equal value, which had lain silenced until then—and lobbied for laws that would protect us. Now, our generation has turned the focus inward. Tellingly, our relationships with our bodies often signal how far we still have to go. It is evident not only in how we treat them, but in how their role continues to permeate our existence and dictate our lives.

So where do we begin? Although "body image" won't make it into Congress, related issues will—for instance, sports, reproductive rights and affirmative action. As young feminists, we can point out how these individual and personal issues are linked to a larger political agenda.

Body image is significant as a rallying focus because it speaks not only to the converted but also to the "I'm not a feminist, but . . . I'm tired of measuring myself against an impossible-to-achieve beauty standard" contingent. It can catalyze our dormant or displaced activism, primarily because it's both a cultural and a political issue—and we are a pop culture–driven generation. Mention teen magazines, for example, and many young women react viscerally, offering stories of how fat/ugly/ethnic/misfitting/self-hating the magazines made them feel. Even young women who don't identify as feminists offer heartfelt and complex emotions on the topic.

Perhaps that's why much of third wave feminism has centered on pop culture, rather than legal and political strategies. Our activism is directed at our most visible "oppressors"—the media and entertainment industries. Rather than holding marches or rallies, many young women create zines, websites, music, films and videos that counter images we deem insulting or dangerous.

In the visual world of the late twentieth century, however, the outside counts as well as the inside. We use our appearance—bodies, clothing, style—to express our inner convictions, our pride, our affiliations, our identities, our insecurities and our weaknesses. In a generation focused on identity issues—and unafraid to show them to the public—our bodies, and how we adorn them, can express who we are.

But, as young women redesign feminism, we run the risk of being misinterpreted as all image, no substance—as having no collective agenda. Too often, image becomes a convenient cover-up for issues we haven't resolved, just as eating disorders often manifest more deeply rooted problems such as childhood abuse.

We have to be careful not to fall into the trap of only having our bodies and our images speak for who we are—what we think, what we feel, what we do. Images and slogans are too easily co-opted and robbed of the substance they have the potential to convey. Instead, we must take this opportunity to seize control of our bodies and the forces that manipulate them—mostly the advertising and entertainment industries.

A feminist world is often where women find themselves when they get fed up with the representation of women in the media. It's a place to express all the rage, realization and healing that follow—and to find a support community of people who have had similar experiences. Once feminists reach a point of understanding that we are not these images—that we don't have to look like Claudia Schiffer to be beautiful—then what? The silence, at that point, is deafening. We're supposed to go out and educate other women about loving their bodies, to save them from eating disorders. But if, as leaders, we dare to expose our own unresolved body image issues, we have to worry about tarnishing our feminist credibility. We're not supposed to have those problems anymore.

But we do. I do. As a feminist, I feel helpless at times, caught in a double standard. At "Ask Amy," my online feminist advice column, I confront painfully honest letters from young women who are dealing with their own eating disorders or body issues. What do I tell them? I could ignore the fact that the women we see thriving are those who fall under the rubric of athletic, attractive, slim, good-looking, fit, healthy. I could forget that, statistically, thin women have a greater chance of being accepted to elite colleges than heavier women do even if their credentials are identical; and that it isn't poverty that causes obesity, but obesity that causes poverty. But I see it as my responsibility to be honest with my correspondents. Body image issues, like most any other painful life experience, become less difficult once an open dialogue begins. So my advice usually includes my own experience. I tell them how I struggled with bulimia and how I eventually realized that developing my own identity is more important than pleasing other people.

The road to a solution is certainly a feminist one. It includes women creating our own beauty standards rather than following those dictated by corporations. It includes pointing out that this problem affects men, too. (Men are only slightly less likely to be concerned about their body image than women are, and a reported 10 percent of those suffering from eating disorders are men.) It means better sex education and more forums to talk about body image. But we can't stop there. We must create a dialogue that extends beyond these forums and into our daily lives, a dialogue that leads us to less shame, less denial and more room for individuality. It's up to the third wave of feminism to make sure this conversation continues and that a support network exists.

american
all-girls

all-american girls:
jock chic, body image and sports
leslie heywood

What did it mean to grow up a girl in white, middle-class America in the 1970s if you didn't want to be a girl—that is, be treated like a girl, with people assuming that you were weak, worth less than boys, that you'd rather be shopping or playing with dolls than kicking some ass? For me, it meant listening to Aerosmith and Kiss and fighting my mother for equal access to Lee jeans and flannel shirts from Miller's Outpost. It meant your mother might be schizo, because for the second time in American history, following those primo babes in Seneca Falls, New York, who first raised the idea of women's rights in 1848, gender equity was being questioned. My mom, raised with traditional family values, tried to impress on me traditional girl-ness—obedience, mildness, acquiescence and servitude. But, in some ways, she was also a feminist and tried to impart values to me that refuted traditional girl-ness, like independence.

The fighters who launched the second wave women's movement

(to whom today's grrrl-jocks owe our lives) nailed an important victory. It was Title IX of the 1972 Amendments to the Education Act, which mandated equal facilities and funding for women's sports in any educational program receiving federal dollars. So if, like me, you thought that girliness was for aliens and had nothing to do with you, you went out for sports.

The work of sports historian Susan K. Cahn shows that the entrance of girls like me into the world of sports was not always welcomed: Many, in fact, "perceiv[ed] women's entrance into sport as an unsettling and unwelcome intrusion into the realm of masculinity." So even as we entered this world, girls had to accept some pretty traditional ideas about gender, which were rigidly enforced. Ideas like: A girl is always less than a boy. And if she wants to excel, she has to be as similar to a boy as possible for anyone to think she is serious about or any good at her sport. When I was in high school, a feature article about me in the local newspaper illustrated this only too well:

> Leslie Heywood is just "one of the guys" as far as the Amphi High School cross country team is concerned. The pretty blonde, blue-eyed junior is the best runner on the girls team, but she regularly works out with the boys team. . . . "I want her to stop thinking like a girl runner," Panther coach Raul Nido said. "Not that I want her to stop being a girl, but because I want her to work and think like an athlete. Right now she's just one of the guys."

Apparently, working and thinking "like an athlete" meant working and thinking like a guy, which I was more than happy to do at the time. I thought it gave me value, made me different—you know, from all those mediocre wussy girls who just ran because they liked it and didn't worry about winning.

Eventually, striving to become one of the guys became really physical for me. As Cahn writes, "Many Americans could not separate the concept of athletic superiority from its cultural affiliation with masculine sport and the male body." So, by the time I entered sports, girls who wanted to be taken seriously as athletes had to have bodies that were as close to a guy's body as they could make them.

I wanted very badly to train with the guys, to be just like them, so when I became the only girl allowed to train with them, I felt like I was special, different, not a *girl*. I was accepted as an athlete precisely because I was different from the other girls, an exception to the "rule" of feminine frivolity, weakness and insignificance.

What did I say about our mothers being schizo? It went for their daughters, too. Even if you were one of the guys, you also had to be a babe. It was extremely important to me that I was the "pretty blonde, blue-eyed junior" (*geez*—I was even a cheerleader), because often it seemed as if looking that way was the only thing that made it okay for me to kick ass. Tough like a guy, but *still feminine.* That meant hot-rollers in my hair before practice, little green and white bows in my ponytail. I had to be like a guy to be taken seriously, but I also had to be like a Barbie doll to be accepted. So where did that leave me with my body? Extremely confused.

I have always been a mesomorph—my body tends toward muscularity. At that time, being a middle- to long-distance runner, I ran 120 miles a week, weighed 110 pounds and had eight percent body fat, yet I still looked pretty big. The whole muscular-woman-as-sex-symbol trend hadn't hit yet—a girl's biceps and quadriceps were still supposed to be small—and I was continuously asked if I was a swimmer—code word for a bruising burly chick who wasn't going to make any splashes in *Vogue.* The femme aesthetic, combined with the valued-for-being-like-a-guy point of view, was lethal. At 110, I

leslie heywood   **203**

was *sure* I was too fat. For an athlete, breasts were *non grata,* and legs had to be rope-tight and very thin.

Coaches reinforced that aesthetic. When I was running on a track scholarship at the University of Arizona, the coach used to herd the team into the training room and weigh us—in front of all the football and basketball players. The trainer would adjust the balance carefully and then shout our poundages out (I've heard the same story over and over in my conversations with other female athletes): "Leslie—*one hundred and twelve!"* It was enough to make me eat spinach for a week. The monthly underwater weighings to determine our body fat percentages didn't help much either. Coach wanted us all under ten percent. Anything higher was occasion for great shame, not to mention a threat to our scholarships.

Yep, we were pretty fucked up. If you wanted to see a bunch of paranoid, catty women who would give you a stomachache for at least three weeks, all you had to do was sit in on one of our team dinners. Strained silence, everyone looking at everyone else's plate, victory to she who ate the least. Veiled, sideways glances at this woman's stomach and that woman's legs. One woman whose stomach was a little puffy earned the snide nickname "Bread Basket." Another woman, whose body looked a little like a spider's, would eat only fresh vegetables she had boiled herself, drinking the leftover water, too. Incapable of such discipline, I ate as little as I could during the week, giving in to ice cream and Captain Crunch binges on the weekend, followed by solitary trips to the bathroom where the good Captain would come back up with a little help from my index finger. Sports a panacea for women? I'm sure glad I had them, but it wasn't exactly a perfect world then.

♌

Is it different now, in the late '90s, the age of the power babe? Maybe.

A report from the President's Council of Physical Fitness and Sports verifies that girls who participate in sports are more likely to stay in school, are less likely to become pregnant as teenagers, and have higher self-confidence.

Nike latched onto those findings and popularized them in an ad campaign in 1995 that went:

> *If you let me play/ I will like myself more / I will have more self-confidence / I will suffer less depression / I will be sixty percent less likely to get breast cancer / I will be more likely to leave a man who beats me / I will be less likely to get pregnant before I want to / I will learn what it means to be strong / If you let me play sports.*

Nike has successfully tapped the growing segment of female athletes—there are enough of us Title IX babies around to comprise a significant demographic—creating a new market for its products and letting us out of the closet and onto center stage.

Part of the credit for putting women athletes center stage goes to volleyball superstar-supermodel Nike spokeswoman Gabrielle Reece. "There used to be two types of women on the big screen," Gabby writes, "moms and sexpots. Now we have the power chick."

The power chick. We don't have to be guys to be taken seriously anymore, right? We don't have to reject our bodies, because today *girl* doesn't mean weak little wuss, *woman* doesn't mean doormat, giving up all your time and dreams for other people. We can have muscles now, and ostensibly what those muscles stand for: power, self-determination, presence, a place in the world. There's been a lot of rhetoric in the late '90s about having it all (again), and what this new body aesthetic means. As Gabrielle Reece's collaborator, Karen Karbo, writes:

The covers of newsmagazines show women with serious snarls, flexed muscles, in their shorts or suits or cleats—look at these jocks!—while the covers of beauty and style magazines give the same basketball players and swimmers and baseball players the female celebrity treatment—makeup artists, hairstylists, air brushistes—rendering them safely feminine (and, curiously, less overtly sexual) but virtually unrecognizable as the Women We Love Who Also Kick Ass.

Karbo points to a double standard: the down and dirty athletic chick, as ready for sex as she is for the field, and the glamourous, done-up, untouchable goddess. Gabby is both.

But oh, pooh! It's totally cool! You can have it both ways, Gabby insists. At least, that's what she tells us in the new Condé Nast magazine *Sports for Women* (now *Women's Sports and Fitness),* where Gabby has her own column:

Femininity and strength aren't mutually exclusive. We can sport strong bodies but be chicks at the same time. I get out of bed, throw on the Lycra, pull my hair back, lace up my shoes and oh-so-deliberately apply my lashes. Then I go out and spike the ball into my opponent's face. This open display of schizophrenia is fun. Men aren't so lucky. They generally aren't allowed to wear lipstick with their work suits . . . true power comes from knowing we have the choice and playing it whichever way we like.

Yeah, well, Gabby, I was doing this back in high school. But it wasn't always a "choice." I won't deny that my power babe body has gotten me a lot of things, from a kind of amazed respect from my students

(I'm now a college women's studies professor) to a very real sense of self-value. But that value is dependent upon constantly working out. As Susan Bordo writes in *Twilight Zones:*

> *My students know that as long as they keep up their daily hours at the gym, they can feel pumped up, look like Madonna and burn enough calories so perhaps they will not have to throw up after dinner. But how, they wonder, can they possibly keep it up their entire lives?*

That's a damn good question. There's a fine line between *just do it* and an endless treadmill that eats up a very large portion of your life. Are glamour jocks more powerful? Let's get real. It takes work to look like Gabby Reece. Put thirty more pounds on her six-foot-three, 170-pound frame, and just see what happens to Reece's "choices" about Lycra and spiking then. A two-hundred-pound woman slamming a volleyball in someone's face is more likely to be called a monster than a babe.

So why do I keep working it myself then? Truth? I'm scared to death to do anything else. As it is for so many women athletes, the idea of fat is scarier to me than any horror movie. So while some things have changed, in some ways, the song remains the same. At five-foot-five and twelve percent body fat, with the pumped-up muscles of the most kick-ass babe, I weigh close to 150. I stopped cringing whenever I got on the scale in about '94. But the power look comes at a price—I still wouldn't call food a friend, and I stick by the ethos that if I ever see an ounce of cellulite on *my* thighs, I'm heading for the plastic surgeon or the hills. Worse, now I've got to worry about aging. Now that I'm more comfortable with my weight, it's the wrinkles on my forehead that plague me—and I'm a feminist professor. People always think this means I won't be worried about my looks. It doesn't. What it does mean is that I'm not stupid, that I know as well as the next woman just how much this culture still values us for our looks, and it's impossible to rise completely above that.

Still, the new attention, and validation, given to female athletes is positive in many ways. If you put aside the media image issue and just look at what happens to girls and women when they play sports, the picture gets a bit rosier.

For example, I compete in powerlifting now, a bench pressing event. At a recent meet, I lifted over two hundred pounds. It broke a big psychological barrier for me, an "oh, a woman just can't lift that much" limitation I had imposed on myself. Bench is the quintessential litmus test of masculinity in gyms. The guys I train with started calling me "Lester" rather than "Leslie" after I lifted those 210-pound weights—I suppose to mark my passage from the land of girly weights to the land of real men. So I delivered an impromptu lecture as we were all struggling with our bicep curls, sweating and straining: "You know guys (curl, gasp), are the words *woman* and *strength* (puff, strain) so incompatible?" And although they laughed and elbowed each other and said "Oooh, big words, the girl's got big biceps *and* big words," it was obvious they got my point.

Despite these vestiges of old-model thinking, eased here with a humor that took away the edge, the powerlifting community is by far the most egalitarian and democratic athletic community I have been in. Everyone's efforts are supported, no matter who you are, no matter what level you are lifting at. When Billy, the guy who first called me "Lester," didn't hesitate the first time I made a move to spot him on his bench, it was a great gesture of respect and trust. He was lifting maybe four hundred pounds, a huge amount of weight, and as his spotter it would be my job to grab the weight from him and get it to the bar should his muscles fail. Many guys assume that a "girl" won't be able to spot them and turn to the nearest guy, but Billy did nothing of the sort. He treated me like any other spotter from the beginning, granting me full group membership. That dynamic says a lot, and these guys—normal guys, not much academic training, the kind of guys you might normally suspect of armchair, beer-swilling sexism—have treated me much better than some men have outside the gym. I train hard, I lift. That's all I had to do to earn equality and respect, and the same respect is extended to other lifters, of whatever race, gender, ability or social class.

As maligned as the word *feminist* has been since it first showed up over a century ago, the current stereotype of feminists as man-hating, unshaven, cargo-pants wearing, shrill harpie "femi-Nazis" has led to academic and media documentation of young women's acceptance of feminist ideals like equal rights and equal pay, but a rejection of identification with the term itself (the "I'm not a feminist, but . . ." syndrome). So what's a girl who really believes in female power to do? A lot of us have become athletes and support other women's efforts to become athletes. The current explosion of popularity the female athlete is enjoying may well be a form of displaced feminism, a kind of late-'90s stealth feminism. The female athlete may serve as the site for feminist ideals no one quite wants to call feminist, a place where feminist ideals can be acted out in a way that is no longer stigmatized. Female jocks sure weren't always "in," but they sure are now. Sports sociologists have cautioned that this new trend marks only an individual agency that can never alter oppressive social conditions as a whole. In fact, they suggest that it may function to reproduce those conditions by turning girls' and women's attention away from the kind of collective action that does change things.

Forms of individual agency like sports participation can affect people's everyday lives. We've still got to do the activism, though. We need to consciously work toward turning that sense of personal, everyday empowerment toward some larger redefinition of social roles, or girls playing sports will be just another Madison avenue coup. We can't forget to take our politics along with our endorphins, our pro-girl activities along with our sweat and reps.

marked for life:
tattoos and the redefinition of self
silja j.a. talvi

Sometime in the midst of the politically turbulent and socially perplexing 1980s, I gathered enough courage to pick up the phone and call Hollywood's legendary Spotlight Tattoo to ask if the poorly self-made, hand-lettered tattoo on my ankle could be fixed. The gruff voice on the other end of the phone belonged to the studio's owner. "Sure," he growled. "Come by next week. Cash only."

At the time, my main concern—aside from the pain—was whether the studio would demand identification. But in a shop that was then populated by motorcyclists, punks and other misfits, no one blinked at the sight of a mohawked teenager getting her ankle retouched. One excruciating half-hour later, I looked down in stunned appreciation. Black, gang-style Old English letters spelled out the word *Sisu*—Finnish for "strength" or "tenacity of purpose."

A week later, I went back for an addition—a traditional red rose picked out from a stack of existing designs. The finished product was nothing spectacular, but it was noticeable. Most important, it said something new about me; this tattoo would serve as a visual reminder of my belief that I was going to make it through a difficult and painful time. By getting tattooed, I consciously took a small step away from my emotional suffering and toward a radical new self-definition.

By Western standards, there is nothing ladylike about being tattooed. Standards of acceptable beauty for women still dictate unblemished skin. The female body can be adorned with ear piercings, makeup and silicone implants, but any form of decoration that radically challenges mainstream beauty standards is sure to raise eyebrows. At worst, the woman who chooses to visibly alter her appearance by having her skin tattooed risks being classified as a freak and treated accordingly. Tattoos in this context can represent a sense of pride in one's ability to survive adverse circumstances; a visible affiliation with a given subculture, and a permanent *fuck you* statement to a larger society that honors beauty only within the parameters of its own rigid definition.

Despite tattooing's growing mainstream popularity, I believe that women who choose to get tattooed usually represent more societally marginalized groups—lesbians, female gang members, punks, runaways, ex-convicts and other groups whose lifestyles or beliefs relegate them to the fringes of society. Assigned a class or social status that designates them as outsiders, they may find a sense of empowerment in their freedom to drastically alter the color and design of their skin.

Owing to a combination of familial, economic, ethnic, political and social circumstances, I have always felt like an outsider, in many senses of the word. My childhood in Scandinavia as a dark-haired Jew from a mixed family primed me for a sense of exclusion I have never been able to shake. When I came to California, the feeling was intensified by the culture shock of life in Los Angeles. I couldn't seem to coexist comfortably with American kids my own age and I retreated further and further into myself, often experiencing chilling waves of self-loathing and depression that I would only later come to understand compassionately. Later, as a teenager growing up in a single-parent home in Los Angeles, I finally found acceptance in the hard-core punk scene. Nothing could match the sheer sense of emotional outrage and sociopolitical defiance that defined the larger punk rock movement of the time.

From the cradle of the punk scene, I soon grew familiar with another genre of music and another subcultural community—reggae and Rastafari. In England, the commitment of so many punks to sociopolitical change and to the creation of original music—which spoke to real-life "sufferation"—had resulted in unlikely political and musical interchanges between Rastafarians and working-class punks. While this phenomenon was not as pronounced in the United States, my early exposure to reggae music and to Rastafari expanded my notions of identity and nurtured my burgeoning spirituality. Two years after making a spiritual commitment to many of the main themes and practices of Rastas, I was finally able to truly turn my attention to my own Jewish ethnic and spiritual heritage. My ensuing adherence to both faiths (which share many of the same principles and approaches toward life) provided me with a much firmer sense of place and purpose in life.

But as a woman who was already on the periphery of society, choosing to get tattooed meant that I accepted the possibility of further ostracism and hostility. Despite this, I've always felt it was worth the risk. But many tattooed women I know have faced ridicule or consternation from their own families, or from male partners (sometimes tattooed themselves) who find tattoos unappealing on women. I've also met plenty of women with poorly designed tattoos that bring them no sense of joy, or whose tattoos are just unhappy reminders of difficult times and abusive relationships. But in a world that offers women few concrete ways to exert control and power over our lives, tattoos can bring a real sense of strength, identity and dignity.

In the essay "Mark Her Words" (*Ms.,* September–October 1996), author Deborah Shouse echoed one of my long-standing beliefs: that tattoos can help women reclaim their bodies in the aftermath of sexual abuse or trauma. Shouse, the mother of a sexually abused young Jewish woman, described how her daughter used tattoos and piercings to mark her reclamation.

One angry reader, equating this girl's body modification with masochism and self-destruction, urged the mother to recognize her daughter's self-oppression, arguing that feminism and maturity were about self-acceptance. Her concerns over the emotional well-being of the daughter in question, it seemed, came from a genuine place of concern. Yet, the reader was simultaneously denying that this young woman's acts of body modification were a valid form of self-acceptance—even acts of her burgeoning feminist identity.

I've come to understand that a young woman's decision to re-claim herself though tattooing is fundamentally *frightening* to some women. Tattooing is an undeniably strong statement and, for many, a disconcerting display of trauma and ferocity. While some feminists may feel more comfortable with healing circles, new moon rituals and writing exercises designed to draw out the "inner child," a newer generation of young women may relate to the healing process in an altogether different way. To be sure, tattooing is not a decision to be made lightly or half-heartedly. But when such a decision is made, it typically marks an important stage in a woman's life—a process of discovering, exploring and learning on the very surface of the body.

Many women seek out tattoos for altogether joyful reasons—to celebrate ethnic, spiritual or cultural heritages; to mark exciting life transitions or to display a lifelong beautification. To dismiss tattoos as a form of self-oppression is to miss out on the fascinating complexity behind each woman's decision to adorn her body with one or more permanent designs. Much of the time, tattoos on a woman truly say something about her character, her life and her spirit.

It would take another decade after being tattooed in Los Angeles before I decided to put ink in my skin again. Having begun to make peace with many of the complexities of my identity—shaped so significantly by pain as well as by an overreaching desire to make a meaningful and worthwhile difference in the world—I celebrated a new chapter in my topsy-turvy existence with new tattoos. Branching out from the older tattoos, I started by having an exquisite rose vine inked around my ankle.

The vine, beautiful in its simplicity, was a statement of closure in my life. Having marked myself before to signify my suffering and my resilience, I now marked myself to acknowledge my progress. The vine, gently reaching out from the original rose and the *Sisu*, transformed the hardness the old tattoo had represented. Over the next few months, I adorned myself with several more tattoos.

Compared to the elaborate and large pieces decorating some people's arms, torsos and legs, my tattoos seem small. But taken together, the images that decorate my body are a confluent mix of sweetness and sorrow, strength and vulnerability. For the most part, they remain concealed under clothing, where I can often feel their energy radiating over my body. I have no burning desire at this stage of my life to show the world what I'm made of—my tattoos are not intended to impress, frighten or impose. On the occasions when warmer weather favors lighter clothing, I'm not always prepared for the curious questions—or the hostility—that my tattoos can provoke. Like my well-kept, past-waist-length dreadlocks, my tattoos are no longer a novelty to me. But I'll be the first to admit that I find other people's tattoos fascinating, and, as such, I tolerate most inquisitiveness about mine.

In some contexts, however, I feel distinctly uncomfortable displaying my tattoos. Out of respect for a different generation and way of life, I have always concealed my tattoos around my grandfather. Although members of my immediate family are aware of my tattoos, I prefer to keep them mostly covered in their presence. After all, it must seem strange to have brought a child into the world whose skin now looks different from the skin of the child they held and cared for.

But the environments in which I feel most conflicted about my tattoos are those that revolve around my ethnic and spiritual identities. In my interactions with both Jews and Rastafarians, I am distinctly aware that being tattooed goes against Old Testament prohibitions regarding the marking of skin. In religious contexts, my tattoos thus mistakenly brand me as an outsider or a wayward soul and may raise feelings of alarm or even disgust in Jews who remember the forcible tattooing of Nazi Holocaust victims. Jewish edicts further prohibit the burial of a tattooed person, a prohibition I learned about only after having been tattooed. The virulently anti-Semitic young man who angrily informed me of this fact intended for me to feel further isolated from a faith he considered to be an evil, archaic force in the world. He was disappointed to find that I did not feel the same way.

I don't regret my tattoos—nor do I apologize for them. Just as with other edicts set down in our holy books and then amended, reinterpreted or discarded altogether, I believe that the prohibition against tattooing should be discussed and re-evaluated. In truth, I am no less committed to my multifaceted spirituality and heritage because of my tattoos, nor do I believe that those who get tattooed are any less worthy in the eyes of the Eternal One. Yet my emotions on the matter are mixed. I do cherish the laws and guidelines by which most Jews and Rastas live their lives. And so, it saddens me that I'm perceived by my own people to have gone against a commonly observed law of the Torah.

Ultimately, the discomfort many people feel over the sight of tattooed women is both intriguing and challenging. Conscientious, radical self-definition—whether external or internal in nature—forces me (and many others) to contemplate my place in the scheme of things. Where do I fit in this pre-existing social order, or where must I carve out a new paradigm for myself? How does my physical appearance affect people's perceptions and, consequently, how they might learn to treat others? How might my steps toward a new self-definition assist the younger generations of women who will seek to carve out their own identities in even more radical and descriptive ways?

In 1917, feminist anarchist Emma Goldman wrote of her perspectives on the true potential for women's liberation:

> *[Woman's] development, her freedom, her independence, must come from and through herself. . . That is, by trying to learn the meaning and substance of life in all its complexities, by freeing herself from the fear of public opinion and public condemnation. Only that . . . will set woman free, will make her a force hitherto unknown in the world, a force for real love, for peace, for harmony; a force of divine fire, of life-giving; a creator of free men and women. ("Woman Suffrage," 1917; reprinted in* Anarchism and Other Essays, *1970.)*

As Goldman knew, no journey in a woman's life is more significant than that which questions and challenges her sense of self, allowing truisms of identity to be reshaped or to crumble and be rebuilt. And so, as I map the inner regions of my mind and soul I pause, on occasion, to mark the passages and triumphs on the other side, on the canvas that is my own flesh and blood.

at home in my body:
an asian-american athlete search-es for self
allison torres

I learned at a young age, as most multiracial people do, to interpret the motives behind squinting stares, furrowed brows and perplexed finger snapping. "What are you?" was an inevitable and tiring question, usually asked by complete strangers. And it was always a toss-up whether they were genuinely interested, or just frustrated that they couldn't figure it out themselves.

A guy once approached me and asked, more bluntly than some, with a bunch of his buddies looking on. Of course, I knew what he was getting at, but I didn't give him the satisfaction until he clarified his question. It turned out that he and his friends had been debating my ethnicity, and they were all waiting to hear. I am lots of things, and although being half Filipino is an important one of them, it is certainly not the sum total of who I am.

It's not that I mind discussing my ethnicity—my parents are both part Filipino and a mixture of other ethnicities, and I'm used to explaining my racial makeup. What I do mind is the naive expectation that my ethnicity alone satisfies such a weighty question. Some say that attention from curious people should be flattering. Personally, I'd much rather be recognized for my accomplishments.

Being around people who were born with similar physical features doesn't necessarily make me feel at home. Even in designated Filipino spaces, like Filipino clubs or the introductory Tagalog language course I took in college, I have still felt out of place. Surrounded by peers who grew up immersed in Filipino traditions, foods and culture, it was obvious that we didn't have the same experiences. They were taking refuge in the familiarity of the culture, while I was only becoming familiar with it. What could I do? I came from an assimilated family. My father was in the military and we moved frequently, making it hard for me to establish roots. We rarely lived in places with any significant Filipino presence. Like most biracial people, I was destined to be a minority no matter where I went, and I grew accustomed to life without a predetermined community.

Then, I joined my college crew team. Crew, or rowing, is an intensely physical, team-oriented sport. Ironically, it also has a history as an old money, old boys' sport. By the time I joined the team, that reputation had changed and Title IX, a 1972 federal mandate legislating gender equity in sports, was finally beginning to take effect and make sports more accessible to women.

Later, Title IX made women's crew at my school a varsity sport, but when I joined the team my freshman year of college, it was still a club sport. This meant that anyone could join—you didn't have to be a star athlete to row, and I was glad. I didn't want to be judged before I had even decided completely that crew was something I wanted to try. All of us who showed up to join the team had little in common at the time, as far as we knew. But what held us there was the one thing we did share: our willingness to try something out, to approach a challenge—without knowing how long, how tough or how rewarding the journey would be.

There was something else that made me stay, even after I discovered that I'd have to commit to regular 5:00 A.M. practices, intensive weightlifting and out-of-state weekend competitions. It was the dawning of the notion that I fully *belonged* somewhere. Crew is a team sport if there ever was one, and I carved myself a niche in the team. It was like a community—everyone had to be in perfect sync with one another to move the long, eight-person boats we raced in. And before I could train my muscles to swing, contract and release with such precise timing, I had to understand my body and what it could do. I had to know who I was as a person, and how I worked best. Practice was never just physical; I was never *just* pumping iron or moving water. I made that boat rip through the water with my legs pounding and my arms burning because I knew that I *could.*

I had to build strong relationships of trust and understanding with my teammates, or my efforts would be in vain. I had to be acutely aware of my power. In this intense team environment, I was not an outsider, but an essential component of a well-oiled machine. Swaggering in the gym, rowing through the mist in the morning, working out past exhaustion, I was an active part of creating a new culture—the culture of my team.

By the end of the first season, I started to look like a rower. My shoulders were broader; I could see my back muscles. Now, people responded to me with a different curiosity. Once, when I was wearing a sleeveless shirt, a man told me I had "swimmer's shoulders" and asked if I swam competitively. The questions about my ethnicity still came up, but now I had a convenient response. *What are you?* An athlete. *What's your ethnic background?* Half Filipino, and the other half is Italian, Canadian, Spanish, Welsh, Danish and Scottish.

At the same time that other people's attitudes toward my body changed, so did mine. Fueled by the confidence of my new identity, I became less focused on the way my body looked and more concerned about what it could do. At practice, I lifted weights until muscle failure. I had a growing collection of medals. I realized that I was at my best when I was proving myself wrong about what I could do. People took me seriously as an athlete because I took myself seriously.

I noticed a change in my teammates' attitudes about themselves, too. One year my boat won at a national championship regatta. After the race, we got out of the boat, in sweaty spandex uniforms, to stand on the medals dock for photographs. Some of the women bursting with pride next to me were the same ones who, earlier that season, were mortified that they had to race in spandex. They used to run to the pile of loose clothing as soon as we got off the water. That day everyone was just proud. After a while, it was easy to stop critical thoughts. *So what if my thighs are big? They can lift a hundred pounds more than my body weight.*

In a women's studies class I took, we talked about the idea of women "being" bodies rather than merely possessing bodies. A reading suggested that women were taught to separate their identities from their bodies, which distorted their self-image.

Before I became an athlete, I would have disagreed. I possessed a body, an appearance, that often belied my cultural identity. I was too many things mixed together to just "be" one of them. There was more to me than what you could see. To me, being a body suggested that I should have an easy definition of myself, a phenomenon that occurred only after I started rowing. Then, my body became more and more indicative of who I was.

At the same time, though, my success as an athlete has depended on a slight separation between my mind and my body. To reach my goals, my mind had to be convinced that my body could do the impossible. Athletic records would never be broken if we all just did what our bodies were comfortable with. I don't believe that extraordinary athletes simply have extraordinary physical capabilities. They also have to know themselves and their limits well. Separating mind from body in the appropriate context, in my case, has led to a better union between the two. I've learned that the limits of my body's strength are as fluid as my ethnic identity. As soon as I discover a limit in people's expectations—or in my own—it pushes me harder to break past it into new terrain.

Moreover, being an athlete has taught me that I must know myself—inside and out—to succeed. I must know where my limits are in order to break them. I've never let my ethnicity stop me from challenging myself, so why should I let anything else? With nothing holding me back, and with teammates pushing me forward, it was only natural to break one more barrier by becoming a serious athlete. And when I graduated, I bought a single scull so that I could keep rowing as a part of my life even after I left my "community."

Being an athlete is now my single most defining identity. Not everyone has to be aware of it, just as not everyone has to be aware that I'm half Filipino. I've realized that what shapes who I am—what gives me my self-image—may not always be outwardly recognizable. But now I'm sure of how I see myself, and this perspective will stick with me. Just as being born half Filipino will always be part of my identity, so will the way I feel about myself and what I can do because I'm an athlete. Even if I never compete or train as rigorously as I once did, I will always be an athlete. My crew team is where I really planted roots of my own for the first time. I chose this community. It was the first time the decision was completely my own.

I'll never know for sure what the next person will see when they look at me. Filipino, white, Latina, mixed? Swimmer, rower, volleyball player? Will they look to my skin tone or my muscle tone for a clue? It's anyone's guess. But when I'm out on the water rowing, and the creases and the colors deepen on my shoulders, I'm satisfied to see how well I've defined myself.

inner visions
christy damio

"The last time I got a good look at myself, I was thirteen years old," I recently told a friend.

She sighed. It was a "tell me about it" sound, the sort of murmur you emit when you smear a friend's sunburned shoulders with Noxzema and feel a sympathy itch. In my case, though, I meant it literally. At age thirteen—a time when many girls become body-conscious—I inexplicably lost my eyesight.

In retrospect, I suppose my friend knew how I felt. After all, I'd made a statement that could probably apply to most American women. With all the fantasy ideals and emerald-cut expectations jockeying for position around us, I can't be the only one who hasn't seen herself clearly since childhood. All of our reflections are clouded by the status quo, tarnished by self-doubt.

I think thirteen is the age when it happens to most of us. Before that, we're girls. We look in the mirror and see girls who are great athletes and poets, girls who can communicate with animals and tell brilliant stories, and girls who carry snappy one-liners in our shirt pockets in the space our breasts will soon occupy. We see girls with talents and goals and excitement—and not much time for looking in mirrors; we've got stuff to do! Then, somewhere around the big one-three, the media is kind enough to clue us in on all our shortcomings and we realize just how fat, gawky, hairy or pimply our miraculous little bodies really are.

It happened shortly before I began high school. I woke one morning from a dream about horses dancing to the song "Love Gun" by Kiss, and I could not see. I called out for my mother, certain she could help. She came right away, and in the familiar herbal smells and unfamiliar shadowy darkness of our home, she found my shoes and led me out to the car.

The lights in the emergency room were bright enough so that I could see a little. I saw a jumble of white—white coats, walls and sheets. I heard a lot of questions and very few answers. And what answers the doctors did give seemed to contradict one another. One blamed my condition on a parasite (yuck); another suggested I'd smoked some laced weed. Still another told me I had a genetic disease—never mind that no one in my family had ever had it. I asked the third doctor what I could do about it, and he told me, "Learn Braille." Like many well-educated men, these guys had a lot to say. But when I returned home that evening, everything still looked blurry and bleak.

My mother spent the rest of the summer ferrying me around from specialist to specialist. In the space of one week, I was examined and treated by a Reiki therapist in Vermont, a Chinese acupuncturist in New York (he jammed needles into the corners of my eyes, then consoled me with little sesame cookies) and a renegade neurologist in Germany. By the first day of high school, my vision had improved slightly (God only knows what did it), so my tenacious, optimistic mother dropped the brochures for blind schools into the garbage. She drove me to Fiorello H. LaGuardia High School of Music and Art and Performing Arts in New York City, where I'd been accepted as a theater student the previous spring.

Don't believe what the TV shows tell you; high school is hard on everyone, not just on the "freaks and geeks." It actually might be a little easier on the weirdos, because we don't have that frightening prospect of a long fall from grace. At an age when the girls' room is full of Olympic hopefuls measuring their waistlines with their fathers' tape measures, debating the relative merits of drawing black lines all the way around their eyes or just darkening the lids, and surreptitiously comparing themselves to each other in the mirror, I was usually grateful just to avoid stumbling into the boys' bathroom again.

Also in blinding contrast (if you'll pardon the expression) to what you see on TV, teenagers can be amazingly kind and generous. With one friend to walk me from class to class and another to help me read my homework, I developed a little confidence and actually did okay in ninth grade. In fact, I did pretty well—academically, at least. Socially, well . . . suffice to say that my accidental visits to the boys' room were the least of my worries.

In high school, when sophistication was the key to the kingdom, I was unsophisticated in that remarkable way that can only come from having no point of reference. Since I couldn't see what the other girls were wearing or how they were doing their hair, I couldn't make my look blend in. I knew that thin was in and stout was out, but I couldn't see the standards well enough to know into which class I fell. One thing I *was* sure of was that other girls were wearing makeup, and—this memory is more painful than the acupuncture needles—I was determined to go from geek to chic with the best of 'em in that area. I bought eyeliner, lipstick and blush, all in day-glo colors that could not have complemented one another less. A word to the wise: If you can hardly see, do yourself a favor. Don't try to choose or apply your own makeup. And don't color your own hair (at least, not without consulting a trusted friend for a quick once-over before you leave the house).

Aside from all the experimenting, I actually didn't give my looks much thought. How could I? I knew appearances were the stylish thing to focus on, but my own appearance had become as foreign to me as Singapore. Realizing that the blotchy skin, the excess weight and the guileless, joyful expression (like a dog in a car) that I'd sported with such assurance in junior high wouldn't fly in my urbane new surroundings, I did the only thing I could. I bought a pair of sunglasses and kept telling myself that if I couldn't see other people, they couldn't see me either. I'd still love to do that sometimes.

But that's high school. I'm sure there were some students with 20/20 vision who looked worse than I did, and that's okay. It's what growing up is all about—or at least that's what our parents tell us. Apparently, overwhelming confusion, abject misery and searing humiliation are as essential to healthy development as are protein and vitamin C. Great.

Without the distractions of male attention (excluding the tasteful flattery I received from the winos down the block from my house), I studied my tiny heart out and escaped from high school in three years. By that time, with a body full of herbal remedies and pinpricks, I could see well enough to walk the streets sans cane, dog or companion (and not get run over, but quite possibly fall into a pothole). I didn't look blind to most people, so they probably thought I was crazy when I asked mannequins for directions or hugged strangers, thinking they were friends.

My mother and some pals helped me pack up the car and drove me half an hour north to the cozy haven of a liberal arts college I'd chosen for its proximity and its intensive writing courses. I loved it right away. It was like something out of a classic novel, and it was different from anything I'd ever known. The grave, cheerful students were mostly wealthy, mostly female and mostly white. Did I mention I'm not? Well, it's about time. I'm the combination of a charismatic black musician/civil rights activist (my dad) and a warm-hearted white professor/civil rights activist (my mom), which never struck me as unusual for a minute—especially when compared with blindness—until college. But, cradled and turned in the sweetly inquisitive, finely manicured hands of my classmates, I became "exotic."

If there's anything that's *not* exotic in this day and age, it's a biracial person. Mixed-race babies make up the largest percentage of births in King County, Washington, and are wearing practically all the little booties and tassled hats in California, too. The 2000 Census even included a box for people of mixed race; that's how many of us there are. However, "exotic" is a matter of context. My enigmatic features might have slid through New York City unnoticed, but on a tiny, wealthy campus surrounded by woods, I was the epitome of difference on many levels—a llama among ponies.

Well, I'm no stranger to yuppie vernacular. Just like *cute* (read: "pretty and short") and *sexy* (read: "pretty and easy") are variations on the word *pretty* (I saw that on *News Radio;* yes, I'm a child of television), *exotic* is a variation on the word *strange.* When it refers to a woman, it means "strange and hot." If a white man calls a woman of color exotic, the pig is objectifying her and should be beaten with a garden rake (I learned *that* in a women's studies class; I'm not all about TV). But when a white woman says something like that to me, it's just a compliment. Or so I was told.

Despite all the "compliments" and the attention I got from my classmates as a whole, I soon found that I was most comfortable with the other accidental nonconformists at school—the mixed-race, disabled or foreign students. Since few of us could slide easily into any of the ready-made categories a college campus offers, we spent time together. It seemed to me at the time that we were the only ones still struggling to understand the world and how we fit into it. Of course, that wasn't true at all. But even now, three years out of college, fully half of my friends are immigrants, disabled or of mixed race. We understand each other and don't ask too many questions.

Conversely, guys in bars seem to love to guess where I'm from. There's at least one in every tavern who has to know. Whatever they guess, I tell them they're right: "Are you Korean?" "Yes." "Are you Peruvian?" "Yes." If you could see me, you'd understand why I have no time for anyone who's ignorant enough to think I'm Korean or Peruvian. But the questions do give me some idea of how I look to others. We could probably all use that kind of mirror.

Now, almost exactly ten years after that first sightless morning, I still don't quite know what I look like. My vision is a little clearer, but I'm still legally blind, and glasses don't help worth a damn. I can see others reasonably well if I get close enough to kiss or spit on them, but the shiny surfaces of photographs and mirrors make it hard for me to see much detail in myself. There are probably few of us who can recognize our best features, the details that make us beautiful, like our mother's eyebrows and our grandmother's fingers.

I'm lucky to be disabled and biracial in a time when people are beginning to understand both of those qualities. I have a fun job as an editor and enough adaptive computer equipment to do it. I have a boyfriend who reads to me. I have friends who tell me I'm beautiful, a gift that eclipses any breast size or nose shape I could want. I also have two thirteen-year-old girl cousins, and they are my heroines. They play basketball and soccer. They do martial arts, play the piano and dismiss boys as "immature." Each of them has a "Girls Rule" T-shirt, and I think they believe it. But any time they look uncertain or afraid, I wonder if Corporate America's lacquered claws have already begun to rend their tender flesh. Every day, I think, "Let them be blind to all the unfair expectations. Let them be free."

Maybe it's better not to see too much, or to believe as I do that it's the mirrors and the atmosphere—not one's own body—that are flawed. I'm not sure about much, but I'm sure that if I were supposed to look different, I would've been made differently. I know I'm thinner than I was as a teen and that my "black-girl butt" is here to stay. I'm told that my skin is much clearer. I can say with some certainty that the mass of black hair that plagued me as a kid has been tamed, or at least sedated. And I'm delighted to hear that I've become a "more glamorous" (read: darker) version of my fierce, vibrant mom. But the last clear self-portrait in my mind remains that of a plump, ebullient thirteen-year-old with pimples and too many curls. And I'm glad about that. I never want to forget her. She had so much spirit.

sizing up
myself

sizing myself up:
tales of a plus-size model
kate dillon

I didn't know I was fat and ugly until I was twelve years old.

The awakening came on my first day of junior high. After carefully applying frosted pink lipstick and electric blue mascara, I boarded the school bus feeling like pretty hot stuff. My peers made it clear that I was mistaken. They jumped up and down on the bus chanting, "Overweight Kate, Overweight Kate." I slumped into the front seat and tried desperately not to cry.

Shortly thereafter, a made-for-TV movie aired and accidentally offered me a golden ticket. It was one of those sensationalized, movie-of-the-week deals, and the lead character was in the hospital for bulimia. There she met a beautiful girl who was being treated for anorexia. I decided to emulate her. Completely disregarding the fact that the anorexic girl *died* at the end of the movie, I thought, *I'll stop eating and be anorexic, too. I'll get cute and skinny, and everyone will like me.*

So I did and they did. I was right. In my seventh-grade year I lost thirty pounds and grew four inches. My weight loss was rewarded with friendship and acceptance. Suddenly, I was popular and invited to all these parties—the connection wasn't difficult to make. Skinny equaled friends and popularity; fat equaled teasing and loneliness. I'd be damned if I'd eat a normal meal again.

Later that year my family moved twenty miles away, and I transferred from my old public school to an elite private school. At the new school, my body wasn't an issue, but everyone thought I was weird because I wore thrift shop clothes instead of the designer outfits they sported like uniforms. I couldn't win.

I think most people assume that anorexics want to be beautiful or to look like models. If I dig below the surface, I realize I didn't care about any of that. I just didn't want to be ridiculed. I didn't want to take up space. I wanted to shrink away from the cute, petite girls I would never be. I wanted to hide from the objectifying, dissecting eyes of all the boys who would never ask me out.

When I was sixteen, life became even stranger: A photographer approached me to model. Although I had created myself in the image of a model to avoid criticism, I had no interest in the profession or the women themselves. I wanted to be a writer. I loved to read; I used to hang out at a cafe in San Diego and talk about books and poetry. I fancied myself quite the intellectual.

But the photographer was persistent, and the next thing I knew, I was signed with a modeling agency in Los Angeles. In 1991, they entered me into their annual "Look of the Year" contest and I placed third, winning a $75,000 contract. It was intensely surreal to walk down a New York City runway that night while hundreds of people watched—among them Donald Trump, Kareem Abdul-Jabbar and David Copperfield. At home, my classmates called me "bag lady" because I wore thrift store clothes. Yet, there I was wearing Alaia

kate dillon   233

couture and making seventy-five thousand bucks for it. Inside, I was laughing hysterically.

I continued modeling while I finished high school, not really sure when I'd work off the contract. I had every intention of going to college, especially since I was accepted to Berkeley, my first choice. But fate intervened: Berkeley accepted me for the following spring, so I had a six-month window after graduation and was free to do as I wished.

Two weeks after graduation, I hopped a plane to New York, planning to stay only those six months. Three months later, I was on my way to Paris, where my career took off. I worked seven days a week, twelve to eighteen hours a day with high-profile fashion photographers. I traveled throughout Europe and to Africa. Needless to say, I never made it to Berkeley.

I realize this lifestyle might sound idyllic, and for obvious reasons, it was. But there was one catch: the modeling industry's weight requirement. The tall part I could handle; I'm five-foot-eleven. But I was expected to be really skinny, and my weight was a constant problem. (By the way, here's an idea of what a "weight problem" is in the fashion industry: At five-eleven and 125 pounds, I was ordered to lose ten or twenty pounds.)

My size was my livelihood and my size was my self-hatred. I'd go to the gym at one o'clock in the morning to try to sweat out as much water weight as I could. On my days off, I'd try to sleep all day so I wouldn't eat.

Eventually, all I thought about was how I looked. If I went to a party and nobody told me I was beautiful, I assumed it meant I was ugly. I was paranoid about my body, and constantly checked myself out in shop windows and mirrors to make sure my stomach was flat. I was obsessed. At night I lay awake worrying that my clothes wouldn't fit the next day.

On one really high-profile shoot with Ellen von Unwerth for Italian *Vogue,* I was dressed head to toe in Versace. Ellen asked me to pose straddling a chair backward. As I lowered my backside into the chair, the skintight Versace pants didn't, um, "stretch and conform." I split the ass out of 'em. There is really no delicate way of saying it. I was mortified.

After one show season—during which I'd been living on coffee and cigarettes—my health failed. I went to see a nutritionist, who helped me to start eating properly. Because I'd starved myself for so long, I gained weight quickly and easily. Clients started complaining about my size, and I began having anxiety attacks and bingeing uncontrollably. The harder I tried to lose weight, the more I wanted to eat. I'd hit a brick wall with dieting. I just couldn't do it anymore.

After seven years of dieting, and a year and a half of professional modeling, something in me snapped. My business manager was giving me hell about my weight, telling me I "wasn't trying hard enough." Suddenly, I realized I'd become victim to society's body ideals. I hated that. I wanted to be the righteous woman I'd always dreamed of being, not the socially programmed putz I'd become. I wanted to live on my own terms. I wanted to set things right with myself and with my body. More importantly, I wanted to stop contributing to the illusions (and delusions) that were at the root of my own self-destruction.

I had a revelation while I was working with Peter Lindhberg for *Harper's Bazaar,* a very exclusive booking. We were all working so hard to create an illusion that *none of us could even live up to*—not the photographer, not the fashion editor, not the models. I realized we were creating an ideal that simply doesn't exist, and I was hurting myself for fiction. I quit and moved back to San Diego to figure out who I really was—behind the image.

I spent two years getting reacquainted with myself. And what I discovered was freedom. Freedom to be whatever it was I needed to be at any given moment. The freedom to be silly, to be stupid, to be brainy, to be ugly, to be beautiful, to be anything at all. And I made some ambitious vows to myself: I would no longer bow to the self-consciousness of external validation, and I would accept myself unconditionally. I would no longer try to fit my body into a cultural ideal. In other words, I lightened the hell up and decided to enjoy life.

So . . . "how did I do it?" How did I go from being the kind of girl who would have looked at my current appearance and thought, *Oh, I'd never want to look like her. It's so unfeminine to be that big, it's so ugly. How could she enjoy her life?* It didn't happen overnight. Believe me, it was hard gaining forty-five pounds when I'd spent the previous seven years associating each pound with shame and ugliness.

Sure, I'd had a great revelation that I wanted to be true to myself, but I didn't have the slightest clue how to get there. My life had so totally flip-flopped. I'd been a highly successful model hanging out in New York City with all the "cool" people. Now I was "fat," delivering pastries and selling books at Barnes and Noble in San Diego. It didn't make any sense! I was so afraid of everything then: of what others thought of me, of what would happen to me. I was afraid I'd never be successful again, and my life would never again be exciting or extraordinary—*that* was a big one. And I hated that I was so scared, because all the people I'd ever admired, like Maya Angelou and Malcolm X, were fearless and bold.

Throughout high school I'd imbibed poetry, literature and movies about freedom. Seizing the day. Making life amazing right now. Being righteous. Being different. I listened to punk rock, got tattoos, dressed in thrift store clothes. I wanted so badly to be an individual. I *believed* in individuality—in theory. I thought I was above all the superficial crap, but I couldn't even embrace the most basic part of myself that is so different from everyone else: the way I looked.

One thing that helped change my perspective was meeting my friend Missy. Missy didn't represent the culture's idea of beauty, but she possessed a more awe-inspiring appeal. Missy had something— the *thing*—I was searching for. She had confidence. She didn't edit her opinions to appease others. She knew she was "different," and rather than try to fight it, she laughed at it. Embraced it. Spoke her mind. If we were at a club and there was a cute guy, I'd try to act cool and coy. Missy would just bust out and tell him he was the cutest boy she'd ever seen.

And it was amazing to watch the responses. Missy came to visit me in New York once, and I took her to see a local band I liked. The room was full of supermodels, and while the band played, everyone stood around, checking each other out. Not Missy. She was jumping around the dance floor doing funny moves. And who did the lead singer hit on? Not the bevy of supermodels on hand, but Missy— because she's got life. It was her attitude that inspired me to forget everything I'd learned about the way you're "supposed" to act or look. The people who were free from all that bullshit were having a much better time.

After living with my parents for two years in San Diego, doing some incredible soul-searching, I knew the time had come to move on. I needed to go find my place in the world with my newfound sensibilities. In 1996, I moved back to New York, intending to go to college and study elementary art education.

A friend of mine suggested I try plus-size modeling. I'd worked with Christine Alt, a plus-size model, once before. I remembered being awed by her courage, thinking, "I could never be that cool. I could never dare to be that different."

When I entered the plus-size modeling world, it was quite a different entity than it is today. Everyone in the industry—photographers, advertisers, designers—was so scared of taking a risk, or making the shoots too racy. I'll just say that. For the most part, they just didn't get it. I'm asked sometimes if I ever felt embarrassed, because I'd work with people who "knew me then" (when I was skinny). It never occurred to me to be ashamed. I'd spent the past two years discovering joy and learning to be comfortable with who I was and how I looked. I knew I was right. I knew in my bones that anyone who couldn't see or understand that beauty was not bound by size, color or anything else was wrong. I just knew it.

I was *inspired*. I wanted to change the modeling industry. And with a lot of help, that change is happening. Much of the credit goes to plus-size retailers like Lane Bryant, Liz Claiborne and The Avenue—and to *Mode* magazine. The visionaries at the helms of these companies have transformed America's image of a full-figured woman.

Ironically, I've had a better career as a big-gal model than most skinny models have in their lifetimes! I've been featured in Gucci's Spring 2000 ads, and I have a beauty contract with Isabella Rossellini's makeup line, Manifesto. My picture has appeared on a billboard in Times Square and I was declared one of the "fifty most beautiful people in the world" by *People* magazine. And the best part is, I did it on my own terms.

I love to witness the moment when someone's perspective shifts before my eyes. It's the moment I go from being "pretty for a bigger girl" to just being pretty. I ask myself often what my life would have been like had I just told those kids on the bus to go to hell. Or if I'd merely smiled at them, thanked them for their opinions, and asked them out for pizza. I mean, what if I'd had that kind of strength?

Would I have gone through the same struggles?

A friend recently reminded me that it's not really about strength, though. Anorexia, as with all eating disorders, is a disease—and a complicated beast. Many factors could have contributed: my personality, being sexually harassed by my P.E. teacher when I was eight, my family's move to weight-obsessed southern California when I was ten. The kids on the bus could have simply been the final straw. What I do know, however, is that I wasted seven years of my life depriving my body of basic nutrients. I risked death, long-term health problems and emotional instability—and I've only recently begun to understand the psychological implications of this experience.

My life is pretty incredible these days, but it would be a lie to suggest that those seven years of self-deprivation and alienation from myself didn't profoundly influence my perception of the world today.

Far too many women and men share the roots of my story. And we spend far too much time and energy contemplating our inadequacies. We forget that we are all perfect in our imperfection.

not of reality

sada mecca

Who are we?
Who do we think we are?
Who are we to say?
Let us close our mouths
Our thoughts are never final anyway.

Cleanse our minds
Poisoned by what we declare
As facts
Only holds our children back.

I am me
Skinny, creamy, funny
A shortie, a cutie that shines
           Because my thinking is pure
No, I won't judge you
I've broken down the wall they've built
Based on what they see
A weak foundation
           Not of reality

size queen:

a gay guy on girth
john chaich

A moment at this year's New York City gay and lesbian pride parade revealed my own pride—and shame—as a short, stocky gay man. Among the rainbow flags, the pink triangles and the occasional pampered pooch walked a living, breathing cornucopia of gay male body types. Go-go boys let us see their thong th-thong-thong-thongs. Leather daddies let it all hang out—literally—in their chaps. The gay swim league and wrestling team slipped and slid in Speedos and singlets. If a float featured flesh, the crowd cheered.

And then came the bears—the self-styled posse of hefty, hairy homos who looked more like lumberjacks than limber jocks. With their grizzly goatees, glistening chest hair and jutting guts, they were here, they were queer, and the audience was not sure what to do. The otherwise enthusiastic onlookers seemed to cheer less and ponder more as these hirsute hulks marched on. By the time the next float full of short-short-wearing, waxed-chest-baring men approached, you could almost hear the collective sigh of relief from the crowd. Or maybe we were all just exhaling the stomachs we'd sucked in when the bears bounced by.

At that moment, I don't know what I felt more ashamed of: how the years of media criticism and body empowerment that I'd preached alongside feminist friends could leave me as easily as a Fleet enema, or how the years of half-and-half in my coffee have settled so obviously in my lower half. And with whose gaze was I most concerned: the buff boys', the beefy bears' or my own?

From the streets to the sheets, gay men faithfully fight and foster the battle of the bulge—both below and around the waist. At thirty, I'd like to think my skin is as thick as my thirty-six-inch waist and I'm comfortable in my own body. Yet, I am most out of sync with myself when I'm feeling sized up by the brave and the shirtless at events like this.

Research shows that on average men are more visually oriented than women. We are more turned on by pictures than stories, prefer saucy shots to love letters. Gay men can look into each other's thighs as easily as we look into one another's eyes—we've crafted the gay male gaze known as "cruising." Gay men spend a lot of time looking at other men in hopes of getting looked at ourselves. Therefore, we spend a lot of time grooming in hopes of some groping. Gay male culture is a highly visual, highly sensory culture, and I'm fascinated by how the gay male body is a site for commodity and identity, flesh and fetish, inclusion and exclusion.

On more than one occasion, I've entered a homo's house to find the same magnet set on the kitchen fridge: Michelangelo's *David*, complete with a variety of outfits to make him a butch Barbie. I don't have this magnet. Instead, I relate more to one that hung at my parents' house for years: a plastic pig that wore an apron reading, "Taste makes waist." Together, these magnets easily symbolize the

john chaich   243

extremes of gay male body culture: the buff and the bear, the fit and the fat, the young and the waistless. Gay men are size queens of our own accord.

As long as it's not on us, gay men seem to have no problem with body fat. From Aretha Franklin to Martha Wash, we like our divas large and in charge. The famed fag hag is often an overweight, overzealous gal pal. Big girls do cry—on our shoulders and at our sides. But do gay men accept weight on women because it makes us look better? Conversely, gay men have also shaped the fashion industry's size standards that have segmented and degraded women for decades. Unlike many of our lesbian counterparts, who seem to wear their weight as easily as their Birkenstocks, are gay men projecting the complexity of our own body image issues onto the women around us?

Gay-created media perpetuates our own physical standards. As in most media outlets, the predominant face is still Caucasian, and the typical body is still as idealized as a Michelangelo statue. Just as a straight woman may pick up an issue of *Vogue, Cosmo* or even *Jane* and feel intimidated by the models and messages that thin is still in, I can pick up a copy of *Out, Genre* or even the *Advocate* and be bombarded with ads for hair removal, plastic surgery, muscle enhancers and the like. To be the "It" gay man that these images idealize, you must have little to no body fat or body hair. When Jack calls Will a "fatty" on *Will & Grace*, I find it an absurd observation yet an accurate representation of how body image influences gay men.

Our body obsession has even spread to our dogs: Recently, a naturally thin and tall friend of mine was walking his terrier around a gay neighborhood in Manhattan and encountered a buff boy walking his. A few minutes into the dog talk, Gary realized that both he and his dog were being sized up when the guy announced to his pup, "See, you don't want to get all old and fat like this doggie, now do you?" Aging—and the accompanying wrinkles around the eyes, hair around the ears and extra weight around the waist—does not settle well with most gay men. From International Male to Abercrombie & Fitch, the gay gaze focuses on eternal youth. To be over thirty, in age or in waist, makes you a not-so-delicious delicacy on the gay food chain.

My youth was a battle of the thick and the thin. In junior high, I was a chubby sissy who wore corduroys from the "husky" section while others wore parachute pants. (During a health class back then, when students were asked to write a compliment for everyone on a sheet of paper, I received the accolade: "You waddle nicely.") As puberty kicked in, my budding homosexuality was peppered with a confused masculinity: I was an overweight introvert who didn't date girls or play sports like the other guys. My sexuality and my perceived lack of masculinity were intertwined with how I saw my physicality.

When I came out in the early 1990s, I inherited generations of body boundaries defined by and imposed upon gay men. In the '70s, rejecting the stereotype of their fey forefathers, gays from West Hollywood to the West Village began to look less like fruit and more like meat. As caricatured as they were, the Village People represented the "macho men" that gays strove to be when they worked out—and then some—at the YMCA. By the 1980s, as AIDS devastated the gay community, once-buff bodies grew emaciated. If AIDS equaled gay, then thin meant sick. Gay men returned to the gym with a renewed fervor, as if lifting weights would lift the burden of fear and loss off their shoulders and their hearts.

Equal parts narcissism and escapism, the buff hardbody became known as the Chelsea Boy, named for the New York City neighborhood that was home to thousands of gay men and dozens of gyms. In the early '90s, Chelsea's famous David Barton Gym summarized the buff-boy phenomenon with an ad campaign that read "No pecs, no sex."

"The athleticism missed in high school," John DiCarlo writes in the *Gay & Lesbian Review*, "is made up for after one comes out. The body of steel, the machine, the citadel, all these hyper-masculine attributes of the muscle body are a part of why many gay men find it an attractive ideal."* Yet to date, I am a full-fledged gym-o-phobe. A few years back, I was so intimidated by the idea of other guys watching me struggle to lift thirty-pound weights that I refused to use a free gym membership and personal trainer session. Instead, my workouts have stayed in the safe confines of women-populated spaces. For two years, I was the only man in an Ohio jazzercize class. Just as I feel more at ease among my female friends and body-positive magazines like *Bust*, I feel more at home among the forty-something, T-shirt-and-leggings-wearing jazzercizers. Over the years, I've even acquired a collection of aerobics videos led by B-level divas like Zsa Zsa Gabor, whose "workout" involved two buff assistants and a chair. (I'm not sure which accessory makes her or me sweat more.)

Richard Simmons is the one exception to my boys-on-the-side workout rule. I own every *Sweatin' to the Oldies* video and have seen Richard Simmons twice in person. He is high-camp yet low-fat, and best of all, for someone who exercises that much, he still has some meat on him. But no matter how short his shorts or how oiled his generous thighs, Richard Simmons is not a sex symbol. He's not even out of the closet. With his shameless weeping and over-the-top antics, Simmons may be as kinky as his hair, but he is not the body beautiful that homos hold high; he's more like a modern-day eunuch.

I may aerobicize, but I am not asexual. Even without the prerequisite pectoral muscles, I've still managed to have my share of sex. And in fact, I would consider myself an expert at equal opportunity sexploitation. I've had sex with men of many colors, shapes and sizes—and in doing so, I've learned to accept my body more. My first boyfriend was a big boy. Around 6'1" and 260 pounds, his physical presence was the security blanket I needed as I nurtured my first love.

My next relationship was with a tall, slender lad of six feet and 180 pounds. At times I felt that he was my trophy boyfriend, but more often I just felt fat next to him. My current beau is my size precisely. Overweight as teenagers, we both joke that we are "FF's"—formerly fats—who have had to work out both our emotional and physical selves to feel comfortable in our own skin.

In between these boyfriends, I've explored how sharing my body with men of different body types has shaped my self-esteem. Not really into bars or clubs, I have met men online. An industrious lot, gay men have formed countless chat rooms and social clubs for like-minded lusts. Peruse the AOL chat rooms, and you will find a selection of men looking for other men, with requirements as specific as they are diverse. There are rooms for muscle men looking for muscle men. Bears looking for bears. Black guys looking for white guys. Husky men for stocky men. A guy can call himself a "chub" online and find "chasers": thin guys who like thick guys. Not suprisingly, in the generic "men looking for men" chat rooms, I've found the body image ideal runs rampant: "Fit only!" "No fats or femmes." I learned this the hard way after a user demanded, "If you're 5'7" and 190, how can you be proportionate?" On the other hand, in a bear or husky chat room, these same stats that brought me scorn become another guy's porn. Online, I've called myself a "cub"—a younger, moderately hairy variation on the bear. I knew it would get me attention if not action. Ultimately, it was a self-esteem booster. We all want to feel wanted.

From the dance club to the health club, from the bathroom to the chat room, gay men are masters of marketing. We can articulate the who, what, when, where and why of the sex we want—in person, on the page and online. Full-figured fags can meet at a Girth and Mirth event. If a buff or waxed chest is the passport to a circuit party, a hairy one is the ticket to a Bearapalooza night. The extent to which gay men

john chaich   **247**

create cultures based on body types will never cease to amaze me. I avoid buff guys but I am not driven to become a bear: I feel most uncomfortable with homogeneity—period. At the same time, I have benefited from marketing myself according to my body type.

But my body and my identity are not commodities. And both buff and bear cultures are complexities that at once celebrate and critique body types. At the end of the day and after another lay, we are gay men because we want to have sex with a man's body. It's clear that how we shape our bodies affects how we share our bodies. Some thirty years after Stonewall, being a "fat fag" makes a queen-sized political statement—perhaps even more than Log Cabin Republicans or Queers for Christ. Ultimately, I've learned to like what my mama gave me—a thick ass and legs, a great smile and hair in all the right places—because I looked for the guys who liked these features. In order to connect with other bodies, I've had to find what makes me feel the most comfortable with my own. I have a choice to lose weight, lift weights, wax my hair or go bear. Through thick and through thin, it's up to me to work on—if not work out—how I handle my love handles.

In fact, I have a vision of designing a T-shirt that says just that: a ring of text across my waist asking gay men at large, "Can you handle my love handles?" I'll take back the fat and wear it at circuit parties, tea dances and pride parades alike to show off among the shirtless. In fact, maybe I'll make it a baby T so my own stomach sticks out. I may get jeers from the queers, but I may also get some bear hugs. And perhaps I'll learn to accept them both.

But it takes more than wearing our pride on our sleeves. Gay men are as notoriously creative as we are bitchy. Perhaps if we transferred some of the energy we spend critiquing each other in person to critiquing the images we create in print, we can create inclusive media representation. I don't know if there will ever be a *Mode* magazine for gay men of girth, but there can be more images of men of all shapes, sizes and colors in gay media. Seeing these, new generations of gay men can come out feeling more confident that every body can be a place to parade our pride.

*John DiCarlo, "The Gym Body and Heroic Myths," *Gay & Lesbian Review* (July-August 2001).

to live and diet in l.a.:
a vegan tour of lipo-land
elisa albert

I grew up in Los Angeles, or La-La Land, as it's aptly called. I came of age with scions of movie stars, entertainment lawyers and their trophy wives, future movie stars and future trophy wives. It was not pretty. Within this milieu there were two commandments: (1) *Thou shalt not eat food according to the dictates and desires of the human body*, and (2) *Thou shalt not try to initiate an intellectual discussion about the politics or implications of commandment number one*.

My oh-so-exclusive high school lacked fat people. Even not-quite-camera-ready, slightly-zaftig-but-not-heinous people were scarce. It was hard to find a zit within a five-mile radius. Poor fashion choices were rare. Plastic surgery was a not-uncommon answer to "What did you do this summer?" At least two of my best friends were hardcore anorexics. I can't account for the ostensibly countless others who were just anorexia dabblers or social bulimics, but these two friends seemed a pretty representative population sample. Food obsession was simply a way of life. You did not eat. If you ate, you ate very little. If you ate a normal meal, you exercised compulsively or induced vomiting. There was always this palpable tension in the air; you could feel it emanating outward from the cafeteria like cartoon radio waves. Lunchtime was fraught with complex negotiations— most people understood implicitly that it was not entirely acceptable to be seen eating nothing whatsoever, so there were tiny concessions to the convention of digestion. A small cup of soup and a Diet Coke, a bowl of steamed veggies picked at listlessly until it was time for class, an apple. Each handled reverently and delicately, like archaeological artifacts from a lost society.

Ah, to live and diet in L.A. My first thought, once I understood the rules, was this: *If only I had the willpower to be anorexic.* My short-lived career as a bulimic lasted only long enough for me to heave unsuccessfully several times into the toilet bowl and then rest my cheek on its cool rim, exhausted and a failure. My mother cheerfully introduced me to the Scarsdale diet in the eighth grade. "We'll do it together!" she said. "It'll be fun!" Female extended family members all had lengthy and cumbersome lists of off-limits foods, and watching them order off a menu or artfully avoid filling their plates at dinner parties sent the message loud and clear: *Food is a scary, dangerous and harmful thing. Partake at your own peril.*

Meanwhile, I was watching my friends waste away. I was watching them construct elaborate lies about having already eaten. I was watching them spend their early mornings and late afternoons in desperate, endless treadmill hikes. And it *pissed me off.*

So I revolted. Or, rather, I took the path of least resistance, which for me meant eating—and digesting—what I pleased and refusing to exercise. Which, of course, did not lead to the ideal Southern California body. I look back now and pat myself on the back for what amounted to years of extended performance art, my body my tool for sociopolitical commentary, my every stomach roll a calculated *fuck you* to the beauty mafia and the culture that nursed it. I cultivated a righteous (if somewhat smug) anger and unleashed it upon anyone unwise enough to discuss the StairMaster or order salad dressing "on the side" within earshot of me.

My rage at these phenomena was deeply connected to my burgeoning feminist consciousness, and I nurtured it protectively. I screamed along with my Ani DiFranco albums: *I am not a pretty girl / that is not what I do.* My favorite T-shirt read "Fuck Your Fascist Beauty Standards," at which most of my clueless classmates knit their well-shaped brows in utter confusion. To beat everyone else to the punch (assuming they were sharp or interested enough to bother), I chose "Phat Albert" as the moniker for my school newspaper column. I knew better than to be ashamed of my body because of its closer proportional proximity to the Venus of Willendorf fertility goddess than to that dumb bitch Barbie.

Basically, I constructed an identity around who I *wasn't*: thin, pretty or working hard at becoming either. I made some sort of peace with myself; I read *Mode* magazine, bought the first edition of this book for everyone I knew, fantasized about becoming a plus-size model (which, I realize, was problematic in its own right—different body types, same emphasis on beauty as power). Eating whatever I wanted, whenever I wanted, was tantamount to guerrilla activism within the confines of Los Angeles. I understood this from the wide-eyed stares of disbelief (and even disgust) I received while freely partaking of party snack foods, unscooped-out bagels, pizza without the oil mopped off the top.

My contempt for anyone who was not overtly flouting the body ideal and its attendant food neuroses was all-consuming. I believed that you could not be a fully realized feminist or human being and concurrently be a slave to carb boycotts or the gym. I understand now that my friends were actually *ill*, that the compulsion to starve yourself half to death is a psychological *disease*, but my reaction to it then was anger. I could not, ahem, stomach the focus and energy so many people around me poured into their diets, and I hated the implicit suggestion that I do the same. I wanted to *enjoy* food, to savor the sensuous pleasure of it. I wanted mealtimes to be relaxed and happy social outlets. Anything less seemed a literal and figurative denial of life.

A few years down the road, once I'd staged a definitive exit from the ranks of Rhinoplasty High, something strange happened. I had never liked meat very much—it seemed intuitively disgusting to eat animal carcasses—and as I began to read about factory farming and bovine flatulence and everything else that goes with mass production and consumption of meat, I morphed into a vegetarian. From there, it was a pretty short leap to veganism, which was for me the only sensible ideological continuation of a committed vegetarian life. In addition to meat, fish and poultry, as a vegan I don't eat any eggs or dairy. It's quite simple, really; the dairy industry fosters almost identical mistreatment of animals and waste of resources as do the meat and poultry industries. There is also often rennet (the lining of a cow's stomach) in cheese. Many vegans also shun honey (bees kept captive) and refined sugar (for which ground animal bones are used in processing). We each draw the line where we see fit.

I am proud of the politics and conscience behind my eating choices, but suddenly I became *that girl*, scanning menus anxiously, looking for something that fits my diet, needing to exert a relatively high level of control over what I eat, where I eat, how I eat. Suddenly, out for dinner with friends or family at an invariably meat-heavy establishment, I found myself picking delicately at the mixed greens salad or the plate of grilled vegetables. Suddenly there could be no casual enjoyment of the dip and chips at the party because the dip might contain eggs or cheese or milk. And there could be no *conver-*

sation about what may or may not be in the dip because that's such a horrible thing to talk about while standing around the freaking dip and chips.

As my eating evolved, I also started practicing yoga, which, in concert with veganism, really changed my body inside and out. Yoga for me was an emotional release, a form of deep thinking, a much cheaper alternative to therapy. I practice because it makes me feel calm, expansive and potent. Weight practically fell off me, which led to a bizarre disconnect between my outward appearance and my emotional politics.

On the surface, I now appear to be right in line with the multitudes of iceberg-lettuce-picking, dessert-denying masses. It's a scary feeling, especially when people seem *impressed* by my willpower or *congratulate* me on having lost weight. The latter is particularly difficult to deal with. For the first time, I'm experiencing public appreciation for and approval of my body.

"You look *fabulous*," some well-intentioned friend or family member will intone, looking me up and down like a beer-chugging frat boy at last call. To this I'm supposed to say, "Why *thank you!*" and be pleased that my body has passed muster.

"How did you *do* it?" the conversation might continue, to which I'm supposed to respond by detailing my idiosyncratic regimen of denial and exercise. Men and women I've known most of my life suddenly feel free to comment on my body, touch me and give me burlesque victory signs meant to unite us in solidarity against the evils of fat. It's a perverse thing, to be applauded for something inadvertent. What did all these people think of me when I was carrying forty extra pounds on my 5'11" frame? Were they, unbeknownst to me, horrified, embarrassed for me, dismissive of my sexual and aesthetic legitimacy in the world? Am I more real for them this way? Do I count now?

Rather than play along with this little game and pretend that, yeah, I happen to have lost some weight and isn't it just the best thing that could ever have happened, I prefer to offer my interlocutor a crash course in veganism. This does the handy job of taking the focus off my body and whatever I've been through to fit into size-twenty-nine jeans, and instead onto the politics of the consumption of animal products. But, funny enough, people don't want to hear about stun guns and rennet, debeaking or hormone injections. Conversations about the Zone, Atkins, stomach stapling or lipo? Bring 'em on. But the minute food becomes something connected to morals, not just aesthetics and/or fat, I may as well be lecturing on the intricacies of West African politics. Yawn.

I wonder, every time I see a picture in *Us Weekly* of a yoga-mat-wielding celebrity vegan, what is it about our culture that demands every lifestyle choice be a grab at the brass ring of aesthetic perfection? Is it possible that yoga and veganism just make Gwyneth Paltrow, Alicia Silverstone and Madonna feel really, really good about themselves? Killer pecs are a byproduct, sure, but can't there be more to it? Or, on the flip side, what strange bedfellows we all are—we of the extensive devotion to yoga and prohibitive diets aimed at living forever, toning our abs, animal rights, looking good at the Oscars, whatever.

At the present writing, I am planning my wedding. The lucky guy is, of course, a vegan. (If "Is he Jewish?" was always my mom's first question, "Is he a vegetarian?" was definitely mine. Since he's a Jewish vegetarian—and tall!—everyone's psyched.) We approached our parents with one large nonnegotiable request: Our wedding feast had to be vegan. This shocked quite a few people. A wedding without meat, they said, could not really be a true celebration. Interesting. Apparently, our community felt emotionally connected to meat as a signifier of joy, celebration and life, and could not fathom an evening denied of it. As a result, we've spent an inordinate amount of the prenuptial period fielding inane questions about our diet. If one more person demands to know how vegans get protein, I hope I have the nerve to smile sweetly and reply, "Cum."

I worry that our wedding day will be overshadowed by angry cries of "*Vat,* no brisket?" from the relatives and friends who gather to celebrate with us, and that we will be forever branded That Strange Couple Who Won't Eat Anything. If no one stops to think about *why* that strange couple won't eat anything, they might easily assume that it is because this is L fucking A and *no one* here eats anything.

Recently, I was complaining to my brother about a family member, a grown woman of maybe ninety pounds, whose anxiety over what goes into her mouth assures any dining companions the unhappiest, tensest meal of their lives.

"She's such a fucking freak," I griped. "I hate eating with her."

"Of all people," my brother snorted, "*you* shouldn't be talking about strange eating habits." In all likelihood, my brother was just being his lovable, contrarian self, but his words haunted me. My worst nightmare is for people to equate my politically, ethically motivated decision not to eat animals or animal-derived products with the extreme neuroses of a constant dieter. And yet, from the outside, I know that any dietary restriction can seem weird, over-the-top or downright neurotic.

The only time food is not an issue for me is when I'm with fellow vegans. Otherwise, my behavior calls uncomfortably to mind that of those long-lost eating-disordered high-school pals. Want some pizza? No. Want some M&M's? No thanks. How 'bout some ice cream? Uh-uh. Nachos? Nope. And now I'm the one sitting out the snacks and meals, watching others enjoy food and live life, holding fast to my convictions even as I wistfully eye the nacho cheese.

The echoes of the socially endorsed eating disorders of my youth in the paradigm of my restricted diet utterly terrify me. So much so, in fact, that I sometimes find myself fudging the boundaries of veganism here and there, ordering the banana cream pie in front of an audience because I *can,* goddamn it, because I am *not* "that girl," all appearances to the contrary.

Mercifully, I've long since lost track of most of the people with whom I endured high school. But they're with me still somehow, whispering encouragement as I order dry toast at the Rose Cafe, winking lasciviously at Fred Segal as I try on a size medium or even, dare to dream, a small. They don't care how or why I'm leaner than ever, but they hiss warnings eternally in my ears, imploring me to stay that way always.

veiled intentions:
don't judge a muslim girl by her covering
maysan haydar

O Prophet! Tell thy wives and daughters and the
believing women that they should cast their outer
garments over their persons. That is most convenient
that they should be known and not be molested.

—The Quran, Chapter 33, Verse 59

And say to the believing women that they should
lower their gaze and guard their modesty: that
they should not display their beauty and ornaments
except what ordinarily appears thereof; that they
should draw their veils over their bosoms and not
display their beauty . . .

—The Quran, Chapter 24, Verse 30–31

I have a confession to make.

258

I've been covering my hair, as is prescribed for Muslim women, since I was twelve years old. And while there are many good reasons for doing so, I wasn't motivated by a desire to be different, to honor tradition or to make a political statement.

I wanted the board game Girl Talk.

When girls from our small, Midwestern Muslim community donned their first *hijab* (headscarf), their families rewarded them with parties and monetary gifts. At twelve, I wasn't nearly as physically developed as a Muslim girl is supposed to be when she starts covering, but I desperately wanted Girl Talk. I knew that if I announced my intention to begin veiling in the board game aisle at Kmart, I could ask for anything and receive it.

My choice of Girl Talk as reward for taking on a religious responsibility is amusing to me now, because it's so antithetical to what veiling is supposed to represent. Girl Talk was the ultimate slumber party game, where players performed gags or revealed embarrassing secrets, then got to choose from four kinds of fortune cards as a prize. My favorite cards hooked me up with the class president, the football captain or a hunky lifeguard who saved me from drowning. And I still have a sheet of "zit stickers," which were meant to punish gamers who failed to share their dirt.

Now that I'm twenty-five and have worn a veil for more than half my life, I can admit to this shallow beginning, which is so far from my reason for veiling today. As an adult, I embrace the veil's modesty, which allows me to be seen as a whole person instead of a twenty-piece chicken dinner. In spite of the seeming contradictions of my life—I'm married to a white man who was raised Catholic, I love heavy metal, I consider myself a feminist, and I sport a few well-disguised piercings—I follow my religion's standard of modesty and appearance. It's only now, after comparing my turbulent teen experiences with those of other women, that I can fully appreciate how much of a saving grace this small piece of cloth was.

Much to my chagrin, many Americans see veiling as an oppressive tool forced on Muslim women by the men in our culture. Yet, the practice of covering hair and body is a choice for many women—and it is not specific to Islam. All the monotheistic religions (Christianity, Judaism and Islam) advocate modesty in dress, though the interpretation of "modesty" varies greatly. Ironically, the population that spends millions on beauty products, plastic surgery and self-help guides is the same one that takes pity on me for being so "helpless" and "oppressed." On a New York City bus a couple weeks ago, I sat with another woman, also veiled, but wearing a traditional *jilbab* (a cloak that women wear over their clothing). A girl two seats over remarked to her friend, while flipping her hair for effect, that she couldn't understand how we could dress this way. "Me, I got to be *free*."

To my eyes, her idea of freedom involved a complicated hairstyle, loads of makeup and jeans she probably had to sew herself into. If anything, I would find that ensemble more caging, more oppressive and more painful than clothes that allow me to walk in front of construction sites confidently, with minimal risk of harassment. (Construction workers may feel obligated to say something to every passing woman, but I often get things like "I like your skirt!" or "Girl, I would marry you!"—harmless compared to the degradation I've heard many women complain about.)

As for freedom, my parents have a healthy understanding of Islam, especially the Quranic verse "Let there be no compulsion in religion" (2:256). Having been raised in religiously different homes themselves (Mom: very liberal, European-minded, not so religious; Dad: religious, culturally structured gender roles and expectations), they only practiced traditions that they understood, accepted and believed. Thus, my mother knew the best way to introduce veiling to me was to emphasize its feminist, forward-thinking reasons: Covering removes that first level of being judged, of being assessed based on my measurements, and it absolves me of the need or desire to be wanted solely for my looks. My choice of Girl Talk didn't showcase a deep understanding of that idea. But reflecting back, I see that wearing a scarf greatly influenced how people viewed me and my goals, before I could ever appreciate that it was having that effect.

In high school, my interactions with the opposite sex were different than the norm. If I hadn't yet been inclined to deal with boys in an unpressured, ungiggly, un-made-up way, the scarf shoved me in that direction. So, without being given handbooks or informative flyers about how they should curb their posturing and come-ons, guys sensed that they should treat me with respect.

I didn't watch boys and girls learn about each other from the sidelines. I have many rich friendships with men, and over the years a good number of them have made a go at becoming "more than friends." I didn't participate in dating games, but I was flattered by the attention, especially since I knew I was being liked for who I was beyond my body. What made me attractive was my ability to relate to everyone in a very natural way, without all the confusing sexual pressure. The weirdness that normally clouds boy-girl interactions was lifted, because most guys automatically assumed I wasn't available for dating. Of course, girls deserve to be treated with respect no matter what they wear. But since we live in a world of mixed messages, I got to bypass a lot of damaging experiences.

The veil bestowed other experiences upon me that I wouldn't quite classify as negative, but definitely educational. Like anyone else who's visibly different from the norm, I encountered ridiculous ideas about what a covered person should be, do and enjoy. If someone overheard me talking about my interests, which included karate and skateboarding, I grew to enjoy their disbelief and shock. I didn't pick my hobbies to prove that stereotypes are often false, but it was nice to make people reconsider their notions of a Muslim girl.

Moving to New York City right after college and living alone was the most affirming thing I've done to solidify my resolve and truly understand what veiling means. Here, for the first time, people believed that I was wearing a scarf because I wanted to, not because my family coerced me into it. On the other hand, New York exemplifies what's wrong with our image-obsessed society. I worked for a couple of magazines and saw the way women acted out to draw attention to themselves. It was especially apparent at my anything-goes dot-com job, where women showed up to work in backless halter tops and were fawned over by male coworkers.

And now, as I write this, I can watch women subjugate themselves on reality dating shows. On a show about aspiring models I heard a woman say that her greatest goal would be to appear in *Stuff* magazine. I can't imagine centering my life on something as fleeting and meaningless as being admired simply for my body.

You might assume that because Muslim women traditionally don't display our bodies, we don't hold them as important or feel connected to them—or that we don't value ourselves as sexual beings. Guess again. While our degree of modesty is high, the value Muslim women place on the bodies underneath our veils is higher. In Sunday school, girls are taught that our bodies are beautiful ("God is beautiful and loves beauty" is a *hadith,* or saying, of the prophet Muhammad) and that they're so valuable that they're only meant to be shared in an intimate relationship: husband and wife, mother and baby, among women and in clinical or safe spaces (for example, with your doctor, among family members). Historically, the most severe-looking coverings used to be limited to the richest women in Arab society; being swathed in so much cloth was regarded as a sign of status.

People who have written about being in the secluded quarters of Arab homes or at their parties often express surprise at the degree to which these cloaked women maintain themselves via fitness, style and decadent rituals. (Let's not even get started on the body hair-removal process in the Middle East.) I'm not one for creams and blushes, but I understand that there are women who enjoy the beauty process, and I see no harm in indulging it for the right reasons. Feminist author Geraldine Brooks, in her book *Nine Parts of Desire,* quotes women across the Middle East who extol the virtues of prettying up for their loved ones. To me, this demonstrates that Western priorities are out of line: American women spend hours getting ready for strangers to see them but don't give the same effort to those who see them in intimate settings.

As for the variation in Muslim women's dress, it demonstrates the wide-ranging interpretations of modesty. I often get asked what the most "right" version is: the Afghani *burqah,* the Iranian *chador,* the Pakistani *salwar kameez,* the Arab *jilbab* or a sweatshirt and jeans. The short answer is that the recommendations for modesty are to be interpreted and applied at the discretion of the woman picking her clothes.

All through high school, I wore a *jilbab* exclusively, because I didn't have to spend any effort worrying about what was in season or what I would be expected to wear to fit in. I now cover my hair, but generally wear jeans and a long-sleeved shirt. My once-strict interpretation of modesty has been adapted to my urban lifestyle. Is wearing an *abaya* (the head-to-toe gown that completely covers the wearer) and a face veil a good idea in New York City? Probably not, since the abaya would likely get stuck in a subway door or pick up the dust off any floor you glide across. But not wearing an *abaya* in Saudi Arabia would probably make getting around very difficult for a woman.

It's utopic and ridiculous to assert that looks don't matter and that by veiling I'm avoiding the messiness—particularly after

September 11th. Now some people hold their breath a bit longer, assuming I'm a fundamentalist or wondering if I'm there to cause them harm. I sense people studying me on the trains, reading the cover of the book in my hand and trying to gauge if I'm one of "us" or one of "them." I grapple with the frustration that I can't reassure everyone individually that my goals have everything to do with social justice and nothing to do with holy war. But I have seen suspicions fade in the eyes of the pregnant woman to whom I've given my subway seat, or the Hasidic man whose elbow I've taken to help him up the stairs.

Though many of the stereotypes and incorrect assumptions people had while I was growing up still prevail (that Muslim equals backwards/oppressed/fundamentalist/terrorist), current events have pedestrians describing their secondhand "expertise" of Islam—the history of Wahhabi Islam, the export of Sayyid Qutb and the Muslim Brotherhood's ideas—or trying to argue that the Quranic requirements for modesty don't include veiling. It's much harder to explain why I cover to those who think they have a full understanding of the culture and the faith than those whose "knowledge" of the Middle East is limited to *Aladdin* and *hummus*.

I do appreciate the status Islam and the Middle East have in the news these days—the interest has generated new scholarship on Arabia's history and anthropology and on Islamic law, all of which I'm interested in and am relieved is being researched. This research includes a pool of female scholars reexamining Islamic texts with a feminist lens, and separating actual religious commands from their long-held, culturally laden interpretations, which often smack of patriarchy.

Forcing women to veil or unveil usually has the opposite effect. When I attended elementary school in Saudi Arabia and flew home to Michigan each summer, a parade of women swathed in black *abayas* would head to the airplane bathrooms once we were safely in the air and emerge wearing short, tight ensembles. Conversely, banning the veil in Syria and Turkey sparked a resurgence in its popularity.

The question of veiling comes up once someone finds out that I've married into a family that celebrates Christmas, with my full participation. "If you have a daughter, what will she wear?" they ask. I haven't yet cracked a pregnancy or parenting book, but I hope that my policy will be similar to the egalitarian way I was raised. If she wants to, she can; if she doesn't want to, then she won't. It's far more important for her to respect herself, her body and her life.

At the heart of my veiling is personal freedom. I dress this way because it has made it easier to get through adolescent phases and New York City streets with no self-loathing, body hang-ups or sexual harassment. I wish more women emerged unscathed; no one should suffer for what they look like or what they wear.

parisian peel
joyce dyer

My skin-care specialist tells me stories about her other clients while she sandblasts my face.

I've had five Parisian Peels to date, and my specialist says I'm a candidate for about three more. Every third Tuesday for the last five months, I've come to this office and snapped on a blue hairnet so a woman in a white lab coat can blast dead cells from my epidermis with an electric utensil that shoots small crystals into my skin. Each treatment takes thirty minutes and costs $125.00.

It feels a little like a small vacuum cleaner is sweeping across my face. There's a sensation of tiny needles accompanied by suction that feels strong enough to pull my tongue right through the wall of my cheek.

The procedure is French, and somehow that seems important. French women all look like Juliette Binoche or Catherine Deneuve and are gorgeous. Once in a while, a stray crystal blasts its way into my mouth. Sometimes I discover it on my way home and chew it, trying to figure out what's in this tasteless thing.

The specialist thinks I have pretty good skin. She can tell I'm not a smoker. "Have you seen the skin of a smoker?" she asks me. Cigarettes kill the capillaries that keep skin healthy, she explains. Smokers have sallow skin that lines early. "You can tell a smoker clear across the room," she says. "You can always tell a smoker." She can tell I haven't been a sunbather either because they get long, vertical lines all down their cheeks, like pumpkin ridges, and I don't have any of those.

One thing about my skin really bothers her, though. She says she'd like to kill the doctor who removed a cyst from my face twenty-five years ago and left a hole about the size of a chad from a paper punch.

"One lady," she told me during the first treatment I had, "came in here with a full beard." The specialist adjusted a pair of yellow tanning goggles over my eyes.

"Poor thing!" I said. I puffed up my lower lip with my tongue when she told me to. She can scrape around my mouth better that way to smooth the small lines.

"It was real dark," she said. "Ran from her upper lip all the way down to her collarbone."

I tasted a string of acid that had suddenly uncoiled from my stomach and shot up into my mouth. My right eye snapped open to a glare of yellow.

"I've never seen anything like that," I said, now moving my tongue under my upper lip, following the specialist's small, sharp tool.

"She wasn't worried."

"I would be," I said.

"Her husband had just let her with three small kids. What's a beard when you're facing a thing like that?"

I had no reply.

"Her kids started to ask where their daddy went as soon as he walked out on them. So she'd point to the beard, sort of stroke it and say, 'I'm your momma *and* your daddy now!'"

Sometime I tell myself I come here because of stories like that one. There seems to be no end of them. It's not uncommon for her to repeat them several times. There are so many women who walk through her door and sit in the leather chair where I'm sitting now that it probably becomes one long, continual conversation for her after a while, like a chant. How can she help repeating herself? And does it matter, anyway?

But I know it isn't the stories that keep me coming to this place in a city just south of where I live. This isn't about my skin-care specialist or about the cosmetic surgery industry.

It's about *me.* I'm not above all this, and I know it. I'm at the very center. *I* made the first appointment, and all the others that have followed. No one forces me to come here on Tuesday mornings, or ties me to this chair.

I'm part of this world now.

I just don't know how I got here.

I haven't told a soul that I come to this place. I make up excuses so that even my husband doesn't know where I go. I say I'm going to the health club or having my hair trimmed or hiking the nature trail close to our house. I guess I lie, if I'm honest about it. It's one of the few lies I've ever told in a marriage of thirty years. If my own mother were living, I'd lie to her too.

I'd lie to her because of the Coty. I remember only two beauty products my mother ever used: a stick of red Coty lipstick and a box of Coty face powder. When I cleaned out the house after she died, there were no additional beauty secrets hidden in drawers or at the backs of cupboards—the way there are in my house. One of my mother's sisters worked downtown in a department store. She sold cosmetics. Cosmetics were all she talked about, especially after her second divorce. She'd bring home little bags of Elizabeth Arden products for her daughter, and for me.

It's the wrinkles on my mother's skin I always remember, but my aunt's skin was smooth—like nylon. Her eyebrows were painted on where there had once been hair, as if the tiny bristles above her eyes were an offense to the perfect smoothness of her forehead and had to be plucked out one by one. My mother tightened her upper lip against her teeth when she put her lipstick on—in order to help her follow the exact line of her mouth. But my aunt always painted something like an extra lip above her real one—and always in a bright pink shade a girl might use.

My mother rarely looked in mirrors and spent practically no time on her personal appearance. She went to the beauty shop every Saturday morning, but I think she went mainly to get away from my father once a week. She liked to hear her beautician's stories.

My mother felt no discomfort or jealousy standing alongside women more beautiful than she was. She seemed oblivious, as if she didn't know they were even there. She would not have understood why I am paying to have the epidermis of my face removed.

But neither do I.

Of course it would be a lot easier to confess that I go to a cosmetic surgical arts center if I could just pretend that I didn't *really* want to be here. If I could pretend it was a world I deplored. If I could sit in the waiting room with absolute disdain for the women who surround me (I haven't seen a man yet in these chairs, except ones waiting for Lasik or cataract surgery, other services the complex offers), or make fun of the skin-care specialist as a sort of Martha Stewart of the skin industry who knows everything about something that doesn't matter at all. About bronzes, retinoic acid, glycolic acid, emu oil, vitamin

E, and antioxidants—products lined up in small green vials behind the specialist's desk, like elixirs of youth. You can get retinoic acid in 0.05 solution, or a 0.1 solution if you really want to burn your skin off fast. The same goes with concentrates of glycolic acid.

The specialist is trying to talk me into a series of glycolic acid treatments after I'm done with the Parisian Peel. "It's perfectly natural," is how she always begins her pitch.

Glycolic acid is found in sugar cane. It promotes the growth of collagen and rejuvenates the skin by removing dead cells *(exfoliation* is the specialist's word for this, and even teenage girls know about exfoliants these days). You can buy Alpha Hydroxy Acids (AHA's) in drugstores and supermarkets, but the level of glycolic acid in store brands is so low and so severely neutralized that it's not going to do much. Even while I'm having the Parisian Peel treatments, the specialist has had me apply a 12 percent—more recently, a 17 percent—glycolic acid solution to my face at home.

You know you're into the real stuff when you push toward that 20 percent mark. It burns so badly that my eyes water sometimes, and I feel as if tiny rats are taking little bites out of my face. After half an hour, I have bright blotches all over my skin, but the burning settles down. It's like that for a couple of days and the skin gets all saggy and rough, and my eyes look the way they did when I cried all the time after my mother died. But then it tightens, forms beads of tiny scabs, and flakes. In a generous light it glows like cellophane.

The in-office glycolic acid treatments she wants to do on my face will be a lot stronger than the 17 percent solution. "We go up to 70 percent," she tells me, proudly. I can't imagine what that would feel like, but I'd like to build up my tolerance and see if I can go that high.

Wrinkles are defined by numbers here. The specialist has noticeable lines around her mouth and she's worried about them. She calls them threes and fours, sucking air through her teeth every time she mentions them, and wincing. She has a number for each wrinkle on her face and points to them like a classroom chart when patients have questions about the fate of their own skin.

"When they get this deep," she tells me, pointing with her pink acrylic nails to a couple of fours, "you sometimes can't depend on acids. You have to go beyond the superficial layers. Go deeper. Lasers."

Today we talked about lasers for the first time, because she thinks someday that's the way I'll want to go.

She doesn't recommend the CO_2 laser because it has a lot of what she calls "down time." That's a euphemism for the blisters and seeping and terrible redness that sometimes accompany this procedure. It means you have to stay in the house because you'd turn people's stomachs if they saw you. "The redness persists," she explains. Not just for a few days or a couple of weeks.

"Persists" is another word that makes the specialist's eyes grow twice their size when she says it. Dermabrasion, she explains, is a good alternative to laser. It's a little like the Parisian Peel except there's also "down time." You remove top layers of skin with a wire brush, but you get a lot of seeping. Parisian Peel is *micro*epidermabrasion, and after the first day of a little redness, your skin is practically back to normal.

Over 300,000 laser resurfacing procedures (called "ablative" techniques since the epidermis and upper dermal layers are removed; I hadn't heard that word since ninth-grade Latin) were performed in 1999 in the United States alone, most of them with CO_2 lasers. A typical full-face procedure requires a patient to be under a general anesthetic for two hours. Dressings need to be applied and changed daily for two weeks. The specialist tells me that 40 percent of all patients experience redness—along with the slightly-less-common scarring and inability to tolerate any sunlight. Occasionally ablative skin resurfacing reactivates dormant herpes virus.

My specialist is excited about a new laser that a product rep just used on her. It's a non-ablative laser technique that leaves the skin barrier intact and targets, instead, deeper layers of the dermis—stimulating new collagen growth and avoiding the risks caused by removing top layers of skin. The rep *did her mouth*, is the way she describes it. She has a "before" picture she shows me every time I visit. Then, she leans close to my face, pushes her lips forward, and asks me what I think, holding the picture close to her mouth but off to the right. The new procedure takes sixty to ninety days to work, and each time I come she asks me what I think. The lines do seem softer to me. She says she wakes up each morning and can hardly wait to look in the mirror. It's like she's turning back the clock, she says.

Sometimes when I'm sitting in that leather seat looking through the yellow glare of my tanning goggles, I imagine that the hands of the wall clock are spinning backward. Time is different in this room. No one ages. If they change, they grow younger, not older—like the specialist, or Merlin. Every time I see her, she looks better than she did the time before. The non-ablative laser treatment she's just had should give her a wrinkle reduction of approximately 1.88. She understands the numbers and knows that's going to make a big difference.

"All you need right now is to fill in a little around your eyes," she always tells me, hoping I'll be convinced to try the new laser she swears by.

She doesn't put cool towels on my face today because I've built up resistance—even to level twenty-eight, the setting she's chosen for my fifth treatment. I'm relieved she hasn't abandoned the facial that always follows the towels. She squirts creams on my cheeks, forehead and chin and rubs the skin, pushing toward my bones with her strong thumbs. She circles patches of skin, making me aware of the muscles in my face. It feels so good that I hope it will never end. But all too soon she pulls the goggles off and presses the button that will raise the chair. Before I rise from my seat, though, a little dizzy, she presses my cheeks until my lips form a fish mouth and says, "Feel good?" It was something my mother used to do to me. I never can answer the specialist, so I smile and laugh. I have no way of telling her how much this means to me, and how eagerly I wait for it each time I come to see her.

As she removes my hairnet and the cotton balls in my ears that block some of the noise of the machine, she always touches the small frown lines on my forehead and tells me once more about Botox. "It was first used to treat twitchy eyes," she tells me. "Small injections of botulism into the nerve with a tiny needle keep your facial muscles from contracting." She tells me crow's-feet and frown lines and laugh lines are called "dynamic wrinkles" because the more emotion you show, the deeper they become.

She tells me I have a very expressive face and people like me can really benefit from Botox. The effect lasts only three months, unfortunately, so you have to keep on a schedule. "It's a little like having a permanent," she says, patting my hair. (Again, I think of my mother.) There's some temporary bruising at the injection site sometimes, she goes on, but you don't even need a local anesthetic and can usually drive home after the procedure.

A little makeup and you're as good as new.

One of the things I get after every Parisian Peel is a 30 percent glycolic acid treatment on my hands. Everyone does who gets the treatment. "The hands and face are the two places where age really shows," my specialist tells me. The solution is so strong that the specialist uses gloves and keeps a Windex bottle full of water right beside the table where she has me place my hands. She keeps asking, "Can you stand it? Can you stand it?" about every five seconds until you can't stand it anymore. And then she squirts my hands off with the water and pats them with a towel. I try not to say anything even when it starts to burn. I want it to burn because if it burns, I know my skin will exfoliate. My hands don't have wrinkles on them—just a few soft lines at the wrist like the ones around my eyes—but I'm worried that they'll look like my mother's one day.

It's hard to explain why I worry about things like this. I don't know exactly when this happened to me.

I always thought I was above the sick ideas about glamour we have in this country. I really did. In my twenties and thirties I used to make fun of women who caked makeup on their faces or had tummy tucks after a pregnancy. They seemed deluded to me.

I liked thinking of myself as my mother's daughter. She was the least vain woman I'd ever known, and I was absolutely certain that was part of the reason for her contentment. Those two simple Coty products that sat on her dresser were all she ever needed.

But now those products haunt me. I can no longer be content with my own beauty, the way she was with hers. I need fifty-dollar products and expensive French treatments. Or I think I do. I take the money for these things from the savings account I've paid a little into all my life. When I make a withdrawal, I feel as if I'm robbing a bank and have a pistol pointed at the teller's head—or my own.

I tell myself I'm not to blame. I go into the drugstore after a bank withdrawal to sip a Coke and settle myself down. I stare across the room at the bright magazines that catch my eye. "Get Gorgeous Skin," "Get Totally Sleek by June," "The Lingerie Issue," "Your Best-Ever Summer Body," "Your Sex Life," "Slimmer Legs" "Kick-Butt Shorts," "What Men Like." Beside every headline is the face of a perfect model, airbrushed to obliterate even the smallest lines that begin to form on human faces by twenty-five. Men's magazines make no attempt to hide those wonderful laugh lines of expressive faces, but women are not allowed to wrinkle.

I imagine makeup artists attending to the lines around the smiles of models after a magazine shoot. As soon as the camera lights shut off, I see them running hard from the wings toward the pretty women in their care, trying not to spill the unguents and creams held on little silver trays in front of them. They pat and smooth lines away on the fragile creatures they serve, and through sacred chants, summon the return of gods Elastin and Collagen. Cheeks tighten into contours of perfect china cups. The artists are always men, because this is what men want so very, very much for women.

From what my skin-care specialist has told me, the only procedure she offers that men desire is hair removal. They like the patches of turf on their backs removed, she tells me. Or, she says, sometimes they like the hair on their necks removed so the follicles don't get infected when they shave.

My specialist has disdain for the men who actually make appointments for the Parisian Peel. "They sit in my chair," she says, "and just stare in the hand mirror I give them at a little mole or something." She can't stand men who look in mirrors.

Of course, some women have laser hair removal performed too. The bearded lady she always talks about was one of them. But my specialist says she has removed her own teenage daughter's dark mustache as well as the dark hair on her daughter's arms. "The procedure works best on really dark hair," she says.

The most extraordinary hair-removal story she's told me is her own. She casually mentioned something one day while she was dancing around my face with her Parisian Peel hand piece. I haven't been able to forget it.

"I don't have any underarm hair," she told me. She had removed it with lasers. Never has to wax or shave now, or worry about a thing.

I've really wanted to ask her if I could look. I keep thinking if I continue the treatments through the summer, she might wear a sleeveless top and I can catch a glimpse when she drapes herself over me. Would it be as smooth under there as it was when she was a little girl? Would the procedure have left it that smooth? And how could you make sure every single hair was silenced? Wouldn't one or two on the edges have survived the assault of the laser? Or is it a perfect weapon, after all?

I've entered a world where women burn or blast their faces off to eliminate wrinkles and use lasers to stop the hair from growing under their arms. It's a world of acids and needles, of knives, and of clocks whose hands spin backward. It's a world seen through a glare of yellow on a blue leather seat.

I can blame the culture for bringing me here. I can blame men for doing this terrible thing to me. I can blame the skin-care specialist for her seductive promises. I can blame my mother for never warning me that her strength would not automatically be my own. I can blame my body for producing less collagen and elastin than it used to when I was younger. I can blame Age. I can blame Death.

There's some truth in all the finger-pointing. *I do* blame these things. I would scream my anger if there were any chance the world would listen. Or care.

But I also know it's more than this. I've said the obvious things, even when I've spoken of death. I will no longer say the obvious, or continue in its care. It houses someone else's meaning, someone else's heart, and not my own.

And I will not recite the lines I've stored away for times like this. Comforting lines about vanity and inner beauty. "Is the jay more precious than the lark because his feathers are more beautiful?" Let the lines stay in the poems and away from me.

What *I* know is this: I am not at peace with my body. And I never have been. And now I'm so desperate to understand it that I'm looking for a magician to explain it all to me. It's the wrinkles, of course, but it's more than that. For one hour every third Tuesday, I can talk to someone about the human body and not feel like a freak. When my specialist tells me about women coming to have the Parisian Peel for their stretch marks, we often speak of birth. I imagine women there, on that blue seat, naked, the machine grinding at their abdomens to take away from their skin yet another mark women must bear.

I'm suddenly not sure if I ever want to shave under my arms again after I hear the specialist delight in her pre-pubescent hairless state.

I smell heavy, flightless emus when the oil of their bodies is rubbed into my temples at the end of my Peel.

We talk about what men like, and women, and we don't shy away from sex. I realize, suddenly, that my obsession with my face may be an obsession with sex that I've never been able to speak about before. But I can here. I ask her why the skin is so soft on my inner thighs and she answers. I memorize the way she rubs my face and hands and repeat her strokes on my husband when I make love to him.

My mother was the least vain woman that I've ever known; it's true. But she was also nearly sexless. I know all children think this of their parents, so I'm careful when I say it. I've sorted through my memory a thousand times for a single clue of my mother's sexuality and failed to find anything at all. I remember masturbating behind sofas and chairs in the living room while my mother watched TV and sewed. She had no suspicion or curiosity about what I was doing behind those heavy pieces of furniture. There were no low blouses, no lace underwear, not a single touch or kiss I remember her giving my father—or any man. There were no jokes about breasts or butts. When she drank an occasional martini at a restaurant, there was no loss of inhibition. When I started my period, she handed me a Kotex, led me to the bathroom, closed the door and waited outside while I figured things out.

I am enormously sexual, but learned nothing at all from my

mother about this part of myself. This is not her fault. It is just the way things were, and what I have come to understand.

I don't mind the wrinkles. But if the wrinkles affect sex, then I am afraid. Sex is deeply connected to trust and hope. As odd as it is, as many years as I've been married, I'm only beginning to understand its power. It is beyond emotion, beyond words, beyond the petty fears and lies that occupy our days. It is the time and place when we get closest to the center of another human heart. What I feel with my husband when we ride the waves of our passion toward the morning shore is so intimate and so important to me that I would do anything, *anything,* to keep it one more day.

I would rip the very skin off my bones.

shrink rap:
what i learned as an eating disorders therapist
jennifer c. panning, psy. d.

When I began my predoctoral psychology internship at a large Midwestern university counseling center, I was asked to concentrate in one area during my residency year. I enjoyed working on women's issues, so I chose the field of eating disorders and body image. I was nervous, imagining my young female clients describing their latest dangerous diet or favorite method of purging. However, I rationalized that I would learn a lot—I could handle it. Little did I realize then how much I would struggle with my own body image issues during this pivotal year in my professional training. I walked in thinking of myself as a person who was comfortable with her body, only to realize later that I was simply disconnected from it.

I'm tall and curvy with a muscular build I inherited from my father. Looking in the mirror has never been a source of great anxiety for me. In high school, I was the "normal" weight for my height, according to the doctor's scale. I ate well and never skipped meals. My metabolism shot up when I joined the basketball and track teams, and I lost a tremendous amount of weight. Looking back at pictures, I cringe at how closely I resembled a girl with anorexia nervosa. Nobody confronted me about my weight loss, and if they had, I would have told them the truth: I was extremely active and had a very healthy appetite. My best friend joked that I could eat more than anyone else she knew.

During my undergrad years, I continued to be active and eat well, and I never really worried about my weight. I was opposed to dieting, and my metabolism allowed me to eat whatever I wanted without gaining weight. I remember hearing stories about women who refused to eat or who threw up their dinners, but I never personally knew anyone who engaged in these behaviors.

I noticed my metabolism changing around age twenty-five. I had just become engaged and had started graduate school, both of which wreaked havoc on my eating habits and contributed to a more sedentary lifestyle. I had also begun exploring my love for cooking, and had discovered a talent for preparing gourmet dishes. I blamed my creeping weight gain on academic pressures and life with my fiancé (now husband) who incidentally hasn't gained a pound since he graduated from high school. I felt more and more insecure about my widening hips and heavy thighs.

By the time I started my psychology residency, I was about thirty pounds heavier than I'd ever been. I had tried a low-fat diet (hungry all the time), exercising regularly (no time when I spent weekends writing my dissertation) and a low-carb diet (good in the short run; really bad after I wanted my pasta back and regained all of the weight and then some). My girlfriends and I mourned the days when we could eat pizza at midnight without a worry. We collectively decided that twenty-five was when it all began going "downhill" and prayed that our thirties would be no worse on our bodies.

I knew from my professional training that a therapist's body issues could be triggered by clients who were dealing with distorted body image and eating disorders. I felt like a hypocrite, counseling young women on how to become comfortable with their bodies when I was often painfully aware of the flesh on my legs spreading out when I sat down. I asked my supervisor how she thought my clients might perceive me, since many of them were underweight and I wore a size twelve. She thought it wouldn't be a problem because I was "naturally curvy." I didn't buy it.

I learned a lot from my clients about eating disorders and their insidious nature. Many seemed the stereotypical face of these disorders: young, attractive, intelligent Caucasian women from "good" backgrounds. I noticed a strong relationship between obsessive-compulsive characteristics and a tendency to obsess about food and weight—many of the young women engaged in such behaviors as restricting food intake and obsessively examining themselves in the mirror, fixating on their perceived flaws. Some of my clients came from very dysfunctional family backgrounds, homes in which they did not receive attention for just being themselves and felt that they had to portray a certain image, look a particular way. Others were involved in sports where appearance and weight were very important and were emphasized as a way to succeed.

One of my biggest challenges was engaging clients in treatment, thus beginning their long, arduous journey toward self-discovery. Initially I would do an eating-disorders assessment to understand their present behaviors and symptom history, along with an important "related concerns" section that took into consideration clients' interpersonal relationships, among other things. I realized quickly that many clients needed structure because they felt out of control in their lives. In my sessions, I attempted to be a grounding presence, helping my clients distinguish reality from their often-distorted perceptions. I needed to educate them about healthy body image and the short- and long-term effects of having an eating disorder. I tried to support them in making life-changing decisions about their health.

I began to see how powerful psychotherapy was in treating eating disorders. It seemed that, for some of the young women I worked with, being in therapy was one of the few times that they felt listened to, supported and encouraged. I balanced this support and encouragement with a reality-based perspective so my clients would understand the consequences, some lifelong, of the damage they were inflicting on their bodies. Additionally, since clients with eating disorders often have such distorted views of their bodies, eating patterns and what it means to be healthy, I included education and reality testing as part of treatment. Also, since eating disorders affect many areas of a client's life, I worked in conjunction with other health practitioners who focused on the medical, nutritional and psychiatric aspects of treating the disorders.

In addition to providing individual therapy, I cofacilitated a support group for people struggling with these disorders. This was an extremely valuable process, yet immensely difficult. One of the hallmarks of having an eating disorder is living in silence and secrecy about it. The women in my support group were both empowered by and terrified of talking about such vulnerable issues. During this process, I also learned about the power of denial: Just getting my clients to *admit* that they had a problem and to address the seriousness of their eating disorders were huge tasks.

Young women today are faced with extraordinary pressures. Many are perfectionists, holding themselves to unrealistically high standards. They expect—and are expected—to achieve a lot. Now more than ever they receive very mixed messages: While we live in a society that "supersizes" everything and has an alarming rate of obesity, women are expected to achieve a uniform thinness. This may explain why binge-eating disorders are increasing drastically—women are, on one hand, comforted by food, yet on the other made to feel that their self-worth and attractiveness rests on attaining an unrealistic body type. College women face added pressures, including a focus on fitting in and being socially accepted (which may include trying the latest fad diet or simply not eating because that is what other women are doing). Additionally, joining a sorority certainly can lead to becoming vulnerable to developing an eating disorder due to an emphasis on competition and appearance.

As I started working with my anorexic and bulimic clients, my own eating habits began to change. En route to work, I had always bought coffee at the gas station. Then I began to grab a chocolate donut as well. Was I eating for my clients? As I saw them refusing to eat an adequate amount of nutritious food, I seemed to be giving in more and more to my cravings for sweets and fat. In retrospect, I think this pattern illustrated my confusion and helplessness at the time: I wanted to help my clients, but I didn't know how. Perhaps subconsciously I thought that by eating more, I could somehow provide more nourishment to them.

As I became more comfortable and competent treating eating disorders and understanding the complex nature of body image, I grew more at ease with gently confronting my clients when they began denying the effects of their behaviors or discounting what they knew to be true. I became more assertive with my clients and trusted my reactions and feelings while encouraging them to trust themselves more. I worked from a strengths-based methodology, encouraging my clients not to compare themselves with the models they saw in women's magazines, but instead to respect and listen to their own bodies. I was dismissive of dieting, convinced that it only increases cravings and sets people up to fail. Chronic dieting is one of the leading risk factors in developing an eating disorder, and for many dieting can be a "slippery slope" leading to restricting entire food groups and compulsively focusing on food and weight. This focus on losing weight and being fit usually begins in an innocent manner, but it can lead to an unhealthy, obsessive use of food to be in control and feel better about oneself. Thus, the development of an eating disorder often begins with good intentions, such as losing weight and becoming healthy, only to result in more restrictive behaviors and unrealistic expectations.

Midway through my residency, I attended a seminar about the effects on therapists' body image in working with clients on this issue. It was both comforting and difficult. I found one guided imagery exercise, led by a psychologist, particularly powerful. First, she asked us to imagine ourselves looking in a full-length, 360-degree mirror. We were to visualize ourselves clothed, viewing ourselves from all angles, noting carefully how we felt during this experience. Then she asked us to imagine removing our clothes and examining our naked bodies in this mirror.

The exercise hit home. I was struck by how much I covered my own body insecurities by emotionally and intellectually disconnecting from my feelings of vulnerability, fear, insecurity and disgust. In fact, every participant in the room appeared visibly upset after we talked about how this experience affected us. The clear message from this experience was that we are all human beings with bodies. Like our clients, we all struggled at some level with accepting our appearance.

After that workshop, I wondered if I became more effective working with my clients *because* I had finally admitted to struggling with similar issues myself. I also owned up to the fact that, even though I sometimes despised my flabby stomach, I kind of liked what I saw in the mirror—even a full-length one. Fortunately, my loving husband reinforced this by constantly telling me I was beautiful. But maybe also, deep down, I knew that my self-worth did not revolve around my dress size.

So I decided, to hell with it, I wasn't willing to diet, and my crazy schedule only allowed me time for work, meals and sleep. I began to think of myself as a role model for my clients. I gave serious consideration to how I could portray healthy body esteem to my extremely self-conscious and critical clients, many of whom still believed that a "perfect" body would bring happiness and fulfillment. I began wearing clothes that accentuated my curves, and while at times this meant emphasizing parts of my body that I wasn't crazy about, I focused on the message I could give my clients if I carried myself with pride and wore clothes that fit me well. That's not to say that I started wearing low-cut shirts or miniskirts to work; I still dressed in a professional manner. I simply stopped hiding behind baggy or ill-fitting clothing.

This simple act dramatically affected my professional comfort level, helping me stay grounded with my clients. As I reflected on their needs, I learned what *I* needed more of: self-acceptance, compassion, humor and, at times, some good chocolate. Interestingly, that year's theme for National Eating Disorders Awareness Week was "Listen to Your Body." The underlying message is that our bodies are something to be honored and valued. This idea is very potent and stirs up many insecurities and questions: If I'm not thin or toned, does my body deserve to be listened to? Do I even know what my body needs? When I am so busy that I forget to use the bathroom, what does my body need to do to be heard?

My residency year is now over, and I've spent a lot of time reflecting on what I've learned from my clients. I've shared their frustration and helplessness at the pervasiveness of body image dissatisfaction in our culture. Through their insights, I've concluded that for now, the best way for women to fight it is to work through our personal insecurities and demonstrate to others—through refusing to complain about our looks or by staying silent when others make similar comments—that yes, we look like real women, and that's just fine.

My work showed me how desensitized I'd become to the barrage of images and messages about the ideal woman's body shape. I am now a critical viewer of magazines and will often point out to anyone who will listen images of underweight young women who would be considered clinically anorexic. These larger cultural pressures are intimidating, at times overwhelming, and seem only to be getting worse.

My clients also have taught me the importance of self-care. For many reasons, I neglected my own well-being during that stressful year. I am even more aware of the importance of being in balance, moving and generally taking breaks to rejuvenate my body and spirit. Many times, a stressful experience, whether it's beginning college, a breakup or a suffering grade-point average, can exacerbate or set the stage for an eating disorder.

Eating disorders, I've discovered, are rarely about food or vanity. The real issues behind these disorders are fear of losing control, perfectionism, relationship difficulties and other emotional problems, such as depression. The biggest hurdle is to establish a solid sense of self and, related to this, a compassion for and acceptance of being imperfect in body and mind.

I feel honored to have worked with each of my clients. I view them as strong, courageous women for having the guts to admit their problems and the insight to see that they cannot overcome their disorders without professional assistance. As I continue my work with eating disorders and body image at another Midwestern university counseling center, I believe I will continue on my own path toward self-acceptance.

cro-magnon karma:
one dude and his
body image issues
chris godsey

Brad Pitt is a beautiful man. I'm male, I'm straight, and I don't mind admitting that Brad's body, especially in *Fight Club,* is an impressive sight. Same with D'Angelo in his powerful, sexual "Untitled" video; he's a put-together dude, and there's no reason to deny it.

But while I'm cool with thinking those guys are gorgeous, I'm bothered by my frequent inability to see them, *Men's Health* magazine or any fitness machine commercial without believing that unless I have 3 percent body fat, a hairless torso and washboard abs, I'm an inferior man. I spent the week after watching *Fight Club* counting calories like Sarah Ferguson; back when "Untitled" was in heavy rotation on *MTV Jams*, I skipped a lot of meals and doubled up on many days' workouts.

Body image issues aren't historically typical masculine concerns, but I'm not the only guy who does this stuff. I've got buddies who are manly men—they would punch me for saying what I did about Brad Pitt—but who get real touchy about what their asses look like in a pair of jeans. I know dudes who go through serious streaks of food-induced guilt and worry that their bodies aren't attractive.

Most men don't openly discuss body image concerns—even crushing body insecurity among guys is hidden or expressed as humor or tongue-in-cheek bravado. But a book called *The Adonis Complex: The Secret Crisis of Male Body Obsession*, by Harrison Pope, Katharine Phillips and Roberto Olivardia, illustrates how a lot of men are abusing their bodies and minds while trying to achieve a bullshit version of the masculine ideal. According to the authors, men are becoming body-obsessed in unprecedented numbers; yet this phenomenon remains a secret because men aren't "supposed" to have such concerns.

Throughout the book, the authors describe dudes whose hang-ups are surprisingly powerful. They write:

> *Millions of men are sacrificing important things in their lives to exercise compulsively at the gym, hoping for a bigger chest or a flatter stomach. Men and young boys alike are buying billions of dollars of "muscle-building" food supplements and diet aids. As many as three million men have taken anabolic steroids or other dangerous black-market drugs to buff up their bodies. An equally large, even more secret group of men has developed eating disorders—compulsive binge eating, dieting, and exercise rituals. . . . Another million or more have developed "body dysmorphic disorder," an excessive preoccupation with perceived flaws in their appearance. They worry, for example, that their hair is thinning, their breasts are fat, or their penis is too small. . . . Unlike healthy men*

and boys, they have an unrealistic view of how
they should look.

The book's authors are all Ivy League psychiatrists or psychologists who study issues that affect millions of men and account for billions of dollars. Through interviews with hundreds of men, they show how guys are striving for physical perfection through steroid use, eating disorders and other obsessions. They identify "a broad and growing group who feel insecure and anxious—even paralyzed—by how they look. Society is telling them now, more than ever before, that their bodies define who they are as men. Because they find it impossible to meet this supermale standard, they are turning their anxiety and humiliation inward." They also discuss unique experiences of gay men and of the female partners of heterosexual men who face body image disorders.

It's obvious that neither the study nor the problem exist on some wacko fringe of human experience—it's prevalent, and it's *real*. Proof of the problem is everywhere, even if most men don't talk about it. Magazines like *FLEX* and *Men's Fitness* and many other popular culture vehicles are perpetuating the ripped, hairless ideal and making some long dough in the process.

I'm one of those guys who are hung up on their looks. After a long time believing that I work out and try to "eat right" for health, I've realized that shallowness and insecurity are my true motivators. Instead of mental and physical fitness, I concentrate on the MTV, Hollywood and *Us Weekly* ideals of masculine value and attractiveness. Instead of working out to feel good about myself, I worry about looking good to other people, and I base my value as a man on how closely my body resembles those of Brad, D'Angelo, and their buff brothers.

chris godsey   **289**

I'm actually in pretty decent shape—about 6'2", 215 pounds and relatively solid. I do a lot of pushups, pull-ups and Pilates, and I run or bike almost every day. Most of the time I eat okay, and while I'm working some back fat and a little extra around the middle, my body's not bad. I'm not ripped, but I'm not flabby, and I'm healthy enough to feel lucky. All but the most superficial standards suggest I have nothing to complain about.

But since high school, I haven't been content. Back then, I obsessed about being *too* skinny. I played football, and I desperately wanted to gain weight. So I ate enough to feed most families, lifted weights and watched the scale and the mirror constantly, aching for the day when I would become "huge." Everything is relative, and now that I just want to work out comfortably and avoid excess pounds, I'm struggling to lose the weight I once thought would make my life right.

For more than half my life, I've been constantly conflicted, never content and remarkably self-centered. But instead of comparing myself to narrow, arbitrary ideas about what we all "need" to look like, I tell myself it's okay if my torso is hairy and my abs aren't defined; I can have visible body fat and still be valuable—even attractive. I'm trying to internalize the belief that every human body is unique, that perfection is a myth and that the only important standards for me are mine. This self-affirmation can be comforting (when I believe it), but what *are* my standards? They're constantly shifting. A few years ago, I had a bodybuilder roommate who was my height, weighed forty pounds more, and had about 4 percent body fat. I felt skinny and soft and subpar that whole year. A couple years later, I lived with a competitive runner who weighed a muscular 140. If I wasn't careful, I started feeling like an oaf, all big and clumsy and excessive. Add those mental processes to the ones inspired by Brad, D'Angelo, *et al.,* and it's obvious how logic and self-confidence can disappear in a mental quagmire.

But why? Why do I spend so much time in front of the mirror, flexing and twisting and prodding and scrutinizing every part of my body that I deem less than perfect? Why can ten minutes of TV inspire me to renounce all food but asparagus and grilled chicken, and commit every waking moment to working out? Why, even though my wife tells me every day that she digs me enough to get goose bumps, can't I be comfortable with how I look? It's like I'm a . . . I don't want to say it, but it's true. It's like I'm a woman. My self-esteem frequently depends on how I see my body, I seldom see my body in positive terms, and I'm susceptible to the messages about men's bodies shouted at me from magazines, movies and TV shows.

The pressure on men has increased in recent years. *The Adonis Complex* explores how images of the masculine ideal in Western popular culture have changed over the decades. Until the 1970s, they say, even the most masculine of men had perfectly ordinary bodies.

> *Stars of the screen like Gregory Peck, Humphrey Bogart, and Clark Gable didn't have to go to the gym every day to be appealing to their many admirers. The Vietnam-era G.I. Joe, the heroes of old-time boys' comic strips, the men in magazine advertisements and television shows of the fifties and sixties—almost all were ordinary-looking guys. But nowadays, boys and men are fed an ideal of masculinity that is virtually unattainable.*

Women have been confronted by unattainable ideals for far longer than men have. The days of Peck, Bogart and Gable were also the days of Ginger Rogers, Jane Russell, Dorothy Dandridge, Grace Kelly and a multitude of other iconic beauties with impossible hourglass figures and perfect faces. (Marilyn Monroe's outsized sensuality, by the way, weighed about 150 and wore a size fourteen.) Male complements to

chris godsey   291

ideal female physiques are a relatively recent pop culture construct. Even the heydays of Raquel Welch, Pam Grier and Farrah Fawcett were relatively free from male icons defined by rippling granite bodies. Now, though, straight women have more to drool over and men have more images to induce insecurity.

Don't get me wrong, though: While feelings of inadequacy are gaining prevalence among guys, we're still relatively immune compared to women. According to multiple studies from the early 1990s, men and boys have 10 percent of all eating disorders—which means that women have *90* percent of them. Guys aren't intentionally puking in the same enraging numbers as women. Few men have died from starving themselves. And relatively few of us fellas are in counseling to combat our adversarial relationships with food.

The most damaging double standards are still directed toward women. Men are still allowed to eat—"Hey, pard'ner, don't you deserve a hearty, *MAN*-sized meal?" Women are commanded and manipulated and criticized without mercy—"Ladies, now there's a new way to get all that rich chocolate taste without all those fat-causing calories!" You'll never see a SnackWell's commercial in which a bunch of *dudes* stampede through a grocery store seeking the latest, greatest, low-fat devil's food cookies or some other synthetic grub that's more dangerous than the full-fat original. Only women are supposed to express (and identify with) food guilt and body obsession, right?

Not for long. Karma's for real, baby, and it's coming to get us. You didn't think we'd get away with making women feel like shit forever, did you? Men aren't immune to suggestive selling tactics. Our insecurity, vanity and newfound need to measure up to popular images make us a marketing gold mine. The recent popularity of the TV show *Queer Eye for the Straight Guy* is evidence enough. As early as the mid-1990s, writer Mark Simpson coined the term *metrosexual*, which has been getting increased play from reputable media sources like the *New York Times* as a description for hetero-sexual men whose desire to look good puts them in a category formerly reserved for gay guys and women.

In Simpson's 2002 Salon.com article "Meet the Metrosexual," he writes of this shift:

> *The stoic, self-denying, modest straight male didn't shop enough (his role was to earn money for his wife to spend), and so he had to be replaced by a new kind of man, one less certain of his identity and much more interested in his image—that's to say, one who was much more interested in being looked at (because that's the only way you can be certain you actually exist). A man, in other words, who is an advertiser's walking wet dream.*

It's that uncertainty around masculine "identity" that rings most true to me. Masculinity used to be simple, but it's becoming as complicated as femininity always has been. Apply double standards to guys like they're applied to women, and it's obvious we've got plenty of reasons to feel rotten about ourselves. We're too skinny. Too fat. Emotionally dense. Oversensitive. Need to be manly men. Need to express our feminine side. Make us believe our pecs are too small, our guts are too soft, and we're sexually inferior, and we'll buy everything from Super Protein Muscle Building Powder to magazines that give *us* images of bodies we'll never have, but that we—and the people we're trying to attract—supposedly should want.

Women, who since the 1960s have been screaming for men to acknowledge inequalities in gender perceptions and expectations, may have reached a social and financial point where they can push men around a little bit. Simpson writes:

chris godsey   293

No longer is a straight man's sense of self and manhood delivered by his relationship to women; instead it's challenged by it. . . . [T]he more independent, wealthy, self-centered, and powerful women become, the more they are likely to want attractive, well-groomed, well-dressed men around them. . . . By the same token, the less men can rely on women, the more likely they are to take care of themselves. Narcissism becomes a survival strategy; apparently, some men actually buy their own underwear and deodorant these days.

While I'm vain and intimidated by my wife's sexual power, I don't consider myself a metrosexual. I live in Duluth, Minnesota, far from true metropolitan influence. I care about my clothes, but in a second-hand, faded jeans and flannel shirt way; I'm about as glossy as sandpaper. More than anything, I'm a deep thinker who too often turns his philosophical gaze inward. What I see alongside all my worries about back fat and body hair is an expanding appreciation for how difficult it is to be a woman.

Although acting on that troubling awareness would be admirable, I don't—at least not in any substantive way. I understand all this stuff on an intellectual level, but I'm still stupid enough to get turned on by *Maxim* and *Playboy* and Cro-Magnon enough to fantasize about what an alpha male I'd be if I could conquer an icon of physical feminine perfection like Halle Berry. Even when I'm out and about with my wife, Shannon, my head snaps in the direction of every good-looking woman. I'm also stupid enough to frequently make comments like, "My goodness, doesn't Salma Hayek have lovely breasts," or "You know, Jennifer Lopez's ass really *is* amazing." Then—and this is where I get *really* stupid—I expect my wife to be perfectly confident about her own body, and I lose my patience when she gets insecure.

I love Shannon. I wouldn't cheat on or intentionally disrespect her. I'm not such an asshole that I criticize her or tell her she needs to look like other women. In fact, I get butterflies just thinking about her shape—she's curvy and feminine and strong—and I constantly let her know how much I appreciate her body and her mind. But when insecurity distorts my good intentions, love succumbs to shallow vanity, and attraction becomes painful.

Here, in simple terms, is what happens: (1) I feel, usually without realizing it, insecure about my masculinity, largely because I'm afraid my imperfect body makes me less of a man; (2) I fantasize (not out loud, of course) about what a stud I'd be if I slept with, say, Rosario Dawson, or I try to assert my masculinity by checking out or commenting on every hot woman within eyesight (basically a subtle way of prowling for the attention that Simpson equates with proof of existence, and which gives me superficial proof of my value as a man); (3) Shannon winds up feeling insecure because I'm grooving on other women; (4) She says something like, "You want someone with dark skin and hair. Why don't you just leave me? I'm fat and pasty and frumpy. You never get to see me naked again."

It's all because I feel anxious and insecure, and before I realize it, I've hurt her feelings and smashed her confidence while trying to build my self-esteem. Even though her insecurity seems irrational (to me), *my* rotten body image makes perfect sense, and now I feel even more rotten because I know I've hurt her. So I respond with something like, "Sweetie, you know I think you're hot. I'm the one who's got a hairy gut." We've had conversations that are nothing but ping-pong games of "You're hot, I suck," back and forth, back and forth, until we've wound ourselves into self-centered spirals of depression.

And here's the worst part: Sometimes in those situations, I start believing the horrible stuff Shannon says about herself. She's twenty-eight, and I look at her powerfully attractive body and then I visualize pictures of her in bikinis at age twenty, twenty-one, twenty-two. I begin to resent her for not being as solid and slim as she was then. Then I realize I'm being mean and hypocritical, but that doesn't change what I'm thinking. Why not? If I know I'm being a jerk, why don't I just stop?

Here's an explanation that borders on trite psycho-babble: For longer than Western society has taught men that there are required physical components for masculinity, it's taught them that the manliest men score the most desirable women. According to this set of standards, guys whose wives and girlfriends aren't attractive in society's eyes are less powerful and masculine than guys whose women are trophies.

There's obviously a lot wrong with that equation. Not only does it reduce Shannon (whose intellect, humor and other mental and emotional traits are beyond value) to the level of a material object or possession, it makes her body responsible for my masculine identity and self-esteem. If her body is socially inadequate, then so is mine, and if I define myself by my body, then I'm inadequate as a person and as a man. If I'm susceptible to messages about what men "should" look like (and I am), it's probable that I'll emasculate myself for not look-ing like Brad Pitt, then make Shannon's inadequacy the excuse for the insecurity my own vanity and shallowness manufactured.

More briefly: If she's not hot, I suck, and she gets blamed for all of it.

Here's a different way to state the same explanation: Shannon and I dated for a year in the early 1990s. Just before she turned twenty, she dumped me for a professional hockey player. Then she dumped him for a richer, more prominent one. After him, she had some other relationships, and then she was single for a while. She and I didn't talk for seven years. I dated plenty of other women—enough that, in retrospect, it seems like I was trying to prove something. She missed me enough that her good friends made her contact me after all that time. She loves me enough to have married me. But the sleek Shannon in those pictures—"I was hot back then," she's said since we were married—*she's* the one who gave herself to guys whose social status was much higher than mine, and who were paid millions of dollars to be physically fit. She's the one who eventually, after she'd become "a fat girl" (in her opinion), came back to me.

In my Cro-Magnon mind, this is all I can think: Those guys got to play around with and claim her body—the body I had for a while, the body that attracted those other guys, who are true social alpha-males, and whose money and fame and physical prowess means they can get any kind of woman they want, the body she says was way better than the one I get. I had her, I couldn't keep her, I got her back when she went downhill. That would never happen to Brad or D'Angelo. They're real men. I'm just a boring teacher with love handles.

I'm not mad or disappointed because she has a rotten body—she doesn't. I'm angry and sad that I lost her to guys I sometimes envy, and whose traditional masculine power sometimes intimidates me. Her body image frustration gets twisted around in *my* mind to suggest that I have good reason to feel inferior to those other dudes. When she liked her body, they got her; now that she don't feel so fly, I get her, because she doesn't think she can do any better.

But do you see how superficially I've been defining my masculinity as well as that of Brad, D'Angelo and the hockey players? What I've been saying (and believing, without realizing it) is that male value ultimately depends on reducing women to physical symbols of masculine superiority—that masculinity is gauged by a man's ability to conquer and control women. What a shallow line of reasoning. It ignores everything substantial about all women, it hurts straight men just as much, and it simply negates gay men.

Pope, Phillips and Olivardia say that assertive women and shifting expectations of men have resulted in "a new emotional problem, unique to modern society, that we call 'threatened masculinity.'" Apparently, men aren't quite sure how to be "masculine" anymore, so they've resorted to the most basic, Cro-Magnon distinction: muscles. "Muscles are one of the few areas in which men can still clearly distinguish themselves from women or feel more powerful than other men. But muscles are a tenuous foundation on which to base all of one's sense of masculinity and self-esteem."

That rings especially true for heterosexual men. These same authors conducted a simple study about male bodies: Men were shown images of men and asked them which ones would be most attractive to women; then they showed women the same images and asked them which ones they actually liked. "In test after test, the results of this comparison have been dramatic. The body that men think women like is typically about fifteen to twenty pounds more muscular than what women actually like." Interestingly, this study works the same in reverse: Women asked to pick the "perfect" female body choose images fifteen to twenty pounds thinner than what men actually prefer.

All these popular images of the ideal male are a ruse. Masculine value doesn't lie in powers of attraction and conquest. It's not about looking like Brad Pitt or achieving any other physical ideal. The few "real men" who exist have the integrity to seek beyond the superficial, into the substantive, and to act on what they learn. They're the ones who realize that strength comes from admitting weakness, that courage means confronting—not denying—fear and that honesty is the ultimate power. And they realize that real women share the same qualities.

the elephant and the ice cream:
emotions, politics and food
loolwa khazzoom

"People tell me I'm an elephant," my adorable second-grade student said one Sunday morning as we walked to class.

"Miriam,[1] that's terrible!" I exclaimed.

"No, it's not," she said. "It's true."

"Why do you think it's true?" I challenged.

"Because I'm fat," she said.

"She's F-A-T," my new classmate announced on my first day of second grade. The other girls nodded in disapproving, sagacious agreement. Twenty-one years later, I still remembered the sting from those words.

I stopped Miriam, kneeling down in front of her so that we were face to face. "Miriam," I said, looking into her wide, little-girl eyes, "you are not an elephant. Nobody has the right to call you that. Your body is fine just the way it is."

"I like my body," she replied. "But I *am* an elephant." She

299

marched past me and into the classroom. *I have to work on her,* I thought to myself as I followed her inside.

Food is connected to so much from my childhood—deprivation, neglect, control and abuse—as well as to the general woman-hating messages of society, as in "less is better." As a result of this madness, I have done it all: anorexia, bulimia, exercise bulimia, gaining thirty to fifty pounds of excess weight (depending on whom you ask), bingeing, dieting and obsessive calorie counting.

When my back went out a few weeks after speaking with Miriam, I could not engage in my usual Amazonesque activities, such as biking up miles of hills and riding around in the forest at the top. During those sedentary days, I was shocked to find I had exactly the same unhealthy relationship to food as I had years earlier. There I was again, eating when I was stressed, eating when I was pissed and eating when I was lonely.

I confided this to my friend Jessica, and we started talking about what food means to me. The conversation made me want the Portofino Mint Bianco ice cream in my freezer. Badly.

"Of course this conversation brings up stuff," Jessica said when I told her about my craving. "But you're not going to eat it. You're going to talk to me until the urge goes away."

"But I want to eat ice cream!" I cried, suddenly bursting into tears. The intense emotions took me by surprise.

I grew up with an obese mother. When I was six, she started stealing my food. I would buy an ice cream bar (Creamsicles, I loved 'em), take a bite and put it in the freezer for a later time. The next day, I would return to the freezer to take another bite, only to find it gone. My mother had eaten it.

I learned to eat food quickly when it was in front of me, never knowing if I would see it again. I developed a panic response to food, which I still have to this day. Fortunately, my mother was a germ freak, so I made a habit of coughing all over my ice cream bars in clear view of my mother. She left them alone after that, but the damage was already done. (My maternal grandmother, I learned years later, used to lock food away from my mother, using chains and padlocks. And we wonder where my mom got her deprivation issues!)

My family was divided down traditional gender lines, but my mother was an awful housewife and a lousy cook. The only meal she cooked was the one my father ate—dinner—and she gave the best food to him. My father in turn "graciously" gave his choice portions to my sister and me, against my mother's protests. This behavior around food contributed to the atmosphere in which my father later sexually abused me: Everything was for Daddy. He came first before anyone else in the family, and we had to be grateful for whatever scraps he chose to give us.

My father was obsessed with saving money. He would buy ten pounds of rotting tomatoes because they were on sale, rather than one pound of good tomatoes. We acted like it was a great idea, putting on huge, ecstatic smiles and jumping around in excitement. But the food he brought home rotted in the fridge. Though we were a middle-class family, we ate like a poor one.

Food was not about nurturance but about ingesting a kind of sickness. My father made "I feel terrible" faces when food went bad. I felt guilty when I did not eat the rotting vegetables fast enough, when I did not find the garbage food appealing, when I did not do my part in supporting my father's heroic efforts to get the best deal for his family. I was manipulated into playing Chase of the Rotting Vegetables, where we ate not the best of the bunch but the worst, to salvage it before it went bad.

Whenever my father traveled out of town, my mother rejoiced:

Finally, she was free! Celebration always took the form of ice cream, hot dogs and potato chips (in that order, because we kept kosher). So I began to associate good times and freedom with junk food. I looked forward to those times. We had so much fun, just the three of us. On those occasions my mother would cook for my sister and me, showing us this form of love normally reserved for my father. She was such a different person when my father was not there! She would spend our meal complaining to us about what an asshole my father was, how he always bossed her around. And somehow, as unhealthy as her complaining was, it felt like a form of female bonding in my family, some kind of a positive ritual.

I began dieting when I was eight years old. My sister put me on an eight-hundred calorie-a-day diet, until I lost enough weight to "earn" twelve hundred calories a day. These starvation diets were given to me as an act of love from someone I loved, looked up to and trusted. The poison of the diet mentality was invisible to us. I learned deprivation young.

Meanwhile, I lived in constant fear that my mother was going to die at any moment. Often she sat in the dark and ate and ate, checking her ankle for swelling. "I shouldn't eat this," she said, noting how much salt the food had, how high her blood pressure already was and what a risk high blood pressure was for stroke. But she continued eating with a zoned-out look on her face.

"Mommy, stop!" I pleaded with her desperately. "Please, please stop!" My mother got angry and told us to leave her alone. Then she ate even more furiously, with a determined zeal, heading toward her own destruction.

I was ashamed of my mother's body—ashamed to bring her to school functions, ashamed to be identified with her. I wanted a mother like one of the neighborhood girls': slim, perky, friendly and glamorous, with store-bought clothes and makeup; not obese, angry, afraid and withdrawn, with hand-sewn, ripped muumuus and no makeup. In retrospect, I think it was cool that my mother never wore makeup. But the way she approached her body was not about self-love and self-acceptance. It was about neglect and self-hatred.

When I was fourteen, my mother went on a supervised fast and she ate only powdered supplements. Our family was ecstatic as she lost 120 pounds. I have mixed feelings about contributing to the pressure to make her take such a drastic step. I remember the family intervention in the living room one afternoon: Everyone looked miserable. My father said he could not take my mother's obesity anymore, and I shared my own desperation about her weight. My mother sat with her hands between her legs and her head hung low. I felt horrible about making these demands on her body. But I was her child, and did she not have a certain responsibility to me as my mother—namely, to be healthy enough to stay alive?

My mother was euphoric when she lost all that weight, and she loved not having to deal with food at all. There was no middle ground for her: She could eat obsessively or not eat. As she lost weight, my mother gained self-esteem. Around this time, she started making and selling art, finally discovering that she was really good at something.

After the fast, my mother continued with the "modified eating" part of her program, where participants were taught that calories were more important than the health content of food: "If you want to eat cake," they taught, "just eat the cake. Don't eat the cake and then eat something you don't want to eat because you need healthy food. Cake has eggs and milk and flour in it, which are nutritious." My mother passed on this information to me as gospel, not distinguishing the fact that this program was for people whose lives were in danger from their eating habits. For me, this information translated not into "staying alive is most important," but rather, "being thin is most important."

So I started to eat like my mother, becoming obsessed with calorie counting. I knew exactly how many calories were in what serving of which food and how many calories I could burn by doing how much of what exercise. I, unfortunately, still remember much of this information. Did you know, for example, that right now you could burn 0.2 calories per step if you read this essay while running up stairs?

In college, I gained not only the "freshman fifteen," but the freshman thirty, bringing me fifty pounds over what doctors recommended as the ideal weight for women of my 5'7" height: 130 pounds. I find that weight to be a ridiculous and dangerous expectation for someone with my body type, and I find it incredibly disturbing that there was no room for variation within that estimate.

Over the next year, I used exercise bulimia to control my weight, bingeing on food, then "purging" by running twelve miles or swimming six miles instead of throwing up. I lost thirty pounds during the summer after my first year in college. I continued my exercise fanaticism for my whole college career. I ate crappy food because it was low-calorie or calorie-free. And for the first time in my life, I was thin. But I never was thin enough.

I then developed mild bulimia, vomiting up my food after eating, until my mother warned me that I could destroy my organs. So I stuck with exercise bulimia until my last year and a half in college, when I literally starved myself. I was anorexic but saw myself as fat at 135–140 pounds. Even in the freezing New York winter, I bought a quart of Tasti D-Lite every day, because it was chocolate and only 320 calories. That was all I ate, every day, except the days I treated myself to the extravagance of a salad, sometimes with a little tuna or the days I was so hungry that I had two quarts of Tasti D-Lite. Tasti D-Lite, after all, had milk in it, and milk had protein and calcium. Based on the model of my mother's program, I thought I did not need to eat anything else.

My mother thought it was great that I was losing so much weight. Everyone else around me responded positively, even ecstatically, to how thin I was. My ex-boyfriend, whom I wanted back desperately at that point, thought it was fantastic how "slender" I looked. I thought being thin would bring him back. And it did, for a while.

The second semester of my senior year, he and I broke up for good. I became deeply depressed. That semester, I also began writing my thesis. And I gained almost thirty pounds. The food I ate was a substitute for the love and the free time I had lost all at once. In the middle of that semester, I began to love my body as it was. I realized that I had been chasing after some male fantasy that never provided me with happiness, no matter how thin I was. I realized that feeling beautiful was about self-acceptance, not fitting into a certain pair of jeans. It is ironic that I came to love myself most and feel most beautiful only when I stopped trying to "be beautiful."

After college, I read *When Food Is Love* by Geneen Roth. Following suggestions in the book, I started to notice how much I ate and why. When I wanted to eat, I would pause just a few minutes to see what would happen. Usually, I would panic.

Over the next three years, I became extremely health conscious, and my food intake normalized. I was not compulsive, I stopped bingeing, and I exercised regularly but not obsessively. I accepted my body as it was and felt pretty good. But still, this "thin" phantom hung over my head. Somewhere in my brain, thinner still was better, and I still was not thin enough. Occasionally, I weighed myself and saw confirmation of how thin I had become. Then the mad desire to be as thin as I could be—to be "good"—kicked in. And in resistance to this sick impulse, I ate and ate until I gained back all the weight, returning me to a "safe" zone, where that thin-crazed mentality was far away.

Although my eating stabilized over the next few years, with my interest being in my own health, nutrition and sensual satisfaction, my athleticism was not based solely on the desire to be strong and to rid myself of stress. I also wanted to remain "fit." In other words, not fat. I wanted to be loved and recognized as attractive.

I did avoid the scale, wanting my relationship to my body to be about my own inner comfort, rather than external demarcations. What is it with allowing an inanimate object to determine how worthy we are, whether we are good or bad, deserving of love or not? When I worked out at the Y, I constantly fought the temptation to weigh myself. Eventually, staff moved the scale from where it was near my locker to another section of the locker room. The walk over to that section gave me the time, on more than one occasion, to talk sense into myself and march right back to where I came from.

When my back went out, I had the opportunity to deepen my understanding of my relationship to food, in all its complexity. As my friend Jessica and I talked about my eating issues, I realized my conflicting needs: I needed an abundance of good, nourishing, tasty, satisfying food in my house, to nurture my body and soul and counter the deprivation I felt throughout my life. But when I had food around, I felt obligated to eat it. I panicked about how much food I had because I did not want to waste it—again, back to childhood issues. I decided that I needed to have a rich abundance of food, to let myself waste. I needed to have the nutritious options without the feelings of obligation.

Following that conversation, I put several pints of ice cream, my favorite cookies and a plethora of healthy food in my kitchen. In response, I went back to my five-year-old tendencies of eating a spoonful of ice cream and putting the carton back in the freezer until the next day. For the first time in my life, I experienced ice cream going bad in my freezer. *Wow*! But it was not easy. I also tried *not* responding to compulsive food cravings that sprang up when I wasn't actually hungry. Sometimes I had intense physical withdrawal symptoms, as well as emotional and psychic pain when I fought these urges. And frequently, I didn't know whether I was actually hungry or not.

What did hunger feel like? I had eaten for so many other reasons, for so long. Sometimes I erred on the side of being too hungry, and I experienced my anorexic tendencies kicking in. Other times I erred on the side of eating too much, and I experienced my compulsive need for food. I cut myself some slack, as I figured out what healthy eating meant to me. I knew I was overcoming a lifetime of issues around this form of sustenance.

In my landmark conversation with Jessica, I shared how much time it would take to deal with these feelings instead of just eating some ice cream. "Of course!" she said, "and that's why people drink. Because it's guaranteed every time that if you take that four-ounce glass of vodka, your mood *will* change. You *will* feel better. It's fast, it's easy. And it doesn't deal with a damn thing." Seeing the analogy to alcoholism made me realize I do not want to use food in that same way. Once I started eating only when I was hungry, I realized how much I had used food to numb myself and how much that had slowed me down, kept me from being alive.

Over the years, my back pain has grown into a chronic (and, I am told, permanent) condition, at times so severe that I did not know which was worse—getting out of bed or staying in it. Often unable to function and deeply depressed from becoming a shadow of myself, I regularly turned to food, my lifelong friend and drug. Today I weigh close to two hundred pounds.

Although at first I was miserable about gaining so much weight, I have come to feel playful and defiant about it: I now find myself wanting to indulge in eating, as a way of actively rebelling against patriarchal madness. Where women have been taught deprivation, I want to practice decadence. Where we have been taught humiliation, I want to practice shamelessness. With a lusty appetite, I want to devour a big, hot, hunkin' piece of chocolate cake with double frosting, topped with a massive scoop of Häagen-Dazs vanilla ice cream. With a hot-as-hell attitude, I want to strut down the streets of Tel Aviv in flashy, skin-tight shirts and hip-hugging low-rider pants, proudly fifty to seventy pounds past the point when a gal is "allowed" to wear that shit.

Inspired by the thick-chick *Mizrahi* women[2] of Israel, who walk around with hot flesh hanging out all over the place, I recently ditched my potato-sack wardrobe and donned new attire, including my favorite item—flashy, gold-striped stretch pants and a black-lace crop top. I am enjoying the challenge and adventure of being fat in a fat-hating world. And yet, despite my political stance on size acceptance, I also want to be healthy.

I am far from having this food thing down. As if I were trying to pick cheese out of an overdone omelet, I am struggling to extricate the emotional and social issues from my reasons for eating, so that I am left with pure nutrition and pleasure.

Meanwhile, however, I have chosen to embrace own my "inner elephant" in all her glory—perhaps what Miriam was doing all along.

1 All names have been changed.

2 Women from North African or Middle Eastern Jewish backgrounds.

over the knife (or why i'll never be carnie wilson)
diane anderson-minshall

I was watching a true-crime show recently, *Cold Case Files*. I'm obsessed with *Cold Case Files* because I like to investigate the relationship between women and crime—as victims, as perpetrators, as law enforcement officers. And since I watch these shows so frequently, very little about murder actually shocks me. Until yesterday, that is. The episode centered on the case of a teenage girl who had been brutally killed years before. For over a decade, her family members had been desperately trying to bring her killer to justice. The man was indeed found, tried and convicted, and while he awaited his ultimate punishment on death row he gained a great deal of weight.

At the end of the show, the family ruminated on this bastard and decided that he had gotten his comeuppance—because he was now *so damn fat*. The man who raped, tortured and murdered their daughter met justice in their eyes, not because of his imprisonment, or impending execution, but because of his unfortunate girth. I was appalled at this premise, but clearly the producers, the family and presumably many viewers were not.

My shock and awe at this particularly low expression of our American obsession with weight was sharply interrupted by a call from a relative who, as usual, asked about my weight rather than my job, my partner or my life.

I'll admit it: I'm one of the forty million Americans who are considered obese. I spent my childhood in Southern California—trapped geographically between the blue-eyed blondes of the beach cities and the willowy, petite Asian girls of Little Saigon. I was neither, and have forever been saddled with a bit of a complex because of it. I know there are new options for fat people nowadays—weight-loss surgery, for one. I've seen it in action on my mom, my aunt, my sister and a handful of other friends. I even toyed with the idea myself—a few hours on the operating table and a lifetime of size-ten jeans. Who doesn't dream of that?

Most of my childhood friends were performers—Ngoc, a Vietnamese dancer; Anne, an Italian violinist; and Rhonda, a Gidget-like surfer who acted, danced and fronted her family's *Partridge Family*-style rock band. I was a chubby, Native-American, working-class kid with little talent, dark features and chunky female role models. I already knew my destiny was of the wide-hipped variety, but still I pined away for a life as a model-slash-actress. I used to clip pictures of svelte, dark-haired girls from the Sears catalogue, paste them together and photocopy them to pass around as my "portfolio." Nobody was fooled. At the rare audition where I wasn't shown the door immediately, I was still never cast as a princess. In *The Wizard of Oz*, Rhonda was cast as Dorothy; I, in my breakout role, was cast as the wicked witch.

I admit, in the back of my mind, I knew I could never be a model. I was short, plump. I wore a bra in second grade and started my period the next year. By the time I hit thirteen, I was almost as developed as I am now. By junior high, I was a bona fide fat girl. I wore clothes from the women's section, always envying my classmates who could wear cutoffs and tube tops year round. I'm a triple-D now—that's two sizes bigger than Lara Croft, thank you very much—which means I've *never ever* worn a tube top.

In high school, weight became the central focus of my skinny friends—a bulimic, an anorexic and a cutter. Though I got called "Thunder thighs," "Amazon" and "Tub-o-lard," I managed somehow to escape with my dignity intact, perhaps because I already accepted that I was the Fat Girl. You know her, the one with the pretty face. I knew I'd never be the It Girl, so I focused on being unique. And smart, and sexy, and successful. To this day, I think I was (and am).

But my family isn't so sure. My father hates fat chicks. It's a cliché, I know, but he really does despise fat women like Roseanne, Oprah and Rosie O'Donnell. He gives me the most encouragement when he sees I've lost a little bit of weight, and he seems to use my size as a warning to my younger sister. Sometimes she calls and says things like, "Dad says I'm going to be as fat as you, and no man will want me." My stepmother, also fat, battles to lose the same fifty pounds over and over again while my father lambastes her for her inability to shape up. I have two half-sisters—my father's other daughter is barely verging on chunky, and my mother's other daughter is nearly 350 pounds. Both young women loathe themselves and spend an inordinate amount of time focused on their weight, their size and their clothes.

I understand. I, too, feel hostage to my family's fears about the intersection between weight, size and desirability. Because of it, I end up doing incredibly inane things, like removing the size tags from clothes before visiting my family. I lie about my weight—to my stepmother, to the DMV.

The truth, though, is that when my family isn't around and I

diane anderson-minshall   **311**

don't have to buy new clothes—something that makes me cry because plus-size fashions are still so damn *unsexy*—I don't feel bad about my size *or* my weight.

Nearly every woman in my family possesses photos documenting her struggles with weight loss. I have them, too. I call them "before shots," and they feature me at a time and age when I thought I was fat, when other kids called me fat, but now looking at them I realize I was not. I have them from nearly every year of my life. I figure all fat people must have these. On a recent visit, my mom showed me one of her before photos—she was thirteen, right before she got pregnant the first time. She was probably a size twelve. Everyone already called her fat, and because of the shame she felt about her body, she found love, and a baby, in the arms of a stranger. At thirteen!

My mom has struggled with her weight all her life. I admit I've tried a few weight-loss techniques, too. I'm only human. I've tried cabbage soup, Slim Fast, grapefruit, fasting and vomiting after meals. None of it worked because I don't like vomit and I do like food. I've never been as devoted to attaining the perfect body as my mother. She's had a tummy tuck, a boob lift, liposuction and gastric bypass. She's tried almost every new diet in the last forty years and was so devoted to NutriSystem at one time that she became a spokesperson. Seeing her—and the other women in our lives—struggle so valiantly with controlling her body's natural destiny has had a profound effect on me and my sister.

My sister—the one who weighs 350 pounds—still tells a story about when she was two years old. My mother picked up dinner for us at Taco Bell. I was ten then. My mother was on diet pills, was skipping meals and didn't realize how much was reasonable for each of us kids to eat. So when I asked for two burritos, she said no. My two-year-old sister and I each got one small burrito. I stole half of my sister's burrito, and according to my sister, she's still hungry to this day. She is terrified of starving and, because of it, has gained so much weight she has violent headaches, vomits daily and is afraid to leave the house. Now she's going to have gastric bypass surgery.

I don't blame her. I know at least a dozen women who've had stomach stapling, gastric bypass or laparoscopic duodenal switch (a hybrid surgery that reduces the stomach and bypasses part of the bowel). I considered surgery myself, very briefly. Not because I think I'm unsexy or want to wear cooler clothes (the latter, though, is true), or because I'm unhealthy. I eat ten veggies a day (count 'em—ten!), go to the gym six days a week and probably can outrun many women my age. I'm not unhealthy, but the more I hear about the long-term effects of obesity, the more I worry about whether I am doing enough to *be* healthy. I worry that while today I'm okay with my size, what if in six years I'm carnival fat and won't be so self-actualized about it all. I worry that maybe it's not okay to be self-accepting. Perhaps somewhere deep inside I still believe what my family has told me: that self-acceptance actually means accepting defeat.

I love the fat-positive movement. I really do. I review movies and interview celebrities for a living, so an inordinate amount of my self-image is culled from the things that movie stars say. I know that most of them are thin because they have trainers and chefs and people who punish them severely when they try to sneak off to the fridge for anything more than an extra carrot stick. But when I talk to a chubby celeb who's cool with it all, I wonder why I ever pondered losing weight in the first place. I spoke with Camryn Manheim a few years ago and asked her if she'd take a pill—if one such pill existed—that could safely make her a size ten. She said yes, but with her answer she reminded me that no such pill exists, may never exist, and that our lives are too fleeting to spend time worrying about getting into a size-ten dress. She should know—she became a drug addict trying to make it happen.

diane anderson-minshall   **313**

So I got off the phone and threw out the Slim Fast and started with my Fat Pride talk again. I do it more frequently than I'd like to admit: I go up and down about the weight issue. Never in public, though. To my peers, my colleagues, I'm always completely proud of my body image, my size. I'm there at the fat chick conferences, watching the movies about chubby girls overcoming obstacles (like *Secret Society*, my new favorite movie about female sumo wrestlers) and generally sending a shout-out to any actresses who dare go bare above a size-fourteen. And I admit, I like fat girls. I think Anna Nicole Smith is about as hot as they come.

Still, even when I feel good, other people have a way of imposing social expectations on me. One respected employer told me my size would always limit my career. An ex-lover proclaimed to be sickened by how I had "let myself go." Sometimes teenagers holler so loud that I look, and they tell me—more than once—that I'm too fat to wear what I'm wearing.

I'm approached constantly by weight-loss devotees. Last summer, on vacation in New Orleans (I happened to have the misfortune of visiting the Big Easy during an Herbalife convention), no less than a dozen women approached me with stickers, pamphlets and buttons that encouraged me to "ask how to lose fifty pounds." I chose not to. Yesterday at the YMCA, a complete stranger in my aquasize class wanted to tell me about her incredible transformation at the hands of Jenny Craig, and last week—after remarking that I look healthier than in the past—my stepmother suggested I try Weight Watchers. These people are always so convinced their weight-loss technique, their guru, is so freakin' good that it will immediately transform me into Jennifer Aniston. What scares me is their podlike persona post–weight loss: I'm scared to death that one of these days my parents will have me kidnapped like some cult member and deprogrammed by Jenny Craig and in the end I'll sound like Carnie Wilson. Carnie, you probably know, was a proud fat activist (and singer) who had gastric bypass surgery, lost over 150 pounds (so she looks just like her sister Wendy), posed for *Playboy* and now insists that she would have died without the surgery. Carnie, who once made a workout video for plus-size women, was on the covers of both *BBW* (*Big, Beautiful Women*) and *Playboy* within a five-year span. She makes it sound like a good thing, but I'm sad to think she had to lose nearly two hundred pounds to be considered sexy. Still, I secretly wonder if she knows something that I don't.

Last year, my grandmother died of weight-related diabetes, and my mother, my aunt and several friends and colleagues each had some form of stomach-reduction surgery. I don't have an insatiable desire for junk food, I'm pretty fit and active, and I have a reunion coming up—all of which, I presume, make me an ideal candidate for surgery. So in the wake of all this weight-loss talk I decided I would at least do some research into weight-loss surgery.

What I found online was a community of fat people waiting for a surgical cure to their inability to fit society's crazy expectations. They have message boards with "before" photos and long diatribes about getting around insurance, how long the surgery takes and what can go wrong. Mostly, though, there are thousands and thousands of postings from unhappy fat people who are waiting for their turn on the operating table, and are willing to risk death in order to stop being treated like a goddamn fat person in America. Some do have health issues—debilitating back pain, diabetes, sleep apnea. Many can't seem to maintain an exercise routine, and even those who have enough willpower to scale back their eating haven't seen a dramatic reduction.

In fact, doctors say that with proper diet and exercise, most fat people will only lose 5 to 10 percent of their excess body weight. That's not much of a drop if you're trying to go from 250 to 120. Most of the folks awaiting weight-loss surgery have had a lifetime of growing to the size they are, and they very much look forward to losing 85 percent of that excess weight in the first year. To them, being fat is so socially stigmatizing that they'd risk death to change it. A new study by the University of California concluded that obese kids feel so ostracized by peers that their quality of life is no better than that of a child undergoing chemotherapy treatment for cancer.* Being fat, kids feel, is *as bad as* dying of cancer!

In reality, though, one out of every two hundred people—about 5 percent—who have a gastric bypass operation *will* die from it.

To my mom, that was a risk worth taking. Her insurance footed the bill, though a lot of people are taking out $30,000 loans to pay for the operation. Thankfully, she didn't have complications from her surgery, but because she is an obsessive eater—a food addict, if you will—she spent much of the first several months sobbing because she could no longer eat the quantities, or types, of food she enjoyed. With her new stomach, she would literally become violently ill if she ate food for comfort or celebration. I could never consciously limit my food choices for the rest of my life—my God, what if my new stomach didn't like sushi?

Death isn't the only risk of gastric bypass surgery, and most of the side effects sound absolutely dreadful. Almost 90 percent of patients suffer post-surgery depression. Recovery is painful (think severe gastric distress) and recuperation takes about three months (which includes a lot of vomiting and diarrhea while you figure out what your new digestive system can handle). Short- and long-term complications can include bleeding, abscesses, leaks and infections, pulmonary embolus, gallstones, dumping (a common side effect that includes diarrhea, vomiting, nausea, bloating and dizziness), ulceration of the small bowel (this occurs in about 20 percent of all patients), bile reflux, arthritis, osteoporosis and hernia.

My online research was disheartening—it's sad to see so many people hindered by folds of flesh—but it did confirm what I already knew: Gastric bypass surgery isn't for everyone, and it certainly isn't for me. A lot of fat activists think it's the coward's way out, making people size traitors, so to speak. I don't, because I understand how much social pressure comes with having a plus-size body. But I like my chunky thighs, huge knockers and giant ass. When I walk out of the dressing room in new size-twenty bell-bottoms and say, "Does my ass look big?" I'm honestly hoping for the answer to be "Yes." I'm never going to look like Calista Flockhart or Demi Moore or even Bridget Jones (who really isn't fat anyway), but when I block out all those other voices and listen to my own, I like myself—just as I am.

*Jeffrey B. Schwimmer, MD, Tasha M. Burwinkle, MA and James W. Varni, PhD, "Health-Related Quality of Life of Severely Obese Children and Adolescents," *Journal of the American Medical Association* (2003) 289:1813–1819.

padding it:
why i don't need a plus-size maxi pad
wendy shanker

I'm pumping up and down on the elliptical trainer at the gym when I see the TV commercial for the first time. A beautiful, bountiful blond woman coos about Always Maximum Protection with Flexi-Wings, a maxi pad designed especially for women size-fourteen and up. She wonders if I know that most maxi pads are designed for a size-six and below.

I stop pumping and start thinking. First: *Cool! Finally a company understands that I belong to a special market with special needs!*

Then: *Do my special needs really include a plus-size maxi pad?*

I have a long list of stuff I'd demand before plus-size pads come into play. Like knee-high boots, for example. Sure would be nice to find a pair at Bloomingdale's or Macy's that fits over my well-muscled calves. Women of all sizes without stick-thin legs want 'em, too.

Speaking of muscles, is it too much to ask for an athletic store to carry sports bras or exercise clothing in a size twelve or higher? America can't wait to supersize my fries, but when I want to downsize my thighs I have to special order from a catalog or website.

My curvaceous sisters would like to try on a sample wedding dress that doesn't cloak them in humiliation. We'd also like to ride in airplane seats that actually accommodate the typical American tushie.

I'd like to buy a bra at Victoria's Secret, but I can barely find a double-D, let alone the E that I need. And I appreciate that the Gap and Old Navy are sizing up a bit, now making sixteens, eighteens and twenties, but could they order more than one per store? According to *Grace Woman,* a plus-size fashion magazine, seven out of ten women buying at their local Gap will be grabbing a size-twelve or larger. Small wonder—60 percent of American women wear a size fourteen or higher.

See? Lots of needs for my size market! So why a plus-size pad? There's no biological connection between body size and menstrual flow. So Always Maximum Protection isn't necessarily designed for a heavier flow, but for a wider diameter of protection, in other words, for extra-large undies.

Can you say offensive? Just because a woman wears a size fourteen or up doesn't mean she's running around in a giant pair of granny panties. That lame image has been the punch line of one too many adolescent comedy flicks. I wear sexy, fitted panties in a wide variety of colors and styles. Sure, my skivvies have a wider waistband than those of the size-six girl, but the strip of cloth that is pad-coverable is pretty much the same minimal width in any pair of panties (except the thong, which is an entirely different type of torture).

A press rep at Procter & Gamble, the parent company of Always, assured me that the product was created in response to demand from a plus-size consumer website. So maybe there are some of you out there who want or need a wider product like this one. But girls, can you say uncomfortable? Walking around in one of those pads, I felt like I had a throw pillow stuffed down my pants.

If Always assumes that a bigger girl needs a bigger pad, what about petite women? Like Sarah Jessica Parker, with her size-zero body? Will Always create a mini pad to accommodate her teeny-weeny vageeny? There's no correlation between dress size and genitalia size. You'd never assume that all plus-size men need plus-size condoms for their plus-size penises—though I'm sure they wouldn't mind if you did.

When I hear *plus-size pad*, I think *plus-size vagina*. And that's a major setback. I don't want anyone to think that hidden in these trousers is a big, fat, crazy vagina that's going to swallow you up if you get too close. We've worked so hard to get beautiful, sexy clothes designed to fit our beautiful, sexy bodies. And when we dress stylishly and walk proudly and speak loudly, we affirm that we may wear a bigger size, but sexually, we're just like any other women. We have the same parts, pleasures, concerns and needs.

So I don't need an extra-large spoon, because I don't have an extra-large mouth. I don't need an extra-large stick of deodorant, because my armpit acreage is perfectly average. And I don't need an extra-wide maxi pad, because I have a perfectly fabulous, perfectly normal vagina.

Thanks, but no thanks.

body image mad libs: uncover your fairy tale
ophira edut

Participants should fill out the answers to these questions without knowing how these answers will be used. After everyone has answered these questions, pass out the answer sheet. If using this in a workshop, the moderator should read from the answer sheet while a selected participant fills in the blanks by reading her answers when directed.

1. **Your name:**

2. **Name of the first person who ever criticized your appearance or made you feel self-conscious:**

3. **What did that person say?**

4. **Your most frustrating or least favorite body part or feature:**

5. **How you feel limited by this body part or feature (e.g., I can't wear miniskirts, I can't go swimming or I'll ruin my hair):**

6. **One thing you'd do if you didn't have to deal with this issue:**

7. **How you'd change the world to be more body friendly if you could:**

(Answer sheet on next page)

body image fairy tale
(mad lib answer sheet)

Once upon a time, there was a beautiful princess named YOUR NAME. She was smart, funny and confident. Then one day, a mischievous wizard named PERSON WHO FIRST CRITICIZED YOUR APPEARANCE came along. He was feeling a bit threatened that day, so he told the princess WHAT THAT PERSON SAID.

Well, you can imagine that those magically *un*delicious words cast quite a spell on the princess. In fact, the spell was so powerful, even the wizard didn't understand its effects. Soon, YOUR NAME began to feel less like a princess and more like an ugly stepsister. Over time, she grew to hate her YOUR MOST FRUSTRATING BODY PART OR FEATURE. She told herself HOW YOU FEEL LIMITED BY THIS BODY PART OR FEATURE and lived as though that were true. At times her obsession was so great, the whole kingdom seemed to be staring critically at her BODY PART.

One day the princess tried to release herself from the spell. She decided to do one thing she'd always believed she couldn't: ONE THING YOU'D DO IF YOU DIDN'T HAVE TO DEAL WITH THIS ISSUE. When she stepped out to do it, she was terrified—she was sure everyone would laugh and point and make cruel comments. But she held her head up, smiled and looked people in the eye. And she discovered something strange: Most people didn't really notice. See, all the people in the kingdom were under their own spells—even the magicians were under a spell. They were too busy worrying about their bodies, too.

From that day on, the princess discovered that she had a choice: She could fight the spell or live under its power. She decided to take on one simple but spell-shattering act to show the world her message: HOW YOU'D CHANGE THE WORLD TO BE MORE BODY FRIENDLY IF YOU COULD. Eventually, people in the kingdom noticed a change in the princess, and a few became inspired to try breaking their own spells. It wasn't

322   curriculum

easy, but it was a lot more fun than the old way.

And they all lived a little less neurotically ever after.

write your own autobiography:
changing the body story in your head

pia guerrero

Here lies Billy Jean.
Her thighs were thin, her legs were lean.

How do you want to be remembered? Our words, actions and thoughts are writing our autobiographies every day. Why not write your own life story and document the amazing things you've created and experienced? Write about the time you got a well-deserved promotion or acknowledgment. Or the time you averted disaster by using your 007-style tenacity. What about your everyday victories—like supporting yourself through college, making a difference in people's lives or fixing just about anything around the house without once wishing you had a boyfriend to do the job? What incredible things have you witnessed? Is there something you've endured that would make the average mortal blush at the thought? What do you think is just really damn cool about yourself? Write down your successes and your challenges and weave a story that's unique to you. When you're finished, type it up and post it on your wall next to your mirror. (Feel free to add photos, glitter, funky fonts or whatever maximizes your enjoyment of it!) Whenever you feel yourself slipping into the abyss of body obsession, stop, take three deep breaths and read your autobiography. It should remind you that you're more than your butt—which, unless you're Jennifer Lopez, nobody will care about after you're gone anyway.

curriculum

quiz: how well do you know the media?

pia guerrero

1. How many ads (television, newspaper, magazine, Internet, etc.)
does the average American view each day?

    a) 50

    b) 200

    c) 3,000

    d) 10,000

2. On average, how many hours of TV do kids watch each week?

    a) 7 hours per week

    b) 14 hours per week

    c) 28 hours per week

    d) 42 hours per week

3. Watching TV is the number-one after-school activity for what
two age groups?

    a) 3–6 years old

    b) 6–10 years old

    c) 10–17 years old

    d) 17–19 years old

4. Do kids spend more time in the classroom or in front of the
TV?

    a) The classroom

    b) The TV

    c) Same

5. How many years has the average seventy-year-old spent in

325

front of a TV?

   a) 70

   b) 10

   c) 40

   d) 5

6. By the end of high school how many violent scenes (on TV, in movies and in video games) has the average person seen?

   a) 1,000

   b) 4,500

   c) 100

   d) 200,000

7. An average of five violent acts per hour are shown on prime-time TV. How many are shown per hour during Saturday morning children's programming?

   a) 1

   b) 7

   c) 15

   d) 26

8. The average child sees twenty thousand TV commercials a year, so by age twenty-one the average viewer would have seen how many commercials?

   a) 95,000

   b) 1 million

   c) 15 million

9. How many hours of commercials will children see if they watch TV for five hours?

a) At least an hour

b) At least 2 hours

c) At least 4 hours

10. Children who watch four hours or more of TV a day have which of the following problems?

a) Poor reading skills

b) Don't play well with others

c) Have no other hobbies

d) All of the above

11. At what age does a person start to understand the purpose of commercial advertisements?

a) 6 months old

b) 6 years old

c) 16 years old

d) 60 years old

12. What percentage of girls who watch TV frequently describe themselves as too fat, even though their weight is normal?

a) None

b) 25 percent

c) 50 percent

d) 100 percent

13. A 1998 study conducted at the University of Central Florida in Orlando found that in a sample of thirty popular video game titles—all manufactured by game giants Sega and Nintendo—21 percent depicted violence directed specifically at women. What percentage portrayed women as sex objects?

a) 8 percent

b) 18 percent

c) 28 percent

d) 100 percent

14. Video games reflect diversity in the American population accurately.

True

False

15. How are teenage girls most often portrayed in the media?

a) Intelligent human beings

b) Obsessed with boys, shopping and looks

c) In a variety of shapes and sizes

d) All of the above

16. Magazine ads showing female models have an immediate negative effect on a woman's self-esteem.

True

False

17. Of the publications that follow, which three have the most cigarette advertisements?

a) *Newsweek, Time, People*

b) *Jet, Ebony, Essence*

c) *Glamour, Elle, Vogue*

18. Advertising for contraceptives and birth control is not allowed on American TV networks.

True

False

19. American TV is extremely sexually suggestive.
☐ True
☐ False

ANSWERS:
☐ 1. c; **2.** c; **3.** b and c; **4.** b; **5.** b; **6.** d; **7.** d; **8.** b; **9.** a; **10.** d; **11.** b; **12.** c; **13.** c; **14.** False (Nearly all the human characters found in young

children's games were white, and female characters were severely under-represented, accounting for only 16 percent of human characters. Additionally, when female characters did appear they were portrayed as props or bystanders 50 percent of the time. Almost all African-American females were victims of violence; African-American and Latino men were typically athletes; and Asian/Pacific Islanders were usually wrestlers or fighters. In addition, there were no Latina characters.); **15.** b; **16.** True (After viewing the "ideal" woman shown in twenty magazine ads, a female focus group responded immediately with depression and hostility.); **17.** b; **18.** True; **19.** True (The average American teen views over 14,000 sexual references annually. Less than 175 deal responsibly with human sexuality.).

Sources: *Deadly Persuasion* by Jean Kilbourne; Center for Media Education; Anne E. Becker, M.D., Ph.D.; Wired.com; Planned Parenthood Federation of America; NOW Foundation; University of Minnesota Children, Youth and Family Consortium; *International Journal of Eating Disorders*; Children Now's report "Fair Play? Violence, Gender and Race in Video Games"

curriculum

a guide to bodylovin' organizations

compiled by pia guerrero

activism & feminism

About-Face

www.about-face.org

This San Francisco group combats distorted images of women in the media by giving popular ads a "face-lift."

Feminist.com

www.feminist.com

This site features a clearinghouse of feminist links, a women-owned business directory and the advice column "Ask Amy" by *Body Outlaws* contributor Amy Richards.

The Feminist Majority Foundation

www.feminist.org

The organization that now publishes *Ms.* magazine offers information on international women's news, politics and organizing efforts. The site features a student activism section and a feminist career center with job listings.

Media Watch

www.mediawatch.com

This organization challenges racism, sexism and violence in the media through education and action. This group also offers lectures and a video to teach kids media literacy.

National Love Your Body Day

www.nowfoundation.org/issues/health/lybdkit

This site provides local information and kits for this national day of action (sponsored by NOW), which encourages people to organize local body-positive projects and to speak out against ads and images of women that are offensive, harmful, dangerous and disrespectful.

News We Can Use

www.newswecanuse.com

This site, updated one to two times a week, gleans women-centered headlines from many major and alternative media sources, and covers politics, health, the workplace, reproductive rights and more. The information is also available in email form.

Women's Sports Foundation

www.womenssportsfoundation.org

This national nonprofit is dedicated to increasing Title IX opportunities for girls and women in sports and fitness through education, advocacy, recognition and grants.

body image and self-esteem

Body Positive

www.bodypositive.com

This site, dedicated to "boosting body image at any weight," offers resources for kids, parents, therapists and educators, and hosts the Health at Any Size web ring.

Love Yourself Now

www.loveyourbody.org

Created by this book's editor, Ophira Edut, this site serves to extend the mission of *Body Outlaws* and to announce new bodylovin' projects.

eating disorders

Anorexia Nervosa and Related Eating Disorders, Inc. (ANRED)

www.anred.com

ANRED provides self-help, recovery and prevention advice for people with eating disorders. The website includes survivor stories and poems, a self-test to check if you're at risk for an eating disorder, advice for parents and partners, sections on obesity and men's eating disorders, and definitions of lesser-known conditions, such as body dysmorphic disorder and compulsive exercising.

Colours of Ana

www.coloursofana.com

This website about women of color and eating disorders is loaded with cutting-edge international research, articles and links. Published by a "black eating disordered woman" in the U.K., the site also features forums, artwork and survivor stories.

National Eating Disorders Association (NEDA)

www.nationaleatingdisorders.org

This activist group sponsors Eating Disorders Awareness Week, along with many other projects, such as the Media Watchdog Program, the GO GIRLS! high school curriculum and a curriculum that teaches kids in grades four through six how to understand and resist unhealthy body messages. NEDA also offers a toll-free helpline at (800) 931-2237.

The Renfrew Center Foundation

www.renfrew.org

In 1985, the Renfrew Center became the first U.S. facility to treat eating disorders, and thirty thousand women and girls have been treated there since. The foundation now offers educational material (some of which can be downloaded free from the website), research journals, counseling resources, conferences and more.

Something-Fishy

www.something-fishy.org

This website about eating disorders, including anorexia, bulimia and compulsive overeating, features live chats with experts, a "memorial wall" with tributes to people who have died of eating disorders and a treatment finder with listings for many U.S. and international recovery centers, dieticians and therapists.

health

Black Women's Health

www.blackwomenshealth.com

Dedicated to "the health and wellness of today's African American Woman," this site provides everything from a physician locator to information on health issues affecting black women.

Estronaut: A Forum for Women's Health

www.estronaut.com

This top-rated women's health website covers a wide range of issues affecting women of all ages and offers weekly health chats at AOL keyword "Electra."

National Alliance for Hispanic Health

www.hispanichealth.org

This resource organization advocates for the health and well-being of Hispanics. Among its offerings are a bilingual website covering health issues by topic, a newsletter and Su Familia, a toll-free family health helpline at (866) 783-2645.

National Women's Health Information Center (NWHIC)

www.4women.gov

From the U.S. Department of Health and Human Services' Office on Women's Health comes a comprehensive website and resource database and a toll-free call center offering reliable health information.

Our Bodies, Ourselves

www.ourbodiesourselves.org

This bilingual site is packed with health resources from the Boston Women's Health Collective.

Planned Parenthood Federation of America

www.plannedparenthood.org

This is the ultimate resource for information about reproductive health, sexuality and contraception.

size acceptance

International Size Acceptance Association (ISAA)

www.size-acceptance.org

This international group's mission is to promote size acceptance and fight size discrimination throughout the world by means of advocacy and visible, lawful actions. This growing organization has chapters in the United States, Canada, Europe, Asia and the Middle East.

National Association to Advance Fat Acceptance (NAAFA)

www.naafa.org

This activist group offers a clearinghouse of legal, health and organizing information about fat people's rights.

Radiance

www.radiancemagazine.com

Radiance: The Magazine for Large Women is no longer in print, but the website lives on, including information about the Kids Project, an initiative to help kids lead happy, healthy lives regardless of size.

Size Wise

www.sizewise.com

This size-acceptance search engine is full of interesting links on everything from dating to entertainment to activism.

cosmetic surgery & the beauty industry

Cosmetic Surgery: The Cutting Edge of Commercial Medicine in America
by Deborah A. Sullivan (Rutgers University Press, 2001)
This book delves into the social and economic payoffs of beauty, the marketing of cosmetic surgery through women's magazines and the effects of the plastic surgery boom on the entire medical industry.

Hope in a Jar: The Making of America's Beauty Culture
by Kathy Peiss (Owl Books, 1999)
Profiling both black and white cosmetic inventors, like Madame C. J. Walker and Helena Rubenstein, this book looks at "how women created the cosmetics industry and how cosmetics created the modern woman."

Venus Envy: The History of Cosmetic Surgery
by Elizabeth Haiken (Johns Hopkins University Press, 2000)
This book traces the twentieth-century development of cosmetic surgery, along with its politics and complexities. It also features outrageous graphics, like an ad for penis enlargement.

eating disorders

The Broken Mirror: Understanding and Treating Body Dysmorphic Disorder
by Katharine A. Phillips, M.D. (Oxford University Press, 1998)

Phillips offers a comprehensive look into the root causes of body dysmorphic disorder, a psychological condition that causes sufferers to obsess over perceived appearance flaws.

Freedom from Compulsion: An Eating Disorder Workbook
by Tim Sheehan, Ph.D. and Sue Hoisington, Psy.D. (Hazelden, 2001)
Clear, concise and easy to use, this workbook helps readers understand and come to terms with food addiction and eating disorders such as anorexia, bulimia, binge eating and compulsive overeating.

A Hunger So Wide and So Deep: A Multiracial View of Women's Eating Problems
by Becky Thompson (University of Minnesota Press, 1996)
Through interviews with women from a range of cultural backgrounds, Thompson takes a rare and vital look at the influence of ethnicity, assimilation, abuse and trauma on the quiet struggle of women of color to feel at home in their bodies.

When Your Child Has an Eating Disorder: A Step-by-Step Workbook for Parents and Other Caregivers
by Abigail H. Natenshon (Jossey-Bass, 1999)
With an emphasis on working with professionals, this book offers practical solutions for parents to help heal eating disorders in children.

ethnicity

Black, White and Jewish: Autobiography of a Shifting Self
by Rebecca Walker (Riverhead Books, 2002)
This compelling memoir is both a personal and an analytical look at the author's journey growing up biracial in a world obsessed with race.

The Flying Camel: Essays on Identity by Women of Middle Eastern and North African Jewish Heritage
edited by Loolwa Khazzoom (Seal Press, 2004)
An anthology of writing by Jewish women from "a world often hidden from view."

I'm the One That I Want
by Margaret Cho (Ballantine Books, 2002)
Korean-American comedian Cho hilariously details her body struggles and the entertainment industry's pressure on actresses to be thin.

Women of Sand and Myrrh
by Hanan al-Shaykh (Anchor, 1992)
Bringing attention to voices seldom heard, this novel highlights the very different lives, feelings and choices of four women living in the Middle East.

Yell-Oh Girls! Emerging Voices Explore Culture, Identity, and Growing Up Asian American
edited by Vickie Nam (Quill, 2001)
This collection of essays, poems and letters by Asian American girls and women ages fifteen to twenty-two replaces myth with new realities, on topics such as body image, interracial friendships, adoption, sexuality and more.

Yentl's Revenge: The Next Wave of Jewish Feminism
edited by Danya Ruttenberg (Seal Press, 2001)
Covering everything from religion to body image to transgender issues to the "JAP" stereotype, these Gen-X women present a new model for what it means to be Jewish and female today.

feminism & activism

Black Feminist Thought: Knowledge, Consciousness, and the Politics of Empowerment
by Patricia Hill Collins (Routledge, 2000)
Based on the author's experience as a black woman and her education as a sociologist, this book considers a modern marriage between feminism and traditional black women's themes, such as hair, gossip food and more.

Colonize This! Young Women of Color on Today's Feminism
edited by Daisy Hernández and Bushra Rehman (Seal Press, 2002)
This impressive array of first-person accounts adds a much-needed dimension to the ongoing dialogue about race and gender.

Cunt: A Declaration of Independence
by Inga Muscio (Seal Press, 2002)
Drawing on research and her own experience, Muscio reclaims the word *cunt* as a source of beauty and power, and provides insight and solutions regarding why women are so alienated from the very thing that defines them.

Feminism Is for Everybody: Passionate Politics
by bell hooks (South End Press, 2000)
This book offers insight into a movement that is often misunderstood.

Kiss My Tiara: How to Rule the World as a Smartmouth Goddess
by Susan Jane Gilman (Warner Books, 2001)
With chapters like "Never Mind a Penis, We'll Take a Bigger Paycheck" and "If You Can't Order Dessert, You Can't Ask for a Raise," *Body Outlaws* contributor Gilman breaks down the real deal on men, body image, money and more.

Listen Up: Voices from the Next Feminist Generation
edited by Barbara Findlen (Seal Press, 2001)
This collection of essays is a must-read for those interested in women's studies and third-wave feminist perspectives on topics such as career, culture, identity, sexuality and gender.

Manifesta: Young Women, Feminism and the Future
by Jennifer Baumgardner and Amy Richards (Farrar Straus & Giroux, 2000)
A provocative exploration of the feminist movement, warts and all, that will leave young feminists with a better understanding of the movement and its evolution.

girls & teens

The Body Project: An Intimate History of American Girls
by Joan Jacobs Brumberg (Vintage Books, 1998)
Citing excerpts from girls' diaries throughout the twentieth century, Brumberg captures the way teenage girls have fixated on their bodies, making appearance into a "project."

Deal With It! A Whole New Approach to Your Body, Brain and Life as a gURL
by Esther Drill, Heather McDonald and Rebecca Odes (Pocket Books, 1999)
This frank, funky gem from the creators of the website gURL.com combines must-know facts, amazing illustrations and excerpts from site members' actual email conversations.

GirlSource: A Book by and for Young Women about Relationships, Rights, Futures, Bodies, Minds, and Souls edited by GirlSource Inc. Staff (Ten Speed Press, 2003)

One of the few books written by and for urban girls, this is a great resource for teens on STD prevention, illegal drugs, getting a job and more.

GirlWise: How to Be Confident, Capable, Cool, and in Control
by Julia Devillers (Prima Publishing, 2002)

Devillers offers a witty and hip book of advice for teenage girls struggling to survive the socially awkward and emotionally trying times of adolescence.

Ophelia Speaks: Adolescent Girls Write about Their Search for Self
edited by Sara Shandler (Perennial, 1999)

This diverse collection of essays, stories and poems by teenage girls provides real insight into the common struggle for identity and acceptance growing up female in American society.

Real Girl/Real World: Tools for Finding Your True Self
by Heather M. Gray and Samantha Phillips (Seal Press, 1998)

This book is a great resource on issues that face teen girls today, like body image, feminism, sexuality and health.

Sugar in the Raw: Voices of Young Black Girls in America
edited by Rebecca Carroll (Crown Publishing, 1997)

A humorous collection of stories from more than fifteen girls on what it means to be young, black and female. Topics include self-esteem, identity, racism, prejudice and relationships.

health

Body and Soul: The Black Women's Guide to Physical Health and Well-Being
by Linda Villarosa (Harper Trade, 1994)
A former *Essence* editor, Villarosa offers a comprehensive health and wellness guide tailored to African-American women.

For Women Only! Your Guide to Health and Empowerment
by Gary Null and Barbara Seaman (Seven Stories Press, 2001)
This hefty and thorough guide covers the history of women's health *and* gives health info, including alternative medicine, preventative treatments and health issues exclusive to women.

Our Bodies, Ourselves for the New Century
by the Boston Women's Health Collective (Touchstone, 1998)
No woman should be without this ultimate resource on women's health and well-being, which has been providing women's health information for decades.

Salud: A Latina's Guide to Total Health
by Jane L. Delgado (RAYO, 2002)
Written by the head of the National Alliance for Hispanic Health and the National Hispanic Women's Health Initiative, this book covers everything from traditional to alternative therapies, from medical to spiritual healing, for a population that is often overlooked by the U.S. healthcare system.

media & cultural criticism

Am I Thin Enough Yet? The Cult of Thinness and the

Commercialization of Identity
by Sharlene Hesse-Biber (Oxford University Press, 1997)
This book provides a look at the economic and social pressures that cause women to be obsessed with the pursuit of thinness.

The Beauty Myth: How Images of Beauty Are Used Against Women
by Naomi Wolf (Perennial, 2002)
In this classic feminist missive, Wolf exposes how media, advertising and cosmetics industries have created an unattainable beauty standard that leaves women hating their bodies.

Deadly Persuasion: Why Women and Girls Must Fight the Addictive Power of Advertising
by Jean Kilbourne (Free Press, 1999)
Tired of scantily clad women advertising alcohol and tobacco? In this penetrating look at the advertising industry, Kilbourne argues that people's attitudes are more influenced by advertising than we realize.

Don't Believe the Hype: Fighting Cultural Misinformation about African-Americans
by Farai Chideya (Plume, 1995)
Filled with statistics and examples, this book reveals stereotypes of African Americans that are perpetuated in our society as a result of media misinformation.

No Fat Chicks: How Big Business Profits by Making Women Hate Their Bodies—and How to Fight Back
by Terry Poulton (Birch Lane Press, 1997)

After losing sixty-five pounds in six months, Terry Poulton became the subject of a magazine cover story. She also destroyed her gallbladder in the process and woke up to the diet industry's manipulations.

men

The Adonis Complex: The Secret Crisis of Male Body Obsession
by Harrison G. Pope, Katherine A. Phillips and Roberto Olivardia (Free Press, 2000)
Think women are the only ones who obsess about their thighs? This book examines how men are now striving to meet a media-driven masculine body idea.

Bears on Bears: Interviews and Discussions
by Ron Jackson Suresha (Alyson, 2002)
This candid collection profiles the thoughts and experiences of gay men who buck the waxed, hardbody ideal and celebrate themselves in their hairy, hefty "bear"-like natural state.

Getting It On Online: Cyberspace, Gay Male Sexuality, and Embodied Identity
by John Edward Campbell (Haworth Press, 2004)
This book provides a look at how online interactions shape gay men's sense of themselves and their bodies.

Making Weight: Men's Conflicts with Food, Weight, Shape and Appearance
by Arnold Andersen, Leigh Cohn and Thomas Holbrook (Gurze Books, 2000)

This is one of the few guides for men on how to heal from body dis-satisfaction and eating disorders.

The Male Body: A New Look at Men in Public and in Private
by Susan Bordo (Farrar, Straus & Giroux, 2000)
This candid analysis challenges Americans to reconsider their puri-tanical views of the male body.

Males with Eating Disorders
edited by Arnold E. Anderson, M.D. (Routledge, 1990)
This thorough book of research on men and eating disorders covers both gay and heterosexual men.

parenting & pregnancy

Breeder: Real-Life Stories from the New Generation of Mothers
edited by Ariel Gore and Bee Lavender (Seal Press, 2001)
This book on motherhood for our generation is a great read with real stories by real women.

The Girlfriends' Guide to Pregnancy
by Vicki Iovine (Pocket Books, 1995)
This must-read for pregnant women provides detailed information on what to expect during the physical and emotional journey through pregnancy and childbirth.

The Hip Mama Survival Guide: Advice from the Trenches on Pregnancy, Childbirth, Cool Names, Clueless Doctors, Potty Training and Toddler Avengers
by Ariel Gore (Hyperion, 1998)
Written by the founder of *Hip Mama* magazine, this hilarious book

relieves modern-day moms of the pressure to be perfect, inspiring them to invent motherhood on their own terms.

Hot Mama: How to Have a Babe and Be a Babe
by Karen Salmansohn (Chronicle Books, 2003)
This cute gift book will uplift any expecting mama who deserves to feel like the goddess that she is.

The Mother Trip: Hip Mama's Guide to Staying Sane in the Chaos of Motherhood
by Ariel Gore (Seal Press, 2000)
In a book that combines self-help, cultural criticism and advice, Ariel Gore bucks the stereotypes of what a "good mother" should be and offers support to mothers who break the mold.

The Ultimate Guide to Pregnancy for Lesbians: Tips and Techniques from Conception to Birth: How to Stay Sane and Care for Yourself
by Rachel Pepper (Cleis Press, 1999)
For the woman who wants to get pregnant without a male partner, this guide covers the gamut, from choosing a sperm donor to protecting your legal rights to enjoying life as either a single-mama or two-mama family.

With Child: Wisdom and Traditions for Pregnancy, Birth, and Motherhood
by Deborah Jackson (Chronicle Books, 1999)
If you believe that it takes a village to raise a child, then this book—infused with childbearing wisdom and practices used by communities of women across the globe—is for you.

bodylovin' bookshelf   347

sexuality

Big Big Love: A Sourcebook on Sex for People of Size and Those Who Love Them
by Hanne Blank (Greenery Press, 2000)
Whether you're fat, thin or somewhere in between, this book will expand your definition of sexy beyond the media ideal.

Dilemmas of Desire: Teenage Girls Talk about Sexuality
by Deborah L. Tolman (Harvard University Press, 2002)
A study based on numerous interviews with teenage girls, this is the first book of its kind to make the case that girls who are in touch with their sexual desires make wiser choices about their sexuality.

The New Good Vibrations Guide to Sex
by Cathy Winks and Anne Semans (Cleis Press, 1997)
The owners of San Francisco's first woman-owned sex toy shop offer an informative classic that covers safe sex, hot talk, erotica, romance, desire, toys and everything a woman needs to know about her own pursuit of pleasure.

Sexy at Any Size: The Real Woman's Guide to Dating and Romance
by Katie Arons (Fireside, 1999)
This book proves that sexiness is about confidence, not calories.

When the Earth Moves: Women and Orgasm
by Mikaya Heart (Celestial Arts, 1998)
Heart discusses the various physical, emotional, mental and spiritual aspects of sex. She reminds us that each of us is unique—right down to our orgasm—and we can learn to enjoy who we are instead of comparing ourselves to others.

size acceptance

The Fat Girl's Guide to Life
by Wendy Shanker (Bloomsbury, 2004)
Comedian and humorist Wendy Shanker proves in this hilarious and
enlightening book that women can take charge and live large.

Fat History: Bodies and Beauty in the Modern West
by Peter N. Stearns (New York University Press, 2002)
Stearns presents a thorough historical look at the way ads, doctors and
media gave women conflicting messages about body size throughout
the twentieth century.

Fat! So? Because You Don't Have to Apologize for Your Size
by Marilyn Wann (Ten Speed Press, 1999)
This fun, fat-friendly book calls on the reader to stop dieting and
love her "flabulous" self. Filled with pictures, charts, testimonials
and clever comebacks, it's a great gift for anyone young, hip and in
need of a body image boost.

*Skinny Women Are Evil: Notes of a Big Girl in a Small-Minded
World*
by Mo'Nique (Atria, 2003)
The star of UPN's *The Parkers* gives a hilarious, if un-P.C., spin on
what the world would look like if the big girls ran the show.

Unbearable Weight: Feminism, Western Culture, and the Body
by Susan Bordo (University of California Press, 1995)
Bordo offers a fascinating glimpse into the tangled web of power and
culture that limits women's views of their bodies and selves.

Wake Up, I'm Fat!

by Camryn Manheim (Broadway Books, 2000)

This book is an inspiring look at this talented actress's life, including her struggles as a fat actress, her perseverance through typecasting and rejection and her triumph as an award-winning TV star.

Well Rounded: Eight Simple Steps for Changing Your Life . . . Not Your Size

by Catherine Lippincott (Pocket Books, 1998)

This guide is filled with self-esteem-building activities and beauty tips for adjusting your attitude not your weight.

Women Who Eat: A New Generation on the Glory of Food

edited by Leslie Miller (Seal Press, 2003)

Women celebrate food in all its caloric splendor, reveling in its nostalgic ties to family, friendship and fun, revealing that perhaps we *are* what we eat.

sports

Pretty Good for a Girl

by Leslie Heywood (University of Minnesota Press, 1999)

Body Outlaws contributor Heywood, a former Arizona high-school track and cross-county star, chronicles the disturbing pressures she faced as a young female athlete fighting for acknowledgment in a male-dominated arena.

Whatever It Takes: Women on Women's Sport

edited by Joli Sandoz and Jobi Winans (Farrar Straus & Giroux, 1999)

The first-ever anthology on the topic, this book's contributors include coaches, athletes, tomboys and more.

Women Who Risk: Profiles of Women in Extreme Sports

by Marilyn Olsen (Hatherleigh Press, 2003)

This book offers inspiring stories of eleven fearless women, among them an Indy car racer, a skydiving mother of two, and a surfer.

veganism & healthy eating

Becoming Vegan: The Complete Guide to Adopting a Healthy Plant-Based Diet

by Brenda Davis and Vesanto Melina (Book Publishing Co., 2000)

Written by two dieticians, this book explores the health benefits of veganism and explains how to get all the vitamins and proteins your body needs, without eating animal products.

Diet for a New America

by John Robbins (HJ Kramer, 1998)

Robbins, the director of the California Institute for Health and Healing and heir to the Baskin-Robbins fortune (which he rejected), links heart disease, cancer and other illnesses to mass consumption of hormone-riddled meat and dairy, and exposes the cruel, unnatural conditions under which livestock are raised.

Fast Food Nation: The Dark Side of the All-American Meal

by Eric Schlosser (HarperCollins, 2002)

You won't be supersizing at Mickey D's after reading this exposé, which reveals what's really in the special sauce, the unsanitary conditions in which fast food is prepared and how fast food has caused obesity and disease in children.

Vegan: The New Ethics of Eating

by Erik Marcus (McBooks Press, 2000)

This book offers one of the best introductions to veganism, covering its politics, practices, health benefits and ecological impact.

The Vegan Sourcebook

by Joanne Stepaniak, Virginia Messina and Carol J. Adams (McGraw-Hill, 2000)

This thorough, easy-to-read book explains the entire vegan lifestyle, from its challenges to its benefits, and includes a menu-planning guide and resource section.

violence against women

The Courage to Heal: A Guide for Women Survivors of Sexual Abuse

by Ellen Bass and Laura Davis (Perennial, 1994)

This practical resource helps survivors break the silence and the cycle of sexual abuse, and begin the healing process.

The Gift of Fear: Survival Signs That Protect Us from Violence

by Gavin De Becker (Dell, 1998)

This book shows how to notice, listen to and deal with the threat of violence, whether from a potentially violent partner or an unstable admirer.

Journey to Wholeness: Healing from the Trauma of Rape

by Vicki Aranow and Monique Lang (Learning Press, 2000)

This thoughtful resource for rape survivors opens the door to recovery by providing facts, information and exercises.

about the contributors

Elisa Albert received her MFA in fiction from Columbia University. Her fiction and nonfiction have appeared in *Pindeldyboz, Response* and the *Jewish Journal of Greater Los Angeles.* She is always up for a cupcake or three from the Magnolia Bakery. She lives in New York City.

Diane Anderson-Minshall is the founder of *Girlfriends, Alice* and *Roxie* magazines. Her work has appeared in dozens of publications, including *Bitch, Bust, Venus, Utne Reader* and *Seventeen.* She is currently the entertainment editor of *Curve* magazine. She lives in California.

Erin J. Aubry is a staff writer for the *LA Weekly.* She was previously a staff writer for *New Times Los Angeles* and the *Los Angeles Times* as well as a contributing writer for the paper's City Times section. Her news stories, arts features, essays, interviews and reviews have appeared in many other sections of the *Times,* including Metro, Calendar, Life & Style, Book Review and the Sunday Magazine. She has also freelanced for such magazines as *Black Enterprise, VIBE, Contemporary Art* and *UCLA Magazine.* A Los Angeles native, Ms. Aubry is a poet and fiction writer whose work has appeared in *Spectrum,* the literary journal published by the University of California at Santa Barbara. She received her Bachelor of Arts in English and Master of Fine Arts from UCLA.

Jennifer Berger is now twenty-seven years old and an editor in San Francisco. She is also the executive director of About-Face, an organization that provides girls and women with tools for thinking critically about images of women in the media. She has not yet found a cure for her food allergies but is hot on the trail.

John Chaich is a self-proclaimed "artivist" and feminist "phag" whose birthday falls between those of Dr. Martin Luther King, Jr., Eartha Kitt, Charo and Dolly Parton. He has presented nationally on AIDS and the arts as well as produced theatrical, curatorial and musical outreach projects. After publishing his own zine, *sway: style + substance for smart sexysomethings,* he became a contributing writer to *Bust* and a columnist for several Midwestern publications. A Cleveland native, Chaich currently lives in New York City.

Jill Corral is a writer, editor and infotech swashbuckler living in San Francisco. She co-edited *Young Wives' Tales: New Adventures in Love and Partnership* (Seal Press, 2001) with Lisa Jervis.

Diana Courvant is a speaker, writer and activist who is known at her day job as the "token radical, transsexual, disabled dyke." She spends five days a week programming and takes as much time off as she can to travel, speak and pay the rent. Courvant lives with her partner in Portland, Oregon, where she researches gender issues and domestic violence, and tries to keep her clothes on whenever she leaves her apartment.

Christy Damio has lent her flair for the bizarre and her pit-bull grip on American vernacular to some of the country's hippest special-interest magazines, including *Latingirl, Today's Child, CMJ* and *Mia.* Christy can be seen in AMP Productions' documentary on interracial marriage, *What About the Children?* She has contributed to a number of books, including *Sex and Single Girls* (Seal Press 2000). An award-winning poet, she lives in Queens, works as an editor for Scholastic and is currently writing a collection of short stories about '80s rock and the freaks who still love it.

Lee Damsky is the editor of *Sex and Single Girls: Straight and Queer Women on Sexuality* (Seal Press, 2000). She lives in New York City.

Kate Dillon is a leading plus-size model and a national speaker body image. Called the "curvy comeback" by *Glamour* and named 1998 model of the year by *Mode,* Kate was formerly a "skinny model." After struggling to maintain an impossible weight, Kate took a two-year hiatus and returned to the business as a full-figured, size twelve Wilhelmina model. Within months, she was featured on a Times Square billboard and landed a national commercial spot for Playtex. Kate is the co-founder of ECHO Prosocial Gallery, a non-profit organization encouraging children to use their creativity to advocate for social change. In 2000, she was named one of the "50 Most Beautiful People" by *People* magazine.

Joyce Dyer is director of writing and professor of English at Hiram College in Hiram, Ohio. She is the author of three books, *The Awakening: A Novel of Beginnings* (Twayne Publishing, 1993), *In a Tangled Wood: An Alzheimer's Journey* (Southern Methodist University Press, 1996) and *Gum-Dipped: A Daughter Remembers Rubber Town* (University of Akron Press, 2003), and the editor of *Bloodroot: Reflections on Place by Appalachian Women Writers* (University Press of Kentucky, 1998). She has published over a hundred essays in magazines, including *North American Review, Southern Literary Journal* and *High Plains Literary Review.* Dyer has won numerous awards for her writimng, including a 1997 Individual Artist Fellowship from the Ohio Arts Council and the 1998 Appalachian Book of the Year Award, and was nominated for a 2001 Pushcart Prize in nonfiction. She is currently working on a prequel to *Gum-Dipped* about Goosetown, the section of old Akron that her mother's German family settled in the nineteenth century, as well as a book about beauty in America. She lives in Cleveland, Ohio.

Tali Edut began her journey into the world of women's publishing in 1990, with a stint on *Sassy* magazine's Reader Produced Issue. She continued to write pieces exploring the effects of body image and cultural identity on women's self-esteem. In 1992, she co-founded *HUES,* a national, multicultural young women's magazine. She is now the CEO of Mediarology, Inc. and an astrologer for *Teen People,* and the co-author, with Ophira Edut, of *Astrostyle: Star-studded Advice* *for Love, Life, and Looking Good* (Simon & Schuster, 2003). She lives in New York City.

Debbie Feit is a freelance writer and a former magazine editor, advertising copywriter and well-rested person. In her present position as Batman locator, sippy-cup refiller and supporter of the Crayola arts, she oversees the daily operation of a Cheerio-encrusted conglomerate known as her family. When her computer isn't being used for a game of Peek-a-boo Elmo, Feit uses it to write feature articles, essays and nasty letters to her insurance company. She has written about language development, wedding gown shopping, interfaith marriage and the disappointment of learning your baby's sex, for such publications as *Bride's, Parents, Good Housekeeping, American Baby, Mode, Bridal Guide, Detroit Jewish News* and *PetLife*. She lives in Michigan.

Susan Jane Gilman is the author of *Kiss My Tiara: How to Rule the World as a SmartMouth Goddess* (Warner Books, 2001). A native New Yorker, she has written about women's issues for the *New York Times, Newsday, Ms.* and *US* magazine, and her fiction has appeared in the *Village Voice* and *Story*, among others.

Chris Godsey lives in Duluth, Minnesota, where he hangs out with local rock stars, runs many miles on forest trails and teaches college writing classes. A version of his essay "Cro-Magnon Karma" first appeared online in the summer of 2000. He and his wife, Shannon, share space with a five-year-old pug diva named Jeep.

Pia Guerrero has worked for over a decade with low-income communities of color focusing on media education, violence prevention and youth development. As program director for Our Schools, Our Media and for the Just Think Foundation, she designed and developed media literacy and youth media programs nationally, and directly taught over four hundred teachers, youth workers and young people. Pia's projects include the website for PBS's critically acclaimed television series *Senior Year* and its widely distributed curriculum guidebook. In 2003, Pia developed violence prevention and media literacy curricula commissioned by the Department of Education to support teachers working with urban elementary-school students. She currently works as the co-director for HOMEY (Homies Organizing the Mission to Empower Youth), a nonprofit that works to provide positive, peaceful alternatives for gang members and youth caught up in the underground economies of street survival in San Francisco.

Maysan Haydar is a social worker in New York City. Like everyone else in Manhattan, she's originally from the Midwest—specifically, Flint, Michigan. She doesn't enjoy sailing, biking and long walks on the beach. She does like heavy metal and books on immigration and refugee policy. She has written and edited for the *Nation, HUES, Spin, CMJ* and *Venus*.

Leslie Heywood is a professor of English and cultural studies and director of graduate studies in English at Binghamton University (SUNY). Her latest book is *Built to Win: The Female Athlete as Cultural Icon* (University of Minnesota Press, 2003). She is a competitive powerlifter and a trustee for the Women's Sports Foundation.

Leoneda Inge-Barry is the Changing Economy reporter at WUNC Public Radio in Chapel Hill. She was awarded a 2003 Gracie Allen Award, presented by the Foundation of American Women in Radio and Television. Her winning entry was titled *Out of Work: Mary Moore*. Leoneda began her professional reporting career in Benton Harbor, Michigan, and later worked as a journalist in Grand Rapids and in Milwaukee, Wisconsin. She holds a B.S. in journalism from Florida A&M University. In 1995, she was named a University of Michigan Journalism Fellow (renamed the Knight-Wallace Fellows at Michigan). While in Ann Arbor, she was an editor and contributor at *HUES*. Leoneda writes and plays tennis in her spare time and lives in Durham, North Carolina, with her husband and two sons.

Mira Jacob is the co-author of Kenneth Cole's memoir, *Footnotes* (Simon & Schuster, 2003), and has written for numerous publications, including *HUES, The Stranger* and the pop-culture handbook *The Mysterious Case of Nancy Drew & the Hardy Boys*. She runs

Pete's Reading Series in Williamsburg, Brooklyn, and holds a B.A. from Oberlin College and an M.F.A. in creative writing from The New School.

Lisa Jervis is the editor and publisher of *Bitch: Feminist Response to Pop Culture,* now entering its eighth year of publication. Her work has appeared in *Bust, HUES, Ms., Salon, Mother Jones* and the *San Francisco Chronicle.* She is the co-editor of *Young Wives' Tales: New Adventures in Love and Partnership* (Seal, 2001).

Loolwa Khazzoom (www.loolwa.com) has published articles in numerous periodicals, including the *Washington Post, Rolling Stone, Marie Claire* and *Health,* and she is the editor of *The Flying Camel: Essays on Identity by Women of North African and Middle Eastern Jewish Heritage* (Seal, 2003). She lives in Israel.

Nomy Lamm lives in Olympia, Washington, and is looking for dates. She hates long walks on the beach but loves swimming, drawing, dancing and singing, and is learning to sew herself fabulous costumes. She recently learned the entire choreographed zombie dance from Michael Jackson's "Thriller." Nomy has self-published her writing and artwork in *i'm so fucking beautiful* and other zines. Her work also appears in *Listen Up: Voices from the Next Feminist Generation* (Seal, 1995), *Present Tense: Writing and Art by Young Women* (Calyx, 1997), *Ms.* and *Seventeen.* In 1997, *Ms.* magazine named her one of their "Women of the Year." She recently toured Northwest college campuses, lecturing about fat oppression. Her long-term goals include writing a novel and a one-woman show, planting a garden and, of course, helping to bring about the demise of capitalism and the American empire.

Dyann Logwood is an Ypsilanti, Michigan, native and the co-founder of *HUES.* The daughter of a Pentecostal preacher, she brings her inherited public speaking talents to numerous women's conferences. Dyann has spoken on issues of race and gender at the National Women's Studies Association, the YWCA and at other national forums. She is currently teaching women's studies and African-American studies at Eastern Michigan University. She has her master's in women's studies and communications from Eastern Michigan University and is working towards a Ph.D. in communications from Wayne State University.

Carolyn Mackler (www.carolynmackler.com) is the author of the acclaimed teen novels, *The Earth, My Butt, and Other Big Round Things* (Candlewick Press, 2003) and *Love and Other Four-Letter Words* (Delacorte Press, 2000), an American Library Association Quick Pick for Reluctant Young Adult Readers and an International Reading Association Young Adults' Choice. Her third novel for teenagers will be published by Candlewick Press in 2004. Carolyn regularly contributes short stories to *Girls' Life, American Girl* and various fiction collections. She has also written for *Glamour, Teen People, Seventeen* and *Shape*. A graduate of Vassar College, Carolyn lives in New York City.

Bhargavi C. Mandava (www.bhargavicmandava.com) was born in Hyderabad, India. She is the author of the novel *Where the Oceans Meet* (Seal Press, 1996) as well as a contributor to *Listen Up: Voices from the Next Feminist Generation* (Seal Press, 2001) and *Young Wives' Tales: New Adventures in Love and Partnership* (Seal Press, 2001). Her poetry can be found in *Another Way to Dance: Contemporary Asian Poetry from Canada and the United States* (TSAR, 1996), *Through a Child's Eyes: Poems and Stories about War* (Plain View Press, 2001) and the forthcoming *Writing the Lines of Our Hands* (Creative Arts Book Company, 2004). She lives in Los Angeles.

Akkida McDowell is the granddaughter of a superhero who left the Earth too soon. A self-described pop-culture queen, she embraces the skin and body she's in and has almost crowned her sometimes plaited glory. The Cleveland native considers herself blessed to have collaborated with *HUES, Sports Illustrated Women, Lifetime,* Scholastic and other word creators. Contemplating thriving Boondocks, chocolate and TV rerun obsessions, she spends her days learning to calm her soul. She lives in New York City.

Meredith McGhan grew up in a decaying industrial town in the Midwest and left it to pursue anthropology studies. She worked at a variety of jobs, some short-lived and unusual, others interminable and conventional, between receiving one degree and entering school for a second. She is currently pursuing a master's in women's studies. McGhan, a fiction, nonfiction and poetry writer, is writing her first novel, a tale of survivalist extremists, disembodied beings and topless bars. She lives in Las Vegas.

Sada Mecca is an East Coast native of Brazilian heritage, and a singer, songwriter and producer. She is the mother of a one-year-old son, and a founding member of the hip-hop group Digable Planets. Mecca is a partner in a new production company and an education center in urban Philadelphia. She is currently at work on her first solo album. She prays for all women to understand their value and to stand firm in what they believe.

Marisa Navarro is a freelance writer living in Washington, D.C.

Jennifer C. Panning is a psychotherapist who recently received her doctorate in clinical psychology from the Chicago School of Professional Psychology. Jennifer is excited to continue to work with young women with eating disorders and body image disturbances and feels that being a therapist is her calling. She lives in Chicago with her terrific husband and their two cats, CJ and Elke. A typical Cancer, Jennifer enjoys nurturing and being a domestic goddess—gardening, cooking, reading and being outdoors.

Amelia (Amy) Richards is a young feminist activist and organizer, and the co-author of *Manifesta: Young Women, Feminism, and the Future* (Farrar, Straus & Giroux, 2000). She is co-founder and executive committee member of the Third Wave Foundation. Amelia is also a contributing editor to *Ms.* and a research, editorial and political advisor to Gloria Steinem. She works on a consulting basis with the Ms. Foundation for Women, Voters for Choice, First Nations Development Institute and for other social justice organizations. She is also the voice behind "Ask Amy," an online activist column located at www.feminist.com. She serves on the board of the Voters for Choice Education Fund, Feminist.com and is a member of the Council or Advocates of Planned Parenthood NYC. Her work appears in *Listen Up: Voices from the Next Feminist Generation* (Seal Press, 2001), *Ms.,* the *New Internationalist* and *Bust.* In 1995, *Who Cares* magazine chose her as one of twenty-five Young Visionaries, and in 1997, *Ms.* profiled her as "21 for the 21st: Leaders for the Next Century."

Graciela (Chely) H. Rodriguez has devoted her life to helping others and giving back what was given to her. She has touched and changed lives by sharing her struggle with body image. She has gone from wanting to be a model and starving herself to the point of hospitalization, to now teaching others about self-love. Her early career as an advocate for healthy living began at Girls Inc. of Carpinteria, California. As a teen she attended several luncheons, traveled to New York and sat on panels. As an adult she has facilitated numerous teen programs. Her undergrad experience at the University of California in Santa Barbara gave her the opportunity to conduct sociological research as a MOST (Minority Opportunity through School Transformation) student. She was awarded the Genesis Grant to conduct research for two years on the influence of mass media on body dissatisfaction. She presented her research at the 2002 American Sociological Association MOST Conference in Chicago. She also received the Greek Woman of the Year Award and the Senior Excellence Award. Chely strives to be an example for other young women and for future generations. She is currently working as an elementary-school teacher and attends graduate school at Asuza Pacific University to earn her credentials and master's in multiple-subject education.

Keesa Schreane is currently president of Schreane & Associates Marketing and Media Consulting, based in New York City. Schreane has her master's in journalism from New York University and has spent several years working with top corporate marketing groups as well as news media companies throughout the country. In addition, Schreane serves on the boards of various media and community organizations.

Diane Sepanski has worked with or around words in Seattle for lo these many years. She has sold books at the Elliott Bay Book Company, copyedited for Seal Press and Sasquatch Books, reviewed tools for Amazon.com, helped the Northwest Independent Editors Guild and the Northwest Bookfest take their first steps, proofread for *Northwest Fly Fishing* magazine and written for the *Seattle Weekly.* She just got back from Cluj-Napoca, Transylvania, Romania, where she taught writing and conversation at Babe Bolyai University. When she returned, she thought it was the jet lag talking, but no, the FDA really *had* approved the use of growth hormones for perfectly healthy children, as if being short were some sort of disease. She is currently writing about her travels in Romania; share her journey at www.roadfork.com.

Wendy Shanker is the author of *The Fat Girl's Guide to Life* (Bloomsbury, 2004). She is the resident humor columnist for *Grace* magazine and is one of *Us Weekly*'s Fashion Police. She has appeared on Lifetime and *The Ricki Lake Show* and hosted a show on the Oxygen Channel. A contributor to *The Bust Guide to the New Girl Order* (Penguin, 1999), Wendy has also written for *Glamour, Cosmopolitan, Marie Claire, Seventeen* and MTV's *TRL.* She lives in New York City.

Silja J.A. Talvi is an award-winning journalist and essayist with credits in over seventy-five publications, including the *Nation, Christian Science Monitor* and *In These Times.* She's currently based in Seattle, where she is the staff writer for *ColorsNW,* a monthly magazine devoted to communities of color. Snowboarding, biking and an obsession with lipstick occupy the rest of her waking hours.

Allison Torres graduated from the University of Michigan in 1997 with a bachelor's degree in English, and worked with *HUES* magazine for two years. She rowed with the University of Michigan crew team for four years, and continues to row independently on northern Virginia waters. She currently lives in Alexandria, Virginia, and works as an editor and web content coordinator for a group of history magazines.

Rebecca Walker is considered one of the most audible voices of the young women's movement, and was named by *Time* magazine as one of the future leaders of America. She was born in Jackson, Mississippi, raised in San Francisco and New York, and graduated *cum laude* from Yale University in 1992. Following graduation, Walker founded Third Wave Direct Action Corporation, a national non-profit organization devoted to cultivating young women's leadership and activism. In their first summer, Third Wave initiated an historic emergency youth drive that registered over 20,000 new voters in inner cities across the United States. Walker is a writer, a contributing editor to *Ms.*, and has been published in *Essence,* the *New York Daily News, SPIN, Harper's, Sassy, VIBE* and *Testimony.* She is the editor of *To Be Real: Telling the Truth and Changing the Face of Feminism* (Anchor/Doubleday, 1995), and the author of *Black, White and Jewish: Autobiography of a Shifting Self* (Riverhead, 2002). A recipient of the Feminist of the Year award from the Fund for the Feminist Majority, Walker currently speaks about third wave feminism at colleges and conferences across the United States and Canada.

Regina D. Williams, a.k.a. Divine Ms. Diva, Gina or GiGi, is proud to be a forty-two-year-old big, beautiful woman. In addition to being the chairperson of the Michigan Chapter of the National Association to Advance Fat Acceptance (NAAFA), she is pursuing a lifelong dream to own her own business. Size acceptance is in her blood, so you can be sure her business will serve the size community. She's also gathering submissions for her book, "Fat Dancing Girls." She plans to continue setting an example for other women of size to follow their hearts and live their own extraordinary lives. She lives in Michigan.

acknowledgments

I wish to thank my family and friends for their ongoing support and encouragement. I also wish to thank my editors, Jennie Goode and Ingrid Emerick, for their creative spirit and insight.

This book is dedicated to my grandmother, Sophie Horn Seligson.

about the editor

Ophira Edut (www.ophira.com) is a writer, designer and entrepreneur who has spent over a decade creating groundbreaking media projects for young women of all cultures and sizes. In 1992, she founded *HUES*, a national, multicultural women's magazine, which was published until 1999. She has been featured in numerous anthologies and media sources, including *Ms.,* the *New York Times,* MTV's *TRL* and *Entertainment Weekly.* Edut lectures at colleges and conferences nationwide about body image and the media. In addition, she now helps people navigate their differences on a "universal" level as an astrologer for *Teen People* and the co-author of *Astrostyle: Star-studded Advice for Love, Life, and Looking Good* (Simon & Schuster, 2003). Edut lives in New York City.

selected titles from seal press

Cunt: A Declaration of Independence by Inga Muscio. $14.95, 1-58005-075-1. An ancient title of respect for women, "cunt" long ago veered off the path of honor and now careens toward the heart of every woman as an expletive. Muscio traces this winding road, giving women both the motivation and the tools to claim "cunt" as a positive and powerful force in the lives of all women.

Listen Up: Voices from the Next Feminist Generation edited by Barbara Findlen. $16.95, 1-58005-054-9. A revised and expanded edition of the Seal Press classic, featuring the voices of a new generation of women expressing the vibrancy and vitality of today's feminist movement.

Colonize This!: Young Women of Color on Today's Feminism edited by Daisy Hernández and Bushra Rehman. $16.95, 1-58005-067-0. It has been decades since women of color first turned feminism upside down. Now a new generation of brilliant, outspoken women of color is speaking to the concerns of a new feminism, and their place in it.

Women Who Eat: A New Generation on the Glory of Food edited by Leslie Miller. $15.95, 1-58005-092-1. More than just great food writing, this long-overdue rebuttal to the notion that all women are on a diet celebrates food with grace, wit, and gusto.

Sometimes Rhythm, Sometimes Blues: Young African Americans on Love, Relationships, Sex, and the Search for Mr. Right edited by Taigi Smith. $15.95, 1-58005-096-4. A tell-it-like-it-is look at black women's tumultuous search for love and partnership in their community.

Without a Net: The Female Experience of Growing Up Working Class edited by Michelle Tea. $14.95, 1-58005-103-0. The first anthology in which women with working-class backgrounds explore how growing up poor impacts identity.

Seal Press publishes many books of fiction and nonfiction by women writers. Please visit our Web site at **www.sealpress.com**.

CPSIA information can be obtained
at www.ICGtesting.com
Printed in the USA
FFHW021806020219
50387535-55526FF

31192021650781